THE OLD RUGGED CROSS

THE OLD RUGGED CROSS

A History of the Atonement in Popular Christian Devotion

Ben Pugh

CASCADE *Books* · Eugene, Oregon

THE OLD RUGGED CROSS
A History of the Atonement in Popular Christian Devotion

Cascade Books
An Imprint of Wipf and Stock Publishers
199 W. 8th Ave., Suite 3
Eugene, OR 97401

www.wipfandstock.com

PAPERBACK ISBN: 978-1-62564-742-9
HARDCOVER ISBN: 978-1-4982-8787-6
EBOOK ISBN: 978-1-5326-1057-8

Cataloguing-in-Publication data:

Names: Pugh, Ben.
Title: The old rugged cross : a history of the atonement in popular Christian devotion / Ben Pugh.
Description: Eugene, OR: Cascade Books, 2016 | Includes bibliographical references and index.
Identifiers: ISBN 978-1-62564-742-9 (paperback) | ISBN 978-1-4982-8787-6 (hardcover) | ISBN 978-1-5326-1057-8 (ebook)
Subjects: LCSH: Atonement | Spirituality—Christianity | Worship
Classification: BT265.3 P844 2016 (paperback) | BT265.3 P844 (ebook)

Manufactured in the U.S.A.   09/28/16

Scripture taken from the New King James Version (NKJV). Copyright © 1979, 1980, 1982 by Thomas Nelson, Inc. Used by permission. All rights reserved.

Chapter 5 has been adapted from my "'Under the Blood' at Azusa Street. Exodus Typology at the Heart of Pentecostal Origins," *Journal of Religious History* 39.1 (2015) 86–103, used by permission.

Parts of chapter 4 have been adapted from my "The Wesleyan Way: Entire Sanctification and its spin-offs—a recurring theme in Evangelical Devotion," *Evangelical Review of Theology* 38.1 (2014) 4–21, used by permission.

Extract from "In Christ Alone" in chapter 6 used by permission: Adm. by Capitol CMG Publishing worldwide excl. UK & Europe, admin by Integrity Music, part of the David C Cook family, songs@integritymusic.com

To Pearl, my wife, remembering the companionable silence we enjoyed together night after night while you worked on your MA and I worked on this, with the children all soundly asleep upstairs (usually!).

CONTENTS

ACKNOWLEDGEMENTS

FIRSTLY A WORD OF thanks is due to the staff of the Hallward Library at the University of Nottingham. I forgot to mention them in *Atonement Theories*, so I now pay my debt and acknowledge the very considerable hours I have spent there using my Visiting Scholar card and dipping into their vast collections of classic texts. While we are on the subject of institutions, my own institution, Cliff College, have played their part: Lynne Firth, the librarian, has put up with me hanging onto books for months on end and my boss Dr. Walter Riggans has been very supportive, allowing me plenty of days out of the office, which I have used to infiltrate the Hallward Library, Nottingham. I am, perhaps, giving the impression here that libraries are places that I most love to be: when I escape, I escape *to a library*. In fact I do have a life and it is mostly made up of my wife Pearl and children Abigail, Gracie, and Reuben. The joy they bring sustains me. A word of thanks is also due to my editor, Dr. Robin Parry, and all the staff at Cascade. This has been the most repeatedly delayed piece of written work I have undertaken to date. Every time I asked for another extension, the response was gracious and generous. The result has been a manuscript that I have not rushed and which I feel quite pleased with. Going back into the mists of my PhD days, acknowledgment is due there too. Parts of this book are based on research carried out for my thesis with Bangor University, via Regents Theological College: "Power in the Blood: The Significance of the Blood of Jesus to the Spirituality of Early British Pentecostalism and its Precursors." My supervisor Dr. Neil Hudson was excellent, as was the then Director of Postgraduate Studies at Regents, Dr. Keith Warrington. While researching for this I also made use of the Donald Gee Centre, a Pentecostal archive at Mattersey Hall, England, of which Dr. Dave Gerrard was then the curator. Finally, my wife, who supported me during my PhD years while I brought home only a paltry income from visiting lecturing, deserves easily the most credit here for making the PhD possible.

PREFACE

A Word about Me

A COMMENT ARISING FROM my first volume on the atonement: *Atonement Theories: A Way through the Maze*, is that I failed to show my hand. I did not divulge my own churchmanship so the reader did not have the chance of picking up on any possible biases. My churchmanship is actually Pentecostal, though my most formative years were spent within an independent charismatic church. However, really I come at all of this from no tradition at all. Until my fairly dramatic conversion as a long-haired art student in 1988 at the age of nineteen, I had had next no contact with any kind of church tradition whatsoever.

In my early days as a Christian I invented systematic theology by putting into separate wallets various insights I had gained by reading the Bible. There was a wallet for God the Father, one for Christ, another for the Holy Spirit, salvation, the church, and the "end times" as I called it. Then I discovered (by acquiring my first Louis Berkhof) that systematic theology had already been invented. I was also quite a prolific songwriter. I soon came across some of the words of hymns that I found not only beautiful poetically but a veritable trip to heaven and back theologically. I discovered *Love Divine* and wrote a tune for it. Then I discovered that a perfectly good tune for *Love Divine* already existed. I think I did the same with *And Can it Be?* You get the picture.

I was four years into my life as a Christian when I felt led by the Spirit to read Romans 3–8 as often as I could, to just keep going with that one section. I had been struggling with feeling tormented in my soul. Yes, I was one of those tormented souls. When I read Bunyan's *Grace Abounding*, for instance, I found in his pathetically self-absorbed, self-loathing monologue a real kindred spirit, though I would not have been given to stuffing my head down rabbit holes to stop myself from blaspheming as he did. Meeting God as a young man had been as frightening as it was thrilling for me. At times my room seemed aglow with heavenly light. I had met him and knew that he was holy: hence my torment. It was while reading Romans that I came face to face with the atonement for the first time. At my charismatic church no one, and I mean *no one*, in the four years I had been there, had yet got around to preaching the cross. To give them the benefit of the doubt, it may have happened at Easter: when I was a student I went home to my parents at Easter. Then, one sunny day, Barrie Taylor, to whom my first volume is dedicated, was allowed to take an entire Sunday morning sermon slot to teach us all about the atonement, with a full set of notes given out at the door after the meeting. This tearful Yorkshireman (he always ended his sermons with at least a quiver in his voice) unwittingly set me on the path I am on now. That was July 1992.

So you see why I say that I am coming at this from no tradition. Even the tradition I got myself into hardly mentioned it. And because I am coming at it all from a blank starting point, I do tend to lack the hushed reverence that a devout Catholic might bring when discussing the medieval saints, for instance. In fact, I am prone to slipping in the odd joke, which I hope you will forgive. The lack of religiosity in my upbringing can be quite a handicap. It sometimes falls to me to lead Communion here at Cliff College. I look upon my Methodist colleagues with envy at such times. I altogether lack the *gravitas* and decorum with which these trained ministers can work their magic. I stand behind the Communion table and lead Communion in the style of Jamie Oliver making a pizza. But, by the same token, I lack the cynicism and weariness of a writer that might have been brought up in church. All the old hymns are like a new discovery to me (well, maybe not quite so new anymore), and so I have created spaces in the book, which I have called "Hymn Breaks." These are places where the analysis stops and we can simply pause to appreciate one of the all-time great hymns about the atonement.

The Purpose of This Book

There can scarcely be anyone in church ministry—of any confessional shade—who does not sometimes stop to ask, "What is the point of all this

jiggery-pokery? To what end this weekly hocus-pocus? Is this really doing anything?" Similarly, it would be a very odd thing if, among Christian
academics attending theology conferences, there were not some in every
seminar who were sat there thinking, "What is the point of this never-
ending talking shop? Just what are we achieving with all our papers and
publications?"

In both settings, of course, what we really want to know is, "Does this
work?" In fact, we want to know this possibly more urgently than we want
an answer to the question, "Is this true?" And it is this pragmatic quest
that drives this second volume of studies on the atonement. In this volume I will be trying to implement a strategy that I have found myself using
sporadically in my forays into Pentecostal studies. In Pentecostal studies
we routinely interact with practitioner texts. We unashamedly take books
by Smith Wigglesworth, Kenneth Hagin, or Joyce Meyer as our primary
sources. Because these are written by non-academics, we know we cannot
simply wade in with our theology or our New Testament acumen and tear
them to shreds. We critique the ideas of practitioners on their own terms,
looking at their own internal consistency, rather than judging them by an
intruded standard of scholarship.

I am calling this technique, echoing the terminology of liberation
theologians, "theology from below." In this book I will be doing theology
from below. I will be listening to the voice of the practitioner, attending
to the lay layer in the Christian tradition. I will be discerning the faith in
a way that (for once) ignores the great middle-aged white male pantheon
of luminaries that pontificated so usefully for me in my first volume. Only
where practitioners are reflecting a doctrine that they know has been given
them by one of the greats will I (reluctantly) reference one of the greats.

And this, I hope will point the way to identifying what works in atonement theology. What we are presented with in church history (as opposed
to historical theology) is praxis: lots of it, never-ending praxis. These are the
men and women who tried out different ways of applying and appropriating
the historical death of Christ and would have said it "worked." The sources
of this information may be slightly off-the-beaten track: I cannot lazily go
to that shelf of the library where I know I will find the works of Martin
Luther or Barth's *Church Dogmatics*. I am going to need to work hard, but
I will be rewarded with a treasure trove of practices all of which were held
to "work" in some way. Even given the great cultural divides that separate
us from most of the historical figures under review here, this surely is not

a bad place to start. Instead of starting with theory and hoping one day to arrive at praxis, like most theology still does, we are here starting with avowedly successful historic practice and then tentatively theorizing our way to possible current practice.

So, what will be my criteria for assessing and retrieving historic practices for today? What is needed is a philosophical principle that belongs to today through which to filter the historical data. The system I have chosen arises from within postmodern philosophy, though it has a history going back to early twentieth century American politics and educational theory. It is called pragmatism. To clarify exactly what I mean by this, I am making particular use here of three principles inherited from C. S. Pierce and William James, all three are really just different angles on the same thing:

1. Any given theory is an *instrument for adaptation*. It is a way of coping. The very reason for a theory's existence is that it facilitates adaptation to changing conditions. Theories of atonement can quickly be left behind by changes in culture. When this happens, the pragmatist "turns away from abstraction and insufficiency, from verbal solutions, from bad *a priori* reasons, from fixed principles, closed systems, and pretended absolutes and origins. He turns towards concreteness and adequacy."[1] This book will explore the way this has happened before and could happen again.

2. Theories are judged by the *consequences of accepting them*. "Our idea of anything *is* our idea of its sensible effects."[2] These pages will tentatively suggest that there have been times when a particular theoretical position brought a consequence that frustrated the worshipper's quest for God more than facilitating it.

3. Ideas are *plans of action*.[3] We evaluate a theory by its fitness for purpose. Does it get us to where we need to go? In this book you will find what I describe as the Participation Imperative. Worshippers must participate in atonement. That is where they want the theory to take them.

By way of parameters, my undertaking will not attempt to be an exhaustive historical description of all forms of devotion to the cross but will

1. William James, *Pragmatism*, 51.
2. Peirce, *The Essential Peirce*, Vol. 2, 132.
3. James, *Pragmatism*, 46, citing Pierce.

focus on concentrations of crucicentrism. At all points, the frameworks I bring will be applied in the most gentle way possible. You will not find me very often revisiting my three pragmatic principles outlined above, for instance: these are merely an angle of approach. Everything will be interpreted with a light touch, and tailored to each particular episode in the story. My tools have ranged from semiotics to sacramental theology: whatever tool is the most sensitive. But the meta-tool is the pragmatism outlined above.

This piece of work is not only an analysis; it is a celebration and I invite you to enjoy with me the many golden moments in the story of Christian appreciation for the work of Christ on the cross.

Good Friday
2016

Chapter 1

———

CRUCICENTRISM

The Search for a Beginning Point

Introduction

So, WHERE DOES IT all come from? When and why did Christianity adopt
the cross as its central symbol? And at what point does it start to venerate
the blood that flowed upon it? We will begin our search within that relatively murky world that is second- and third-century Christianity.[1] It is the
part between the death of the last of the apostles at the end of the first century and the emergence of a Christian Europe under Constantine following
the Edict of Milan in AD 313. We leave that first world, the New Testament
world, anticipating perhaps that the resurrection is destined to become
the great centerpiece of Christian proclamation and worship, or that the
mystical union with Christ will be the center. We enter the Constantinian
era with two things that would ensure that it would be the death of Christ
that would occupy an increasingly important central place within the
Christianity of Christendom. These two things, in roughly chronological
order, are the elevation of the Eucharist in the churches and the veneration
of the cross as the main visual symbol of the faith.

---

1. Very helpful here (though not focused on the cross specifically) is Siker, "Christianity in the Second and Third Centuries," in Esler (ed.), *The Early Christian World,*
1: 231–57.

The Eucharist

The Story of the Eucharist in the Early Church

The trend in scholarship, since the discovery of a number of new manuscripts, has, until very recently, been towards less and less certainty as to the true origins of the Eucharist. As with similar scholarly problems such as the quests for the historical Jesus (to which the quest for the historical Eucharist is not unrelated), the desire to answer the un-answerable generates very large volumes of literature. The nature of this literature tends to become more and more detailed, less and less meaningful, and more and more filled with assertions that "certainty is impossible," accompanied by lists of obstacles to that certainty. The reasons for the caution, however, are well stated by McGowan: "The standard account is teleological—an 'intelligent design' theory of liturgical history, reading back to produce a picture amenable to the conclusions assumed."[2] Dearly held confessional standpoints have, ever since the days of Gregory Dix brushing aside the *Didache*, tended to result in fingers in ears and loud singing while evidence has steadily emerged of almost no uniformity or clear chronology in early Eucharistic practice.

In current scholarship,[3] the point of widest agreement is that the Eucharist as we know it today is not the Eucharist that Jesus instituted as such. The assumed direct link between the Last Supper and the Lord's Supper is, unless some new evidence comes to light, undiscoverable, and quite possibly non-existent.[4] This may sound shocking and writers try to lessen the shock of that by emphasizing that the Holy Spirit was at work as much in

2. McGowan, "Rethinking Eucharistic Origins," 174.

3. The most accessible introduction to Eucharistic origins is that provided by Maxwell Johnson, "Worship, Practice and Belief," in Esler (ed.), *The Early Christian World* 1: 480–84. Dominating the field in the mid-twentieth century and still often referred to was Dix, *The Shape of Liturgy*. The most prolific writer on the subject currently is Paul Bradshaw: *The Search for the Origins of Christian Worship* and *Eucharistic Origins*. See also the very significant recent contributions by Stringer, *Rethinking the Origins of the Eucharist*, Spinks, *Do This in Rememberance of Me*, and O'Loughlin, *The Eucharist*.

4. Daly, "Eucharistic Origins: From the New Testament to Liturgies of the Golden Age," 4: ". . . unless a lot more data from the first Christian centuries can be recovered than is presently available, that full story may never be told." Also Meier, "The Eucharist and the Last Supper: Did It Happen?" 335–51. As early as 1893, a certain F. Sptta was proposing a "Double Origin" of the Eucharist, contrasting the fellowship meals of Acts 2:42, 46 and the Pauline Eucharist of 1 Corinthians 11: Fuller, "The Double Origin of the Eucharist," 60.

the postbiblical formation of liturgy as he was in the inspiration of Scripture[5]—something many within the Protestant traditions would doubtless find unconvincing. Be that as it may, what we in fact have are a number of different sources of influence that are largely up-for-grabs since there is no fail-safe way of placing these different Eucharists into a big story: first this, then that, as Chilton attempts.[6] Indeed, a lot of scholars are content to say that throughout the second and third centuries a variety of Eucharists existed.[7] However, I have been bold enough to arrange Eucharistic origins into two chronological phases, more or less following McGowan, and then further divided the discussion into first one of practice and then one of theology, which follows O'Loughlin.[8] And it is hopefully going to be this theological discussion that will be especially suggestive to us of answers to our quest for the origins of crucicentrism.

Mediterranean Banqueting Habits: Jewish and Greco-Roman

GRECO-ROMAN STRANDS

McGowan[9] points out how ubiquitous was the banquet to all forms of voluntary association in the first century. People gathered for all sorts of reasons, drawn together by family and by profession, and by religious and charitable ties.[10] Indeed, it is inconceivable that the early church would not have met together in precisely this form: the banquet or symposium,[11] and Christians had an even stronger reason for doing so: the precedent set by Jesus in his practice of table fellowship. So, gathering around a meal would have happened regularly even if there had been no tradition of an institution saying and a last supper. Probably some churches were aware of this Last Supper tradition, and others not.

---

5. "[O]ne does not need to be able to trace eucharistic praxis back to the historical Jesus or even to the New Testament in order to legitimate it." Daly, "Eucharistic Origins," 17.

6. Chilton, "Eucharist: Surrogate, Metaphor, Sacrament of Sacrifice," in Baumgarten (ed.), *Sacrifice in Religious Experience*, 175–88.

7. Stringer, *Rethinking the Origins of the Eucharist*.

8. O'Loughlin, *The Eucharist*.

9. See also Smith, *From Symposium to Eucharist*.

10. McGowan, "Rethinking Eucharistic Origins," 179.

11. Ibid., 180, 183.

Two ubiquitous elements of these feasts would have been bread and wine. Wine, though varying in quality was not a bourgeois drink, but universal to all such suppers.[12] Similarly, it was customary for each guest to bring their own loaf (perhaps resembling the modern Western custom of guests bringing a bottle). The key difference in Christian feasts, if the Corinthians are anything to go by, was the use of one shared loaf rather than everyone bringing their own. The one shared loaf broken and distributed to all was clearly laden with symbolic significance for the early Christians. Another difference would have been with the god that was invited. Paul spoke of how, though idols invited to pagan feasts were "nothing" or "no-gods" yet there was a demonic power behind them activated by the "participation" in them. Such spiritual participation was implied by the fact of eating with the supposed god. It was even customary to pour a bowl of wine for the god to drink. In the Christian love feast, the deity invited was Jesus and he would set the tone for the evening. Such a meal is a participation in the body and blood of Christ, a receiving of a share in Christ.[13]

THE JEWISH STRANDS

We can logically go no further back in the search for the start of a ritualized Christian meal than the very widely acknowledged importance to Jesus of table fellowship. Though what I am about to say seems quite foreign to us, this habit of his was designed to *say* something. The closest we come in Western culture to making meals into statements is when we host a dinner party purely to show off our social status or culinary skills rather than to be friendly. Similarly, but pointing in the opposite direction, Jesus was deliberately saying something by being completely indiscriminate about his choice of guest and host. He wasn't just being friendly. And what he was saying by eating with sinners and marginalized people in this way was not only about this present age but about the age to come, the time of the Messianic Banquet: "A willingness to provide for the meals, to join in the fellowship,

---

12. Ibid., 185.

13. The Jewish Passover, which almost certainly helped to shape even the gentile Eucharists, also had strong participatory overtones that added a present-time dynamic to its memorialism. The Rabbis taught that, "In every generation one must regard himself as though he were himself come out of Egypt with the fathers." *Mishnah Pesahim* 10:5, cited in Fuller, "Double Origin," 69.

to forgive and to be forgiven, was seen by Jesus as a sufficient condition for eating in his company and for entry into the kingdom."[14]

Such meals were normally accompanied by some sort of liturgical giving of thanks such that, for Jesus to have taken the cup and the bread at some point during his last meal with his disciples and to have invoked a Jewish thanksgiving prayer, would not have been unusual, even if this were not a Passover meal.

What seems to be a further development of this domestic Jewish strand is what Chilton describes as the "Petrine" type of Eucharist.[15] Under the leadership of Peter in the homes of the young church in Jerusalem, we find that people are "breaking bread from house to house" (Acts 2:46), but this, in contrast to the last meals of Jesus, was an uncontroversial affair (hence, it attracted the favor of outsiders). It was not challenging the temple sacrifices like Jesus meals might have been perceived as doing, as I will shortly explain, and these Petrine Eucharists also seemingly gave precedence to the bread over the wine.[16]

As for the Last Supper itself, despite Jesus' inattentiveness to purity laws in his eating habits, all might have been well, so the story goes, had he not tried to occupy the temple during the cleansing of the temple episode.[17] It was this, according to a great deal of current Jesus research, that ultimately got Jesus crucified. The authorities did not act immediately, however. They feared Jesus' popularity with the people. But, in response to the failed takeover of the temple, Jesus began to regularly use bread and wine as suggestive of an alternative to the sacrifices of the temple: "Jesus' meals after his failed occupation of the Temple became a surrogate of sacrifice."[18] This act was a "deliberate break with Judaism."[19] Jesus thus adds to the coming kingdom dimension of his meals the scandalous note of sacrificial "blood" and "body": enough to finally stimulate his arrest.[20]

---

14. Chilton, "Eucharist: Surrogate, Metaphor, Sacrament of Sacrifice," 181.

15. He accords this its own status as a third type following table fellowship and Last Supper: Ibid., 182.

16. Ibid., 181.

17. Daly, "Eucharistic Origins," 10.

18. Chilton, "Eucharist: Surrogate, Metaphor, Sacrament of Sacrifice," 182.

19. Ibid., 176.

20. Ibid., 179.

According to many, however, this is felt not to involve the Passover,[21] or even a paschal meal on the eve of Passover, but simply a meal that Jesus adapted that involved a single ceremonial cup and leavened bread, as opposed to the unleavened bread and the four cups of Passover. It seems that Jesus gave a special meaning to his sharing of the bread and cup and accompanied this with an eschatological prediction about the coming kingdom.

A POSSIBLE SYNTHESIS

There seems to be no reason to choose between a Greco-Roman symposium and a Jewish style of feast. There is enough common ground in the grammar or language of feasting. Meals in both contexts were designed to say or assert something that ran deeply into the participants' sense of identity and belonging. The Mediterranean meal in the first three centuries was a way of articulating the values of a group. McGowan puts it aptly: "Better to think of Greco-Roman meals, including Jewish ones, as a whole system or language of sorts, wherein various meanings could be conveyed and enacted in specific choices made by hosts and diners."[22]

This, perhaps, gives us pause for thought when it comes to the Eucharists of today. These too have a language, a grammar, but it is questionable whether they any longer are bearers of the same kinds of loving fellowship and community that the earliest Eucharists were.

From Supper to Snack: The Abstraction of the Elements from the Feast

> [H]ow was it that the earliest Christians gathered in houses for substantial meals or banquets, but less than three hundred years later the characteristic ritual of the Christian community was a token sacramental meal with a public or civic character?[23]

21. According to McGowan there are no features of the Last Supper in any of the Gospel narratives that can indubitably be linked to the ritual features of a Passover meal: McGowan, "Rethinking Eucharistic Origins," 186. Fuller, while not trying to prove that the Last Supper was a Passover, was open to the idea of a Christian reinterpretation of the Passover that may have developed in the immediate wake of the crucifixion, and which perpetuated the memorial element of the Passover, making Christ's death the new exodus. And parallels with the Passover Haggada can be cited. Fuller, "Double Origin," 67–68.

22. McGowan, "Rethinking Eucharistic Origins," 181.

23. Ibid., 175.

Over the next couple of centuries the Eucharistic meal became separated from the wider feast, a phenomenon that became essential post-Constantine due to the vast numbers of people that now came to partake. The location also would change from home to basilica as a result of that same Constantinian transition from persecuted underground cult to mainstream state-approved religion.[24] Post-Constantine there was also an increased emphasis by the clergy on the fearfulness of partaking in an unworthy manner. The priests were trying to correct the awful behavior of the by now mostly nominal communicants. Communicants were encouraged to set their lives straight by becoming non-communicants for as long as that took. The unintended result of this, far from encouraging reformation of lifestyles, was to increase the numbers of non-communicants. These, it seems, were quite happy to let the priests perform the ritual on their behalf while they sat at the back. This in turn led to the allegorization of the drama of Eucharist itself into episodes from the passion and resurrection of Christ, a process that created what we now know as the Mass.[25] Soon enough the evening Love Feasts of earlier times were looked upon as subversive in deference to the formal, gathered morning ritual overseen by the bishop.

This abstraction of the elements from the wider meal might seem quite extraordinary given the sheer ordinariness of the elements. McGowan even claims that the sacralizing of such extremely mundane elements as bread and wine is "paradoxical," or "ironic."[26] Such a claim, however, is only made fully possible if one ignores from the outset the elephant in the room: the Gospel narratives and the decisive role these must have played in the sacralizing of bread and wine, much as their isolation from a wider meal would not have been the original intention.

---

24. Though see recent scholarship that queries the received wisdom that the early churches were *only* house churches before Constantine: Adams, *The Earliest Christian Meeting Places: Almost Exclusively Houses?* Even before Constantine it seems that churches met wherever they could. Venues could include town halls, synagogues, temples, and even a few purpose-built basilicas. Some of their venues could accommodate well over a thousand people and could lay claim to be the first megachurches. A case can clearly be made however, that meeting in homes was probably the commonest way for churches to meet (Rom 16:5; 1 Cor 16:19; Col 4:15; Phlm 2).

25. By the thirteenth century, there were some people who, so taken by observing the dramatic elevation of the host during Mass, would travel from church to church just to witness the moment of consecration as many times as possible: Bynum, *Wonderful Blood*, 87.

26. McGowan, "Rethinking Eucharistic Origins," 185.

The Theology of the Eucharist

A number, perhaps three or four, distinct though superficially similar liturgies developed around the Eucharist as early as the second and third centuries. Uniformity, after all, would have been impossible in such a fragmented and unorganized body of people dispersed over such a vast geographical area. However, one development that can definitely be said to have taken place is a shift of emphasis in the underlying theology. The emphasis that we find in the apostle Paul is the giving of thanks to the Father in union with Christ. Bread and wine, the two most prosaic and ubiquitous elements of Mediterranean meals, were then used to make the remembering of the Father's love gift more concrete, just as Jesus had done before his death. But the act was a giving of thanks. In this respect Paul seems to have intended a sharp contrast with the sympotic feasts that his gentile converts had been used to. As we saw, in those feasts, to which the deity would invariably be invited as guest of honor or host, and to whom libations of wine would be poured, there would be a *koinonia* or sharing in the deity. Paul allows a parallel *koinonia* with Christ at the Corinthian love feasts but seems keen to direct the participants' attention to God the Father. There was clearly a concern that the Corinthians would celebrate their love feasts idolatrously: venerating the emblems in the way they would once have venerated any physical artefacts of the gods they would once have honored at symposia. For Paul, it is participation in Christ that gives access *to God the Father*. The focus was not Christocentric but theocentric.

This emphasis on giving thanks to the Father can be seen in the late first century *Didache* where it is God who is blessed in grateful thanks for the food and drink, not the food and drink that is blessed or consecrated in any way.[27] It is also of note that the *Didache* makes no association between the death of Christ and the Eucharist.[28] By contrast, the *Apostolic Tradition*, dated at AD 214, evidences a deeply crucicentric approach to the Eucharist, though this liturgy too is clearly focused on giving thanks to the Father:

---

27. *Didache* 9. O'Loughlin, *The Eucharist*, 44–45.

28. Larsen, "Addressing the Elephant That's Not in the Room: Comparing the Eucharistic Prayers in *Didache* 9–10 and the Last Supper Tradition," 253. Mitchell believes the *Didache* represents a community, probably based at Antioch, who were deliberately non-crucicentric, so striking is the avoidance of any reference at all to the death of Christ throughout the entire document: Mitchell, "Washed Away by the Blood of God," in Dreyer (ed.), *The Cross in Christian Tradition*, 56–57.

> We render thanks unto thee, O God, through Thy Beloved Child Jesus Christ, . . . Who fulfilling Thy will and preparing for Thee a holy people stretched forth His hands for suffering that He might release from sufferings them who have believed in Thee; Who when He was betrayed to voluntary suffering that He might abolish death and rend the bonds of the devil and tread down hell and enlighten the righteous and establish the limit and demonstrate the resurrection: taking bread and giving thanks to Thee said: Take eat: This is My Body which is broken for you. Likewise also the cup, saying: This is My Blood which is shed for you. Doing therefore the "anamnesis" of His death and resurrection we offer to Thee the bread and the cup making eucharist [giving thanks] to Thee because Thou hast made us worthy to stand before Thee and minister as priests to Thee.[29]

O'Loughlin reckons an understanding of the Eucharist as an encounter with Christ rather than merely a giving of thanks would have been set in motion from the time that the Institution Narrative was included in Eucharistic liturgies.[30] The words of institution appear to have acquired greater importance from the fourth century onwards owing to the need to catechize the untaught masses who had started to attend.[31]

Developing from the growing Christocentric focus, we eventually see the onset of what would later be termed "transubstantiation," which seems to tentatively begin with Cyprian's (200–258) insistence upon the sacrificial nature of the Eucharist.[32] Even before him, realistic language had begun to be employed that described how the elements were now the body and blood

---

29. *Apostolic Tradition* Part 1, iv. 4 and 7–11.

30. O'Loughlin, *The Eucharist*, 39. However, apart from such suggestive early evidence as the *Didache*, which lacks any reference to the Institution Narrative (and O'Loughlin considers the *Didache* to be of prime importance: 90–91), we cannot conclusively claim that there was such a thing as a Eucharistic liturgy that was ordinarily devoid of any reference to it. It is better to say, (as O' Loughlin himself does: 158) that forms were not fixed. Extempore prayers were still common.

31. E.g., by Cyril of Jerusalem: Barrington Bates, "The Holy Eucharist in the Early Church: Material for a Small-Group Discussion, an Adult Forum, or a Reading Course," 404.

32. The language of "sacrifice" when referring to the Eucharist is all over his *Letter to Caecilius, on the Sacrament of the Cup of the Lord* (dated to AD 253) where his intention seems to be the clearest at 14: ". . . that priest truly discharges the office of Christ, who imitates that which Christ did; and he then offers a true and full sacrifice in the Church to God the Father, when he proceeds to offer it according to what he sees Christ Himself to have offered." *Ante-Nicene Christian Library*, 218.

of the Lord: "For them [the Fathers] it is natural to think of the symbol as in some way embodying the reality which it expresses. . . . This makes it natural for them to speak in strongly realistic terms of the outward sacramental forms."[33] Some have claimed that transubstantiation can be traced back at least as far as Tertullian and his references to the Eucharist as "*oblatio*" and "*sacrificium*."[34] However, the notion that the elements were being offered in the manner of a sacrifice upon the altar does not emerge until later.[35] The Old Testament book of Malachi was sometimes invoked for its references to offering a perfect offering, yet this is not to be misunderstood. The offering was initially a sacrifice of human praise to God, not the offering of the elements.

Interestingly, although Cyprian seems to have brought Eucharistic practice closer to transubstantiation, a move that would later result in the Mass becoming more and more of a miraculous spectacle or drama, there is yet in Cyprian a strong participative element. It comes out in his explanation about using wine as well as water:

> For because Christ bore us all, in that He also bore our sins, we see that in the water is understood the people, but in the wine is showed the blood of Christ . . . , therefore, in consecrating the cup of the Lord, water alone cannot be offered, even as wine alone cannot be offered. For if any one offer wine only, the blood of Christ is dissociated from us; but if the water be alone, the people are dissociated from Christ; but when both are mingled, and are joined with one another by a close union, there is completed a spiritual and heavenly sacrament.[36]

Similarly, in the fourth century Julius Firmiens Maternus would say this: "We drink the immortal Blood of Christ and Christ's blood is united with our own. It is the salutary remedy against your crimes, a remedy which daily keeps the deadly poison from the tainted people of God."[37]

Also on the participative theme we have Hilary of Poitiers (300–368), reflecting on John 6:55–56: ". . . according to the statement of the Lord

---

33. Wiles, *The Christian Fathers*, 110.

34. Rohling, *The Blood of Christ in Christian Latin Literature before the Year 1000: A Dissertation*, 8.

35. So Kilmartin, "Sacrificium Laudis," 268–87.

36. *Letter to Caecilus*, 13.

37. Maternus, *The Error of the Pagan Religions*, 91.

Himself as well as our faith, this is indeed flesh and blood. And these things that we receive bring it about that we are in Christ and Christ is in us."[38]

A further interesting observation concerning what was understood to happen spiritually during the Eucharist is the difference between the Eastern and Western churches concerning which aspect of the rite is the thing that consecrates the elements. In the West it was firmly believed that the words of institution are what do the consecrating.[39] These words were along the lines of the institution narratives in the Gospels and the invocation of these in 1 Corinthians 11. Initially this repetition would have served a catechetical function: informing or reminding the communicants about what they were doing, but later these words spoken over the elements were understood to themselves be the power that transforms the elements. In the Eastern rites it was understood to be the epiclesis that consecrates. In other words, the consecration is entirely a work of the Holy Spirit coming upon the gifts at the moment of the laying of the priest's hands over them.

Summary

We have seen that there was a variety of Eucharistic practice during the first centuries of the church, all rooted in the banqueting habits of ordinary Mediterranean people, whether Jewish or gentile. Some of these practices remembered the death of Christ, and used bread and wine to do so, many did not. Many Eucharists had a more eschatological flavor, some reversed the order, others were bread only; others still involved bread and water (until forbidden by Cyprian). Over time, the ritual element was separated from the wider feast so that an evening love feast that was a complete meal was replaced by a morning sacrament involving only small portions of the elements.

With this transition from banquet to sacrament there was also, it seems, a shift of emphasis from thanking God the Father to partaking of Christ via the elements. Along with this transition to Christocentrism there

---

38. Hilary of Poitiers, *On the Trinity* 8:14.

39. A teaching which Rohling dated back to an anonymous work of the fifth century, *De Sacramentis libri sex* (Of the Six Books of the Sacraments). The author asks, rhetorically, how the bread can become the body of Christ, to which his answer is by consecration. He further asks whose the words of the consecration are, and answers that they are the words of Christ. The words of the institution narrative, when these are quoted during the Eucharist, were understood to be of an entirely different quality, having the power to "produce the sacrament." Rohling, *Blood of Christ*, 43–44.

was a shift to crucicentrism as the elements of the Eucharist, now isolated from a larger meal, become the sole focus and their consecration the real climax of the service. This crucicentrism becomes more profound with the widespread adoption of transubstantiation. And it is this maximalized awe and veneration of body and blood dispensed by an elite priesthood that becomes such a familiar feature of the medieval church and which places limits on the participative aspect of the Eucharist. And it may be that these developments created a yearning among the faithful for a lost participation in the redemptive suffering and death of Christ, which might in turn go some way towards explaining some of the more baroque devotional practices that developed as time went on.

Other Crucicentrisms

Staurograms

The very earliest evidence we have of Christograms—cryptic symbols of Christian faith—are occurrences of the "*tau-rho*," not, as is commonly assumed, the "*chi-rho*." And the earliest of these are not freestanding symbols but appear rather as symbols in place of the words "cross" (*stauros*) or "crucify" (*stauroō*) in some very early New Testament manuscripts.[40] The *tau-rho* or Staurogram is made from the Greek "*tau*" or T with the Greek "*rho*," which looks like a P. These two Greek letters are made to overlay one another. The result is a cross with what looks like Christ's head—the loop of the "P."

Interestingly, this way of taking two letters from a word and combining them into a symbol is a pre-Christian habit, the *chi-rho* for instance, having already served as an abbreviation for Chronos, the snake-like god of Greek mythology. This weaving together of two letters is known as a ligature.[41] The earliest Christian usage of the *tau-rho* that we know of dates to AD 200, where it appears in P66, part of the Bodmer Papyrus of the Gospel of John. Here, it occurs at references to the crucifixion: "cross" (John 19:19, 25, 31) and "crucify/crucified" (John 19:6, 15–16, 18). In the same collection, P75 has the *tau-rho* at Luke 24:7. A third papyrus, P45 of the Vienna Fragment, dated AD 200–250, has it at Matthew 26:2. Hurtado assumes that the *tau-rho* must predate these occurrences and must already

40. Hurtado, *The Earliest Christian Artifacts*, 135–36.
41. Ibid., 136–39.

have been a regularly used written symbol in order for it to appear in these places and be received and understood by the readers.[42]

Constantine is commonly considered to be the originator of the cross as the central Christian symbol, yet it is clear from this evidence that a crucicentric habit of mind in early Christianity is firmly pre-Constantinian. It is possible that there was some element of isosephy, that is, the study of the numerical value of letters as a way of gaining some spiritual meaning from them. There is evidence, for instance, that the *rho*, which had a numerical value of 100, was sometimes a symbol of good fortune (because the Greek for good fortune—*ep Agatha*—was of the same numerical value), and sometimes of help (because the Greek *boëthia*, help, also adds up to 100). More likely, however, is the simple and obvious fact that it is specifically these two letters, when placed over one another, that give a crucifix: not an empty cross but one upon which is the head of Christ at the top of the *rho*. In effect, this is the very earliest iconography and the very earliest visual depiction of the cross.[43] And it would not be long before these written crosses in manuscripts would become freestanding crosses in all manner of locations.

The purpose, then, of these little icons in the New Testament manuscripts was to make the reader reverently pause to give thanks for Christ upon the cross and not thoughtlessly move on from that place in the text.

Making the Sign of the Cross

Just as the earliest occurrence of the pictorial depiction of a cross, the *tau-rho*, dates back to AD 200, so also the earliest reference we have to the act of crossing oneself, whether over the forehead or over the chest and head, dates back to around the same year. It comes from the pen of Tertullian:

> At every forward step and movement, at every going in and out, when we put on our clothes and shoes, when we bathe, when we sit at table, when we light the lamps, on couch, on seat, in all the ordinary actions of daily life, we trace upon the forehead the sign.[44]

42. Ibid., 142.

43. Ibid., 151–52.

44. Tertullian, *De Corona* (or *On the Military Garland*, or *On the Soldier's Chaplet*) III. Roberts and Donaldson, *Ante-Nicene Christian Library: The Writngs of Qintus Sept. Flor. Tertullianus* 1: 336. This last phrase is often amplified into: "We Christians wear out our foreheads with the sign of the cross," and mistakenly given as though this was another

He is referring here to the sign of the cross in its most ancient form: the tracing of it with the side of the thumb over the forehead. By the sixth century, this small cross had been supplemented by the large cross, which, in the East involved using the left hand to trace the cross from forehead to heart, and then from the right to the left shoulder, while the West used the right hand and carried out the actions across the shoulders in reverse order. The hands were then drawn together. Throughout the actions a simple prayer was said: "In the name of the Father (head), the Son (heart) and the Holy Spirit (shoulders). Amen (hands together). In time the five fingers would become symbolic of the Five Sacred Wounds of Christ: the two hands, the two feet and the side wound.

The significance of making the sign appears to be its power to invoke the victory of the cross. In Anglo-Saxon England, Aelfric of Eynsham (c. 955–c. 1010) was confident that, though "[a] man may wave about wonderfully with his hands without creating any blessing" if he makes the sign of the cross, in this case the large cross, "the fierce fiend will soon be frightened on account of the victorious token."[45] And there was a strong belief that its use in baptism prevented the entrance of the devil, who becomes "speedily much discouraged," when the sign is made.[46]

The Cult of the Martyrs

Wave upon wave of increasingly organized and increasingly lethal persecution against the church was combined with the fact that the faith of the church held the murder of its founder to have a special significance to create a spirituality of martyrdom. Because of Christ's own exhortation to his followers to take up their own crosses and follow him (Matt 16:24; Mark 8:34; Luke 9:23), there was an "evangelical call" to share in the sufferings of Christ.[47] Added to this were the unintended implications of Paul's preference for death over life (Phil 1:23) and his positive view of sufferings in this life (e.g., 2 Cor 6:10). These helped to form what Middleton describes as a "radical martyrdom" movement in early Christianity,[48] something that he very plausibly claims to be an entirely new phenomenon with neither

citation in addition to this one.

45. Aelfric of Eynsham, *The Homilies of the Anglo-Saxon Church*, 1: 462.

46. Stevens, *The Cross*, 29, citing Wulfstan, *Homilies*, 33.

47. Middleton, *Martyrdom: A Guide for the Perplexed*, 57.

48. Middleton, *Radical Martyrdom and Cosmic Conflict in Early Christianity*, 146.

Jewish nor Greco-Roman precedents.[49] Origen (184/185—253/254), like Irenaeus before him, was quite clear that martyrdom was the highest form of spirituality.[50] Origen's *Exhortation to Martyrdom* of AD 235, written during the persecution of Maximinus, rallies the Christians of Alexandria:

> Let us each remember how many times he has been in danger of dying an ordinary death, and let us consider that perhaps we have been preserved so that baptized with our own blood and washed of every sin we may pass our existence with our fellow contestants near the altar in heaven. . . . As sons of a forbearing God, and brothers of a forbearing Christ, let us show "forbearance" in everything that happens to us.[51]

So highly regarded was martyrdom that there were many cases of voluntary martyrdom:[52] Christians who "enthusiastically and willfully courted arrest and death,"[53] a practice condemned by some, though not all. In fact, by the time Eusebius wrote his *Martyrs of Palestine* (not long after 311) at the end of the Great Persecution of Diocletian, it is estimated that as many as two thirds of the martyrs listed had not been sought out by the authorities.[54] Martyrdom was the ultimate moment of participation in the cross of Christ, as well as the ultimate demonstration of hopeful participation in his resurrection. Indeed, the very courage of the martyrs said as much about their certain hope of resurrection as it did about their desire to suffer with Christ in his death. As Middleton so aptly puts it, far from the early Christians having a morbid preoccupation with death, for them, "embracing death was rushing towards life."[55]

A devotional consequence of persecution was the cult of the martyrs, which began in the form of honoring them in their burial places, a practice which Augustine refers to: "It had been my mother's custom in Africa," he tells us, "to take meal-cakes and bread and wine to the shrines of the saints

---

49. Ibid., 123.

50. McGinn, et al. (eds.), *Christian Spirituality I: Origins to the Twelfth Century*, 39.

51. Origen, *Exhortation to Martyrdom* 39; 43.

52. De Ste Croix, "Aspects of the Great Persecution," 75–113 (also in: de Ste Croix, *Christian Persecution, Martyrdom, and Orthodoxy*; Buck, "Voluntary Martyrdom Revisited," 125–35, Middleton, "Early Christian Voluntary Martyrdom: A Statement for the Defence," 556–73.

53. Middleton, "Early Christian Voluntary Martyrdom," 558.

54. de Ste Croix, "Aspects of the Great Persecution," 101–2.

55. Middleton, "Early Christian Voluntary Martyrdom," 560.

on their memorial days."[56] In this practice lay the beginnings of Christian veneration of saints. For a particular city or town to be the custodian of a saint's miracle-working relic was a high honor and there was much rivalry.[57]

Pilgrimages and Stations, Relics and Grails

Pilgrimage and the Stations of the Cross

Before long, the veneration of saints' relics was extended to include New Testament relics and to the belief that these had greater miraculous powers than saints' relics. Despite the urges of some preachers, by the later fourth century, the masses who were flocking to the churches were also heading off on pilgrimage in great numbers to visit the biblical holy places.[58] And it seems clear that by no means all of these pilgrims were the ignorant, unlearned, and superstitious who had set off before anyone had had the chance to catechize them properly.[59] It seems that identifying the sacred with specific localities was a hangover of pagan religion.[60] It was now being transformed into "a process of locating the Christian collective memory."[61]

Yet the plain fact of the matter was that only a minority of people had the means or the leisure to engage in such exploits.[62] As early as the fifth century, architectural replicas of the key stopping places along Jerusalem's Via Dolorosa began to appear.[63] The earliest example appears to be a complex of seven chapels that were built as part of the Church of San Stefano in Bologna, Italy founded by St. Petronius (died AD 450). The intention was to replicate as far as possible the Church of the Holy Sepulchre in Jerusalem. Indeed, this complex, which has been much rebuilt and added to over the

56. Augustine, *Confessions* Book IV.2:2.

57. Stewart, "Christian Spirituality during the Roman Empire (100–600)," in Holder (ed.), *The Blackwell Companion to Christian Spirituality*, 84. See also 83.

58. Gonzalez, *The Story of Christianity Vol. 1: The Early Church to the Dawn of the Reformation*, 125–26.

59. Bitton-Ashkelony, *Encountering the Sacred*, 2–3. She helpfully reviews the literature here.

60. Ibid., 26, and her excellent preceding discussion of possible Jewish precedents.

61. Ibid., 29, following Halwachs, *La Topographie Légendaire des Evangile en Terre Sainte*.

62. Thurstan, *The Stations of the Cross*, 2.

63. Storme, *The Way of the Cross*; Murphy-O'Connor, "Tracing the Via Dolorosa," in Murphy-O'Connor (ed.), *Keys to Jerusalem*, 107–17.

centuries, is referred to as the Nuova Gerusalemme, the New Jerusalem.[64] The modern fourteen stations,[65] all expressed in miniature reliefs, seems to have developed only gradually,[66] while the principle of going on pilgrimage without travelling far has its origins in these early centuries.

The spiritual drives that propagated devotion to the Stations of the Cross are revealed in the most popular liturgical formulas that have been used to aid the worshipper passing from one station to the next. While private devotion to the stations, with or without set prayers and meditations, has always been common, two devotional texts for public worship emerged as especially important.[67] One was the medieval *Stabat Mater Dolorosa*, which came to be useful as something to sing while making one's way from one station to the next, and the other was the eighteenth-century meditations of St. Alphomsus Liguori. Both arise from the Franciscan tradition. Here is an extract first from Edward Caswall's translation of *Stabat Mater Dolorosa* ("At the Cross Her Station Keeping"), which displays the style of passion piety that we shall encounter more of in chapter 2:

> Holy Mother! pierce me through,
> in my heart each wound renew
> of my Savior crucified:
> Let me share with thee His pain,
> who for all my sins was slain,
> who for me in torments died.

---

64. Ousterhout, "The Church of Santa Stefano," 311–21.

65. 1. Jesus is condemned to death, 2. Jesus carries his cross, 3. Jesus falls for the first time, 4. Jesus meets his mother, 5. Jesus is helped by Simon of Cyrene, 6. Veronica wipes the face of Jesus, 7. Jesus falls for the second time, 8. Jesus meets the women of Jerusalem, 9. Jesus falls a third time, 10. Jesus is stripped of his clothes, 11. Jesus is nailed to the cross, 12. Jesus dies on the cross, 13. Jesus is taken down from the cross, 14. Jesus is laid in the tomb. Tradition has it that this sequence, though it has evolved considerably over time, was originally based on the path that Christ's mother regularly took as she remembered her son's sufferings. At any rate, the Jerusalem Via Dolorosa was well established by the fourth century, with many pilgrims visiting it: Thurstan, *The Stations of the Cross*

66. The first significant spread of stations came about via the Franciscans owing to their custodianship of the Holy Places during the days of the Crusader Kingdoms. The second impetus came via St. Leonard of Port-Maurice, known as the Preacher of the Way of the Cross, who was said to have built 572 stations, including the one in the Colosseum in Rome. On St. Leonard of Port-Maurice: Bihl, "St. Leonard of Port Maurice," In *The Catholic Encyclopedia* [accessed online 07/01/2016]: http://www.newadvent.org/cathen/09178c.htm.

67. Walsh, "Stations of the Cross," in Bradshaw (ed.), *The New SCM Dictionary of Liturgy and Worship*, 450.

Let me mingle tears with thee,
mourning Him who mourned for me,
all the days that I may live.[68]

For now, we note the very strong note of longing to participate in as authentic a way as possible in the events of history. Emotion takes the place of physical relic or biblical holy place as the medium through which participation is secured.

Liguori maintains the delicate balance between the mournful assuming of responsibility for the crucifixion of Jesus and the grateful acceptance of the salvation it procured:

> My dying Jesus,
> I devoutly kiss the cross on which You would die for love of me.
> I deserve, because of my sins, to die a terrible death;
> but Your death is my hope.
> By the merits of Your death,
> give me the grace to die embracing Your feet and burning with love of You.
> I yield my soul into Your hands.
> I love You with my whole heart.
> I am sorry that I have offended You.
> Never let me offend You again.
> Grant that I may love You always; and then do with me as You will.[69]

St. Helena's Pilgrimage and the True Cross

St. Helena (AD 230–330), mother of Constantine, encouraged the trend in actually visiting the Holy Land with her pilgrimage in AD 326–28. It was a quest to find the True Cross. This trip seems to have been on Constantine's initiative, his interest in the cross having been stimulated so momentously at the Battle of Milvian Bridge, which we will come to shortly. It seems that, at some point in AD 327, Helena, having arrived at Golgotha, ordered the destruction of a Temple of Venus that had been on the site since AD 132.[70]

---

68. Caswell, *Hymns and Poems, Original and Translated*, 76.

69. From the Response at the Twelfth Station: Jesus Dies on the Cross: De Liguori, *The Way of the Cross*. http://www.ecatholic2000.com/liguori/stations/cross.shtml#__RefHeading___Toc362635538 [accessed online 07/01/2016].

70. http://www.holysepulchre.custodia.org/default.asp?id=4072 [accessed online 14/

This had been erected by the victorious Emperor Hadrian during the Second Jewish War.[71] Sure enough, underneath the old temple were found Christ's tomb and three crosses, together with the nails of the crucifixion, plus the *titulum*, the placard that had been above Christ's head, though this was no longer affixed to the cross. All that remained was to decide which cross was the cross of Jesus and which two crosses belonged to the two criminals who were crucified with him. Macarius, the bishop of Jerusalem, was able to assist by means of a test. There was a lady he knew of who was very ill, on the point of death. Once she had died, one of the crosses was brought into contact with her body, accompanied by a prayer. There was no result. Then, another cross was heaved into position: still no sign of life. Finally, the third cross touched her and she was immediately restored to life and ran around with considerably more energy than she had before she fell ill—and probably a lot more energy than the men who had been carrying full-sized crosses to the woman's deathbed all morning.

By AD 335, the elaborate Church of the Holy Sepulcher was inaugurated. And this was just one of a number of churches that Constantine built in an attempt to spread Christianity across the newly conquered Eastern regions of the Empire. Naturally, particular attention was paid to the Holy Land itself with churches erected on every major site. The ageing Helena's role appears to have been mainly supervisory.[72]

The Feast of the Exaltation of the Holy Cross was celebrated on 14 September AD 335 to commemorate the consecration of the Church of the Holy Sepulcher. This was followed by the Feast of the Invention (=discovery) of the True Cross on 3 May. These feasts were widely adopted throughout the Empire and propagated with them the story of Helena's discovery. All this time, a portion of the True Cross remained lodged within the Church of the Holy Sepulcher, with other portions kept in other important cities. Unfortunately, the Holy Sepulcher portion was captured by the Persian king Khosrau in AD 628, but then his not very loyal son assassinated him a year later and returned the piece of wood to the Emperor at Constantinople: Heraclius II. He, in turn, returned it to Jerusalem. But there was soon an alarming proliferation of splinters. They multiplied still further following

---

12/2015].

71. This version of events is based on the oldest account, though there are as many as seven: Drijvers, *Helena Augusta*, 79. Eusebius' account of the founding of the Church of the Holy Sepulcher does not include the legend at all, other accounts include it but do not associate the discovery with Helena.

72. Drijvers, *Helena Augusta*, 65.

the sacking of Constantinople by crusaders from the West in 1204. The city was seemingly a treasure trove of splinters, each finely decorated and bejeweled, greatly adding to the dissemination of this type of relic all over Europe. John Calvin would famously remark that, if all the splinters of the True Cross were gathered together, they would be "a whole ship's cargo."[73] This remark has gradually transmuted into the more common form that if they were all gathered together, one could build a battle ship from them: equally true.

Besides the Exaltation and Invention festivals, the apocryphal but very widely read *Gospel of Nicodemus* (with the *Acts of Pilate* as an appendix in the Latin version), probably originating in the fourth century,[74] seems to also play a large part in the formation of legends surrounding the wood of the cross. It is from this that the name of the lance-bearer who pierced Jesus is discovered to be Longinus and that of the two criminals crucified with Christ to be Dimas and Gestas. A Latin version also contains the earliest version of the Veronica legend. Crucially for the splinters-of-the-cross tradition, the *Gospel of Nicodemus* became the basis of a lengthy story in wide circulation by the Middle Ages, which was part of the enormously popular *Golden Legend* compiled by Archbishop Jacobus de Voragine.[75] The story of St. George and the dragon is one of many hagiographical gems that have their origin in this collection. Within volume 1 is a story about how the wood of the cross originated as a twig from the Tree of the Knowledge of Good and Evil which ended up being planted in Jerusalem where it grew into a tree that was cut for Solomon's temple. However, it proved too ill-fitting to be useful so was discarded in the Kidron Valley, where it lodged itself as a foot bridge. The Queen of Sheba refused to walk on it predicting that one day it would cause the end of the special covenant of God with the Jewish people. In response to this it was thrown into the pool of Bethesda to which it gave the healing powers evinced in John's Gospel. Finally, when Christ was on trial, it handily floated to the surface and was used for the upright of Christ's cross.

So what are we to make of these legends? Thiede and D'Ancona's exasperation with "the (astonishingly rigid) view that the entire Helena

---

73. Calvin, *A Treatise on Relics*, 173.

74. Reid, "Acta Pilati," *The Catholic Encyclopedia* 1. [Accessed online 21/03/2016] http://www.newadvent.org/cathen/01111b.htm

75. De Voragine, *The Golden Legend, Volume I: Readings on the Saints*.

legend is, by definition, nonsense,"[76] and the "pathological skepticism"[77] of the scholarly world towards the legend is well placed if the legend is true. Scholars seem to be either non-committal or negative about the historicity of it.[78] However, Thiede and D'Ancona's sensational journalism does not seem to have done much to support the historicity. It seems to me highly unlikely that there would be any earthly trace whatever of the earthly life of a Jewish rabbi who, at the time of his ignominious death, had but a handful of followers, all of whom would have been too distraught to think of preserving bits of his life and death for a Christian relic fetish that was yet to exist. Besides, the pursuit and preservation of relics surrounding the death of a man who came to destroy death and bring life seems to be a colossal exercise in missing the point. However, the important thing for our purposes is to situate the True Cross tradition alongside other traditions that were seeking to achieve similar things, and then to attempt to define just what it is, in terms of folk atonement theology, these traditions were trying to achieve for the devout. Such a task will be attempted at the end of this chapter. For now, we will continue our odyssey.

Blood, Grail, and Shroud

As early as AD 649,[79] a blood relic[80] tradition emerged, with vials of sacred blood being discovered at fairly regular intervals from then on, especially during the Carolingian era.[81] Following the First Crusade a large number of blood relics found their way to Germany, and one found its way to Westminster where it became important in bolstering Henry III's claim over against the French Louis IX (who only had a piece of the cross).[82]

Grail legends are mostly unrelated to the blood relic tradition and have their roots in Arthurian legend. However, there is a link between the

76. Thiede and D'Ancona, *The Quest for the True Cross*, 3. Parenthesis original.

77. Ibid.

78 Borgehammar, *How the Holy Cross Was Found: From Event to Medieval Legend*; Borgehammar, "Heraclius Learns Humility," 145–201; Drijvers, *Helena Augusta*; Pohlsander, *Helena: Empress and Saint*; van Tongeren, *Exaltation of the Cross*; Harbus, *Helena of Britain in Medieval Legend*; Baert, *A Heritage of Holy Wood*.

79. Bynum, "The Blood of Christ in the Later Middle Ages," 692.

80. Rubin, *Corpus Christi*, 164–212. Also: Beckwith, *Christ's Body*, 33–37; Devlin, "Corpus Christi."

81. Bynum, "Blood of Christ in the Later Middle Ages," 692–93.

82. Ibid., 693.

Blood of Hales (located in Hales Abbey, Gloucestershire) and the Grail, there being an almost identical story surrounding their origin.[83] Though the figure of Arthur is sixth or seventh century and set in the conflicts between Celts and Anglo-Saxons, the literary history of the quests for the Holy Grail does not begin until Chrétien de Troyes' *Perceval* of 1190.[84] And even then, the Grail itself does not yet begin to play the central part in the story. Following *Perceval,* which was an unfinished work, there were numerous re-workings and a surge in the popularity of the Arthur legend throughout the Middle Ages. By the fourteenth century, King Edward III was portraying himself as the new Arthur.[85] There was a second surge of interest in the nineteenth century, and today, it is the inspiration behind countless Hollywood productions.[86]

The process by which the Grail itself takes on a more central place in the narratives culminates in the thirteenth century with Robert de Boron's use of the *Gospel of Nicodemus* and, within that, the *Acts of Pilate,* which we encountered a few moments ago in connection with the True Cross. The *Acts of Pilate* mentions Joseph of Arimathea being imprisoned by the Jews after he had gone to Pilate to request the body of Jesus.[87] This story is then developed by de Boron into a tale in which Joseph, just before being imprisoned by the Jews, obtains from Pilate not only the body of Jesus for burial but also the cup used in the Last Supper.[88] Pilate specifically asks Joseph to use it to collect some of the blood of the crucified Christ. This explains the many medieval paintings in which Joseph is portrayed holding a chalice near to the dead Christ on the cross collecting a spout of blood from Christ's side wound. In this version of events, Joseph, once imprisoned, is visited by Christ himself who explains the meaning of the Grail.[89] The story of how, in the literature, this Grail then finds its way into a hard-to-find

83. Braswell, "The Search for the Holy Grail," 476. It is mocked in Chaucer, *Canterbury Tales* 6: 955.

84. Juliette Wood, President of the Folklore Society, gives the complete history: "The Holy Grail," 169–90.

85. Braswell, "The Search for the Holy Grail," 469.

86. Wood also lists quite a number of modern novels: Wood, "The Holy Grail," 181. Barber provides a more detailed review of modern Grail-based novels: Barber, *The Holy Grail,* 321–55.

87. *Gospel of Nicodemus* 12:1.

88. Braswell, "The Search for the Holy Grail," 470.

89. Wood, "The Holy Grail," 177.

castle which must be located and is steeped in magical powers took, and continues to take, a dizzying array of different forms.

By far the most famous relic of all time has been the Turin Shroud. Although shroud legends are known from late antiquity, in particular the Mandylion or Edessa image, which is mentioned from the sixth century onwards,[90] the strongest of the shroud legends, the Turin tradition, originated in the fourteenth century. The literature, both academic and popular, is vast and it continues to generate huge media interest, even since the carbon dating exercise of 1988 appeared to show that the shroud originated between 1260 and 1390.[91] It continues to be the "single most studied artifact in human history."[92] Recent popes have been deeply moved when they view it and describe it as an icon,[93] though the scientific and archeological analysis of the shroud seems to be the main way in which people today express their fascination with this relic. The most recent major stir in the real-or-fake debate was that generated in 2009 by paleologist Barbara Frale around an analysis of traces of a supposed death certificate that had become very faintly imprinted near the head. She claimed that the words read:

> In the year 16 [i.e., AD 30–31] of the reign of the Emperor Tiberius Jesus the Nazarene, taken down in the early evening after having been condemned to death by a Roman judge because he was found guilty by a Hebrew authority, is hereby sent for burial with the obligation of being consigned to his family only after one full year.[94]

---

90. Bortin, "Science and the Shroud of Turin," 114–15, referencing Sox, *File on the Shroud*, and Sox "Authenticity of the Turin Shroud," 250–56.

91. Damon et al., "Radiocarbon Dating of the Shroud of Turin," 611–15.

92. Currie, "The Remarkable Metrological History of Radiocarbon Dating [II]," 200.

93. Allen, "Pope Francis and the Shroud of Turin," *National Catholic Reporter* (April 1, 2013): http://ncronline.org/blogs/ncr-today/pope-francis-and-shroud-turin [accessed 21 Dec 2015].

94. First published in *La sindone di Gesù Nazareno*. Her work is available in translation via various popular press articles at the time (e.g., *Times Online*, November 21, 2009), as well as via a translation of her whole work: *The Shroud of Jesus of Nazareth*. Many have queried the way such indistinct and incomplete lettering could reliably point to anything, especially given the suggestiveness of the context: Sheeb and Jordan, "Effects of Contextual Information on Seeing Pareidolic Religious Inscriptions on an Artifact" 1427–30.

Over two million people saw the shroud during its 2015 exposition.[95] The urge to travel great distances to reconnect with the death and resurrection of Christ is clearly an urge that is not restricted to the pilgrims of late antiquity and the Middle Ages. What is more, the evidences gathered over many years from the type of cloth used, the type of stains made upon it (which are clearly not painted or printed on), the biblical and historical plausibility of the type and number of wounds that are evident, the coins or shards that were placed over the eyes, and the traces of pollen discovered lend this relic an unusual credibility, locating its provenance in first-century Palestine. Even the inconsistency with John 20:7 (the separate head cloth as opposed to the single length of shroud at Turin) could possibly be explained by the discovery that a length of fabric had been sewn to the side of the shroud which may originally have been wrapped around the head. The only "but" is the big "but" of the carbon dating carried out in 1988 independently by three leading universities, all of whom agreed a medieval origin. Yet plenty of credible researchers have been willing to contest even this.[96]

The Battle of Milvian Bridge[97]

Notwithstanding the earlier discussion about staurograms, it seems beyond doubt that the Battle of Milvian Bridge was a decisive trigger for the very widespread adoption of the cross as the central symbol of Christianity. Not until this point could the cross have been associated with anything other than shame and scandal and agony, hence its coded and concealed use within New Testament manuscripts. The Christians had reverenced the cross and identified themselves with it as a way of inoculating themselves against the pain of rejection and misunderstanding by the wider society

---

95. http://shroudstory.com/2015/06/26/more-than-2-million-people-saw-the-shroud-in-2015/ [accessed 21 Dec 2015].

96. For example, a study which affirms: "radiocarbon testing cannot deliver a final verdict for science and cannot erase all other data, substantially better supported, from other areas of science." Casabianca, "The Shroud of Turin," 422, and a statistical study which insists that: "The statement of Damon, Donahue, Gore, and eighteen others (1989) that 'The results provide conclusive evidence that the linen of the Shroud of Turin is mediaeval' needs to be reconsidered . . . ." Riani et al., "Regression Analysis with Partially Labelled Regressors," 551–61.

97. For a recent discussion see van Dam, *Remembering Constantine at the Milvian Bridge*. Also: Liftin, "Eusebius on Constantine," 773–92.

and the waves of increasingly vicious persecution from Rome, giving rise to the cult of the martyrs. Now, the cross was potentially transformed in a single stroke from an emblem of noble defeat into a banner of miraculous victory.

The event, which has become enormously famous, took place on 27 October AD 312 on the eve of battle. All that stood between Constantine, already emperor in the far West of the empire, and a reign that would extend to Rome and the central territories were the greater forces of his brother-in-law Maxentius. Reports of exactly what happened on that day differ. Lactantius[98] describes Constantine having a dream in which he is commanded by God to emblazon Staurograms on the shields of his soldiers, while Eusebius[99] describes Constantine marching with his soldiers during the day when he sees a cross above the sun and with it the words: "*En touto nika*," "In this sign conquer." He and his soldiers were amazed by the sight, and to this was added the explanation from Christ himself in a dream that night that he was to use this sign to defeat his enemies. The result was the hasty construction of a military standard in the shape of a cross but with a *chi-rho* on the banner. Eusebius also adds the important detail that Constantine believed himself to be up against magical forces that had been recruited to the aid of Maxentius.[100]

Sure enough, Maxentius' forces were routed with their backs to the Tiber, the Milvian Bridge itself having been put out of action by Maxentius himself as part of an earlier siege preparation. In its place was a makeshift pontoon bridge that promptly collapsed sending Maxentius to his death. Constantine entered Rome victorious.[101] Early the following year came the famous Edict of Milan, drawn up jointly with Licinius who, for now, still ruled in the East. They agreed that "it was right that Christians and all others should have freedom to follow the kind of religion they favoured,"[102] which followed on from the Edict of Toleration of AD 311. By AD 324, with the defeat of Licinius in the East, Constantine was the sole emperor of the

98. Lactantius, *On the Deaths of the Persecutors* 44.5.

99. Eusebius, *Life of Constantine* 28–29.

100. Ibid. 27.

101. See Litfin, "Eusebius on Constantine," 773–92 for a recent attempt by a theologian to harmonize and explain all the differing accounts. He mentions many of the options along the way, as does van Dam, who lists all the modern attempts at explaining away the vision here: van Dam, *Remembering Constantine*, 4.

102. Lactantius, *On the Deaths of the Persecutors*, 48.2–12.

entire Roman Empire, and would soon (AD 330) move his capital there to Byzantium and rename it Constantinople.

The defeat of Maxentius already resulted in an edict that the cross was no longer to be used as a method of execution, and so all previous associations with horror and shame slowly faded away. This was also the point at which the cautious and veiled visual suggestions of *tau-rhos*, *chi-rhos*, anchors, swastikas (a reclaimed Teutonic religious symbol), and lambs holding crosses—cryptic and subtle with a view to avoiding charges of "staurolatry"[103]—slowly gave way to the open representation of crosses in countless ways. Bejeweled and golden crosses for altar and archiepiscopal procession, cruciform foundations for church buildings, stone crosses for the departed, and gestured liturgical crossings were all set to multiply considerably.

This transformation was also, of course, accompanied by the momentous change in the status of Christianity in the Roman Empire owing to what appears to have been something like a conversion on the part of Constantine, who prior to Milvian Bridge had been a Sun worshipper. Today, the terms "Constantinian Christianity" and "Christendom" have become interchangeable in some circles when referring some of the more lamentable ramifications of this moment in the church's history. Whether for the better or for the worse, Van Dam rightly says:

> The Battle of Milvian Bridge, including Constantine's vision, has become a shorthand reference for momentous change in religion, society, and politics. In this perspective, "nothing counts for more than the year 312."[104]

The Cross and Icons

What stone crosses and relics were to the West, icons were to the Greek-influenced image-loving East.[105] Even in the East, however, full-blown Christian art was slow to develop and is virtually non-existent in the Ante-Nicene church. As late as the fourth century, Eusebius could confidently assert that there was no such thing as Christian art.[106] Yet he also reported

---

103. A word I found here and nowhere else: Stevens, *The Cross in the Life and Literature of the Anglo-Saxons*, 7.

104. Van Dam, *Remembering Constantine*, 4.

105. Stevens, *The Cross in the Life and Literature*, 93.

106. Turner, *Imagine*, 24.

the existence at that time of some portraits of Jesus, Peter, and Paul.[107] The Christian use of painted images of Christ, often portrayed as the good shepherd, also began to appear in the catacombs. However, with Constantine on the throne, Christianity could move out from the shadows, exchanging meetings in people's homes before dawn for huge services in basilicas fashioned after municipal buildings. The trappings of pagan and imperial cults were also emulated in an effort not to disappoint pagan worshippers who would naturally expect shrines and images of key people on display in the place of worship.[108]

The earliest known pictorial representation of the crucified Christ is the famous second-century Alexamenos Graffito of Rome, a blasphemous representation of Christ crucified with the head of a donkey.

There is also a small carved carnelian stone held at the British Museum which is fourth century and depicts Christ on a T-shaped cross with the twelve apostles standing in a line behind.[109] The shape of a cross is on the ceiling of the Sts. Peter and Marcellinus catacomb in Rome, which dates to the early fourth century.[110] The earliest *painting* of Christ on a cross dates to AD 586 and is to be found as an illustration in a Syrian manuscript.[111]

107. Forest, "Through Icons," in Begbie (ed.), *Beholding the Glory*, 84.

108. Turner, *Imagine*, 25.

109. See the image online: http://www.britishmuseum.org/research/collection_online/collection_object_details.aspx?objectId=59062andpartId=1.

110. Sergeev, "Crucifixion Painting," 26.

111. Stevens, *The Cross in the Life and Literature*, 20.

One of the earliest crucifixes, that is, one of the earliest three-dimensional crosses with Jesus portrayed upon it, dates to AD 815 and was a present for Pope Leo III from Charlemagne.[112] It is clear that portrayals of Christ crucified are very rare until the seventh century,[113] a fact that is probably accounted for by a lingering revulsion and scandal surrounding this method of execution.[114]

During this period, when Christ is portrayed at all he is marked out by the trappings of royalty and divinity: robed in purple and sporting a halo, and when he is on the cross, these trappings remain with him,[115] as though to prevent the portrayal being misunderstood as an "ordinary

112. Sources on passion depictions in art include: Schiller, *Iconography of Christian Art, Vol. 2*; Brown, *Religious Painting*; Marrow, *Passion Iconography*; Kupfer (ed.), *The Passion Story*.

113. Jensen, "The Suffering and Dead Christ in Early Christian Art," 22.

114. Christians may have had a lingering sense that to portray redemption in the form of a crucified and dead Christ was somehow profane: Jensen, "Suffering and Dead Christ," 23, citing Syndacus, *Early Christian Art*, 103–4 and van der Meer, *Early Christian Art*, 120–22. Also: Gough, *The Origins of Christian Art*, 18.

115. Sergeev, "Crucifixion Painting," 26–27.

human death."[116] Not until the Eastern iconoclast-iconodule controversy would there be a theological impetus for images of a crucified Christ.[117]

While in the Western tradition we can speak of "iconographies" of the passion in the art historical sense (i.e., as a recurring theme in Christian art that always has the same basic features, varying little from artist to artist), in the East, we use the terms "icon" and "icon-veneration" to describe a phenomenon that was and is of the utmost importance to Orthodox spirituality. The biblical premise for the use of icons, as the decades-long iconodule-iconoclast controversy (726–87, and 814–43) worked out, was the incarnation: if Christ used matter to become visible and tangible then we too may use matter to make him seen. More specifically, John 1:14 and Colossians 1:15 were adduced. The one presents Christ as *Logos*, Word, the other as *eikon*, image, hence, "we meet him not only with our ears but also with our eyes."[118] Indeed, during the controversy, it tended to be the opponents (the iconoclasts) who struggled to accept that Christ was fully God *and* fully human. They believed that his humanity was so subsumed into his divinity that to make an icon was to make an idol.[119]

The key iconodule argument was won (by John of Damascus) by reference to a more properly Nicene doctrine of the incarnation. In the end, icons were not only permitted but insisted on as the right way to engage ordinary worshippers with this incarnational truth. The Old Testament prohibition on making graven images did not avail here since an icon is not a merely human making visible: God has already made himself visible, and an icon merely represents and celebrates that. And the same God that gave Moses the commandment prohibiting the making of images also gave him detailed instructions about the image-making that was to go into

---

116. Jensen, "Suffering and Dead Christ," 24.

117. Ibid., 24. And preceding this was the Council of Trullo of 692, called by the Eastern Emperor Justinian II. Canon 82 decreed the following: "In order therefore that that which is perfect may be delineated to the eyes of all, at least in coloured expression, we decree that the figure in human form of the Lamb who takes away the sin of the world, Christ our God, be henceforth exhibited in images, instead of the ancient lamb, so that all may understand by means of it the depths of the humiliation of the Word of God, and that we may recall to our memory his conversation in the flesh, his passion and salutary death, and his redemption which was wrought for the whole world." http://www. newadvent.org/fathers/3814.htm [accessed online 26/01/2016]. This further helps establish the theological reasons for what would, centuries later, come to dominate Christian art: portrayals of the crucifixion.

118. Forest, "Through Icons," 84.

119. Brand and Chaplin, *Art and Soul*, 84.

the tabernacle furnishings.[120] Further, the icon user is not guilty of idolatry since through the icon he or she contemplates and hence worships God and does not expect that the icon will do anything more than provide a window into the divine. This is far from the polytheistic practice of praying to blocks of wood for protection or provision. Hence the Seventh Ecumenical Council ruled that "each time, while gazing upon them, we are made to remember the prototypes, we grow to love them more . . . the honour rendered to the image goes to its prototype, and the person who venerates an icon venerates the person represented."[121]

The icon "completes the liturgy and explains it, adding its influence on the souls of the faithful."[122] Iconographers see art as the "mirror of God" to the point where, for art to deviate from its iconic sacred function is for it to take a "sterile path."[123] The icon was left unsigned by the artists and was "totally submitted to its religious function,"[124] and its painter a mere channel or medium of divine communication,[125] whose job it was to reveal the image already there, building it up from a gold base until it appeared.[126] Icon painting was and is seen as a profoundly spiritual act,[127] requiring a soul that is cleansed. The painter's work would then be, it is hoped, as Spirit-inspired as any great sermon,[128] and part of the function of icons, as in Western church art, involved reaching out to the illiterate.[129]

It is this attachment to a very visual form of faith that is part and parcel of Byzantine spirituality's love of "beauty and celebration."[130] However, it is this very love that naturally draws it to celebrate Easter Sunday rather than dwelling very long on Good Friday. Yet, the iconodules also felt a theological urgency about portraying the real humanity of Christ. The result is a twofold tradition. On the one hand, there is the tradition of the *Christus Triumphans*, the image of Christ on the cross, but with eyes wide

---

120. Brand and Chaplin, *Art and Soul*, 79.

121. Cited in Forest, "Through Icons," 90.

122. Andreopoulos, *Art as Theology*, 21.

123. Ibid., 19.

124. Ibid., *Art as Theology*, 20.

125. Ibid., 22.

126. Williams, *Lost Icons*, 2.

127. Andreopoulos, *Art as Theology*, 23.

128. Ibid.

129. St. Nilus of Sinai cited in Andreopoulos, *Art as Theology*, 21.

130. Louth, "'Beauty Will Save the World,'" 76.

open and looking out at the viewer. Two very early examples in the East occur as illustrations in manuscripts of the Psalms: the Chuldov and Pantokrator Psalters of the ninth century which portray the human Christ on the cross and dead and yet looking fresh as a daisy.[131]

On the other hand was the *Christus Patiens* tradition, in all of its minor variations, which would later be influential on the West in the wake of the emergence of the Franciscans in the thirteenth century. It is this tradition that gives us a dead Christ with, on one side of the cross, the apostle John expressing grief with his right hand on his head and, on the other side of the cross, the Virgin Mary gesturing towards her Son and his saving work. It would be the medieval West that developed this tradition to its fullest extent, transforming crucifixion scenes into portrayals of an "actual event," as opposed to an "amplified symbol."[132]

---

131. See Chase, "A Note on the Theological Origins of the Iconography of the Dead Christ," 58–64.

132. Brown, *Religious Painting*, 8.

Anglo-Saxon Developments

Having already looked at the Byzantine iconographical developments in devotion to the crucified Christ, it remains to give due space to Anglo-Saxon spirituality. This was the spirituality that developed among the Germanic peoples who invaded Britain following the withdrawal of the Romans from there in AD 410. As far as Christianity is concerned, the story really begins with their conversion, which followed the arrival of Augustine of Canterbury in 597. The Anglo-Saxon era does not really come to an end until the Norman invasion of 1066. Throughout this time the Anglo-Saxons continued an uneasy coexistence with the natives of Britain, the Celts, who had continued practicing a form of Christianity received during the Roman occupation. There were occasional battles with the "Welsh," a Celtic people who were by no means limited to Wales.

The Battle of Milvian Bridge appears to have made a very deep impression upon the Anglo-Saxons. Indeed, according Bede (c. 672–735), one of their own victories over the Welsh happened in a very similar way, this time involving King Oswald and his victory over Cadwallen at Heavenfield in 633 or 644, in Northumbria. Oswald erected a cross and commanded his soldiers to bow to it. This procured a decisive victory and, following this, he had a church with a cruciform layout built on the site. This layout for churches only later become the standard and was relatively uncommon at so early a date.[133] From this time onwards, the Anglo-Saxon view of the cross as a banner of victory, or victory-token, seems to have become firmly embedded. Indeed it became, "almost a national emblem."[134]

The Anglo-Saxons shared with the Celts a strong attachment to the cross as a physical symbol. In particular, they seem to have learned from the Celts the habit of erecting huge stone crosses in commemoration of fallen chieftains.[135] The famous interlacing designs originated in Ireland, as did most of the artwork of the Anglo-Saxons. The use of the cross as a headstone for every Christian burial place also originated in Ireland and, in England, only partially replaced the simple rectangular slab.

Altar crosses were also common, but the one thing that they all had in common was the absence of a dead Jesus. Crosses were always either empty or held a living and reigning Christ with his head up and crowned with a diadem, looking, as with the Byzantine portrayals, perfectly happy to be there.[136]

Passion Poetry

It is as we look at the poetry of the Anglo-Saxons, however, that we can see that devotion to the cross took deeper root among them and at an earlier point than any of the other peoples of fledgling Europe.[137] Easily the most outstanding piece of Anglo-Saxon poetry, bar none, is the late Anglo-Saxon,[138] anonymous (and originally untitled), *The Dream of the Rood.*

---

133. Stevens, *The Cross in the Life and Literature*, 16.

134. Ibid., 83.

135. Ibid., 39.

136. Ibid., 18.

137. So ibid., 77–78, and Huelin, *The Cross in English Life and Devotion*, 19.

138. The date is uncertain, though it would have to be before 1100 when Old English transitioned to Middle English. McPherson also believes that the poem must predate Anselm's *Cur Deus Homo* and its "confining logic." McPherson, "Spiritual Combat," 167. However, Anselm's satisfaction theory was probably not widely known until the early thirteenth century, in which case this is not relevant.

It is outstanding in its subtle and terse use of language, its dignified and
deliberate pace, and its emotional restraint. Everywhere, even in its most
triumphal moments, there is the melancholy[139] so typical of the period:

> Hark! Of a matchless vision would I speak,
> Which once I dreamed at midnight when mankind
> At rest were dwelling. Then methought I saw
> A wondrous cross extending up on high,
> With light encircled, tree of trees most bright.
> That beacon all was overlaid with gold;
> And near the earth stood precious stones ablaze,
> While five more sparked on the shoulder-beam.
>
> No cross was that of wickedness and shame,
> But holy spirits, men on earth, and all
> The glorious creation on it gazed.
> Sublime the tree victorious . . . .
>
> A long time lying there I sadly looked
> Upon the Saviour's cross, until I heard
> Resounding there a voice. That wood divine
> Then spake . . . .
>
> I beheld the Master of mankind
> Approach with lordly courage as if He
> Would mount upon me, and I dared not bow
> Nor break, opposing the command of God,
> Although I saw earth tremble; all my foes
> I might have beaten down, yet I stood fast.
> Then the young Hero laid his garments by,
> He that was God Almighty, strong and brave;
> And boldly in the sight of all He mounted
> The lofty cross, for he would free mankind.
> Then, as the Man divine clasped me, I shook;
> Yet dared I not bow to the earth nor fall
> Upon the ground, but I must needs stand fast.
> A cross upraised I lifted a great King,
> Lifted the Lord of heaven; and dared not bow.
> They pierced me with dark nails, and visible
> Upon me still are scars, wide wounds of malice,
> Yet might I injure none among them all.
> They mocked us both together; then was I
> All wet with his blood, which streamed from this man's side

139. Quennell, *A History of English Literature*, 12.

When he at length had breath the spirit out . . . .

Now mayest thou know, O hero mine, beloved!
Unutterable sorrows I endured,
Base felons' work. But now hath come the time
When, far and wide, men on earth, and all
The glorious universe doth honor me,
And to this beacon bow themselves in prayer.
On me a while suffered the Son of God;
Therefore now full of majesty I tower
High under heaven; and I have power to heal
All those who do me reverence.[140]

This poem, though set against the familiar story of the discovery of the
True Cross and its bejeweled fate as an honored and venerated object in the
Church of the Holy Sepulcher (which is where the poem begins and ends),
jolts the reader out of their familiarity by placing the cross at the center of
an inversion.[141] It uses paradox to create a metaphor from a symbol. The
power of any metaphor lies in its ability to powerfully bring into relationship two things that are otherwise characterized by their dissonance, one
from the other.[142] Paul Ricoeur describes such a "kinship" as "a calculated
error," yet it is in this very "error" that "metaphor discloses a relationship
of meaning hitherto unnoticed."[143] A good metaphor thus has a revelatory
feel; it says something new about life,[144] and *The Dream of the Rood* is a
particularly brilliant example of the paradoxical bringing together of two
disparate things: defeat, suffering, shame, and death on the one hand; victory, glory, honor, and life on the other. The poem ushers us into a new
world in which the first pole of the paradox: shame and death has become
the necessary pathway to the new order of triumph over death.[145] The poem

---

140. This translation from Stevens, *The Cross in the Life and Literature*, 71–72. A very
extensive literature on this poem exists, which is reviewed here: Mize, "The Mental Container and the Cross of Christ," 131–35.

141. Jones "The Metaphor That Will Not Perish," 63. Anglo-Saxon readers would
have had no difficulty recognizing the allusions to the Invention of the Cross legend. In
some towns the story of St. Helena's discovery was re-enacted every year: Bennett, *Poetry
of the Passion*, 2.

142. Jones, "The Metaphor That Will Not Perish," 63.

143. Ricoeur, "The Metaphorical Process," 78–79.

144. Ibid., 80.

145. Jones, "The Metaphor That Will Not Perish," 71.

lifts the cross from any possibility of domestication or sentimentalization[146] as the bold Germanic-style warrior, stripped for battle, ascends an instrument of execution to save humankind. Despite the shame of the cross, the warrior is "all courage and command."[147] Even as the corpse is taken down, the Warrior is not portrayed as defeated, but as battle weary: "They laid the limb-weary one down, they stood at his head; they looked on heaven's Lord, as he rested there a while, spent by struggle."[148] Underlying the poem there is also the paradox of all paradoxes for the Christian faith: the God who is totally God and yet who is also more fully human than anyone: the great Chalcedonian conundrum. The writer plays freely and movingly with the fact that it is "God Almighty" who is the warrior mounting the cross: "Creator and created are one."[149] This oneness is represented by the fact that the Savior's sufferings become the cross's sufferings. In fact, the cross bears a greater burden of pain in the poem. We find ourselves immersed in the central Christian mystery of the incarnation.

The paradoxical qualities of the poem probably owe their influence to the Anglo-Saxon tradition of telling riddles. McPherson demonstrates this relationship by summarizing the content of the poem in the form of a riddle: "I am the most precious object in the world; I am the most shameful instrument ever made. Who am I?"[150]

Besides this particular poem there are a couple of other significant examples of Anglo-Saxon precursors of medieval piety, which Fulton emphasizes as crucial to understanding what would soon transpire. The first is an example of the early expectation that the Lord would return in the sky but would return as the crucified Lord still on the cross:

> There shall sin-stained men with woe of heart for their lot behold the greatest of sorrows. Nor shall it bring them grace that there, present before all peoples, standeth the cross of our Lord, brightest of beacons, with the blood of the King of heaven bedewed, drenched with His pure blood. And it shineth resplendent over the wide creation. Shadows shall be dispelled where the radiant tree casteth its light on men. Yet shall it become an affliction, a woe unto the nations, unto all such as working iniquity knew no

146. McPherson, "Spiritual Combat," 166.

147. Ibid., 172.

148. Translation from McPherson, "Spiritual Combat," 174.

149. Bennett, *Poetry of the Passion*, 3.

150. McPherson, "Spiritual Combat," 170.

thanks to God, for that He was hung upon the holy tree for the sins of men.[151]

The other example gives us a window into the growing use of drama which would one day blossom into the passion play. Anglo-Saxons, it seems, had their own additional cross feast: the ceremony of the Adoration of the Cross, which took place on Good Friday every year. Following the ceremony of the Adoration of the Cross was an additional, optional ritual that offers a fascinating window into the theatrics of ritual, which I reproduce here almost in full:

> [A]n image of a sepulcher was made on a vacant side of the altar, and a rail drawn around it, where the cross was laid until it should have been worshipped. . . . The deacon's bearers wrapping it in the places where it had been worshipped, i.e., kissed, brought it back to the tomb, singing certain psalms, and there laid it with more psalmody. There it was watched till the night of Easter Sunday, by two, three, or four monks singing psalms. On Easter Day, the seven canonical hours were to be sung in the manner of the canons; and in the night, before matins, the sacrists, because our Lord rested in the tomb, were to put the cross in its place. Then during a religious service four monks robed themselves, one of them in an alb, as if he had somewhat to do, came stealingly to the tomb, and there, holding a palm branch, sat still till the responsory was ended; then three others, carrying censers in their hands, came up to him, step by step, as if looking for something. As soon as he saw them approach, he began singing in a soft voice, "Whom seek ye?" to which was replied by the three others in chorus, "Jesus of Nazareth." This was answered by the other, "He is not here, he is risen," at which words the three last, turning to the choir cried "Alleluia, the Lord is risen." Then other men, as if calling them back, sang, "Come and see the place," and then rising, raised the cloth, showed them the place without the cross, and the linen cloths in which it was wrapped. Upon this they laid down their censers, took the cloths, extended them to show that the Lord was risen, and singing an anthem, placed them upon the altar.[152]

---

151. Cynewulf, *The Christ* II.1080–93.

152. Stevens, *The Cross in the Life and Literature*, 24, citing Fosbroke's translation of the *Regularis Concordia Monachorum*, attributed to Ethelwold.

Making Sense of the Data:
Sign, Symbol, and Metaphor

To begin with, we need to clarify what the materials are that we have been looking at in our survey of First Millennium crucifixion piety. I will be looking at the data through a lens that, as a former artist, is familiar to me: art, and in relation to that, the discipline of semiotics. Because such a lot of the crucicentric devotion we have seen utilized the arts for its expression, this seems an especially relevant lens to use.

I will organize my thoughts around a discussion of sign, symbol, and metaphor.

Sign

Ferdinand de Saussure showed that there are always three things that make a sign function: the *signifier* (the physical gesture, object, or vocalization itself), the *signified* (the thing that this physical thing or action is standing in for), and the *signification*, which is the effect that takes place when the viewer, audience, or hearer is able to relate the two together.[153] Because a sign stands in for the thing signified there need not be any obvious resemblance between the two. An obvious example of this is words. The fact that different languages tend to have entirely different sounds that signify "tree," for instance, is a case in point. Signs can accrue an almost arbitrary feel about them, so embedded within custom that we never even think about them, and they in turn lack the power to make us think. We do not pause in front of a "no entry" sign, ponder its symmetrical form and prohibitive content and then look at our own life with new eyes.

Some signs have always been signs while other signs actually started out with far richer content having once been attributed to them. A sign might be what we end up with when a metaphor has become so over-used it becomes a commonly accepted symbol, and then the commonly accepted symbol becomes so universal that it is part of the grammar of a culture, it has the immediacy of a language. However, even with a mere sign, sometimes all that is needed is a change of context and a new metaphorical richness can occur. A person running towards an open door is a fire exit sign in one context, the opening scene of a great novel or a great play in another: it has become a full-blown metaphor. A cross hanging from the wall of a

153. Sebeok, *Signs*, 5–6.

church is a piece of furniture in one context, the subject of the most wonderful piece of Anglo-Saxon poetry in another.

Symbol

The classic example of a symbol, as opposed to a sign, is a national flag. It is more than a sign because, for the people of that country it evokes a whole host of inexpressible feelings and shared history. The viewer participates in it. Begbie explains:

> as we look at the flag, we are picked up by the symbol, we become involved, we participate in it, we surrender ourselves to it—it "carries us away." The flag gathers together our inchoate experiences so that they are *embodied* in the flag.[154]

In order for such a symbol to work there needs to be a shared perspective, a common understanding that is easily evoked by the creator of the symbol. The image-maker is merely tapping into a really big feeling that is already at large. This leads to the first fate that can befall a symbol: it may not even have the privilege of sliding into a tired old sign through over-use. It may simply become indecipherable to the vast majority of people. These days, many Christian symbols: water, wine, bread, the numbers 3, 7, 12, or 40, and the triangle as a symbol of the Trinity, and, of course, the cross, will be decipherable only to some. Symbols, when they lose their power and significance to people and become labored or misunderstood, are basically "dead."[155] Yet Christians have inherited a peculiarly rich fund of symbols. We certainly do not wish to jettison them. Here is Paul Tillich:

> [Christians are] unaware of the numinous power inherent in genuine symbols, words, acts, persons, things. They have replaced the great wealth of symbols appearing in the Christian tradition by rational concepts, moral laws, and subjective emotions.[156]

Symbols often have the advantage over straightforward communication. They can potentially open up for us feelings not accessed by more straightforward verbal means.

---

154. Begbie, *Voicing Creation's Praise*, 236. Italics original. See also Whittle, *Christianity and the Arts*, 7.

155. Whittle, *Christianity and the Arts*, 8.

156. Cited in ibid., 7.

The second danger is that if symbols do retain their success, their very success can become their downfall, like the over-exposure that certain celebrities get: their very humanity ends up submerged beneath an image of them that has been endlessly replicated, simulated, and commodified (remember Warhol's *Marilyn Diptych*?). A successful symbol can lose its power to rouse us and we start merely reading it like a word rather than feeling it like a national flag. The cross can become a mere logo, having nothing more compelling about it than a "no entry" sign. We read it and it says "the religion called Christianity," but nothing more. Yet the root of this symbol is an ancient historical event, recorded in a wonderfully rich document that is full of metaphorical ways of communicating atonement: the New Testament. There is thus always the possibility of renewal, and always the possibility of finding new ways of making it speak with an arresting voice to people to whom it has come to mean nothing at all.

For the people making their way to Jerusalem on pilgrimage to walk the Via Dolorosa or for those who stayed at home and gazed upon icons and stations, the compelling and participative power of the cross as symbol was renewed.

Metaphor

Begbie believes that the one thing that distinguishes art from other forms of communication is that it speaks in metaphors.[157] Its cognitive content, including any theological content, is held in its metaphors.[158] He takes his cue from Janet Soskice's *Metaphor and Religious Language*. Begbie insists that the crucial difference between a symbol and a metaphor is that whereas, in a symbol, it is only the thing signified that is of interest, in a metaphor, both the sign and the thing signified are interesting to us.[159] For example, a flag is a symbol because only the thing signified is relevant, the cloth that makes the sign is nothing to us. By way of contrast, the writer of *The Dream of the Rood* makes the wood itself into the main actor, and then this actor goes on to say some profound things. It is metaphor because it brings sign and signified together in an arresting way. But the metaphor only works when,

157. Begbie, *Voicing Creation's Praise*, 233.

158. Ibid., 234.

159. Ibid., 237. Begbie borrows the language of "tenor" and "vehicle" from Michael Polanyi's philosophy, mainly found in his work jointly authored with Harry Prosch: *Meaning*.

in our imaginations, we are able to join the two together as a total, and perhaps very powerful, experience:[160] the wood supports Almighty God as he achieves redemption for humanity.

Another thing to note about metaphors is that they are "irreducible."[161] They cannot be converted into a bare proposition without incurring an actual loss of content,[162] rather like explaining a joke. Likewise, a poem whose meaning has been explained in prose is a poem that has, to all intents and purposes, lost its meaning.[163] Even the New Testament metaphors of atonement, once they get into the hands of theologians, well, need I say more? Metaphors have a revelatory quality about them, they are not merely another way of putting something. They say something as though for the first time.[164] They can, however, be explained (in some sense) and evaluated for their competence and power, otherwise we would conclude that they had failed to communicate.

What This Means for Crucicentric Piety

In crucifixion piety we see the cross emerging as a powerful symbol of victory in the wake of Milvian Bridge, and then of Heavenfield, but as it becomes over-used in church décor and architecture, and in headstones, it starts to become dead. It had the power, once, to participate in the thing signified: victory over death and hell, and hence it had the power to rally the faithful, to galvanize loyalties too deep for words: like a national flag or anthem. Then it started to become something more like what we would call the logo for Christianity. Yet the devout could not afford to simply allow the symbol to die and become a mere sign, a logo. The ideal thing to do in order to prevent the symbol sliding into a sign is to make it into a metaphor. And this is where Christianity's long and profound relationship with the arts has its true beginning point. The fact that most of these artistic developments belong to the latter half the first millennium lends weight, perhaps, to my suggestion. The cross does not grow tired until then. But at that stage there is the slow proliferation of efforts to renew the symbol in crucifixion iconography and Anglo-Saxon poetry such as the *Dream of*

---

160. Ibid., 237.

161. Ibid., 238, echoing Polanyi.

162. Ibid., 238.

163. Ibid., 249.

164. Soskice, *Metaphor and Religious Language*, 89.

the Rood, which, quite literally, makes the dead symbol come alive again. The goal in all of these efforts was to reconnect the devout with the thing signified: the actual crucifixion and resurrection of the Son of God, so that they could participate in it afresh.

Conclusion

We have now surveyed a number of concentrations of crucicentric piety during the first thousand years of Christianity. We began by looking at the variegated development of Eucharistic practice and its underlying theology. It started as a communal thanking of the Father for Christ's redemption with an increasing participative element: the meal was increasingly about participating in Christ. Then, post-Constantine and with the multiplication of non-communicants, the Mass became a spectacle: congregants were encouraged to look on in awe and fear as the miracle of transubstantiation took place before their eyes. Alongside this, the element of gathering to offer a sacrifice of praise to God the Father for the provision of Christ's redemption receded somewhat in the face of a growing emphasis on offering up of the body and blood of the Lord, echoing the original sacrifice for sin.

We then looked at the gradual and initially cautious introduction of the cross as a visual symbol, the pivot transforming it from veiled and cryptic references to a symbol of victory was the Battle of Milvian Bridge and Constantine's appropriation there of the cross as his means of conquest over the demonic powers that had been summoned to Maxentius' aid. A whole catena of further developments seem to take place as spin-offs from this one crucial about-turn in history and in the fortunes of the church in the Roman Empire. The habit of making the sign of the cross over one's body develops, so that the large cross made across head and shoulders takes over from the small cross traced over the forehead. With the closing of the age of the martyrs, the cult of martyr relics is soon transformed into a quest for New Testament relics, deemed many times more powerful. The relic of all relics was, of course, the True Cross discovered by St. Helena on her pilgrimage to the Holy Land. Her pilgrimage, combined with the growing interest in relics, inspired the pursuit of pilgrimage as a central aspect of Christian faith. The Stations of the Cross arose as a compensation for those not able to make the journey to Jerusalem and pause at the actual stations of the Via Dolorosa. Other means, too, were soon available for those who wished to renew the power of the cross as the central symbol of their faith:

they could enjoy the growing body of poetry devoted to the passion or, more commonly, watch or perhaps take part in a local passion play. Alternatively, they could engage with a growing amount of iconography which sought to portray various scenes from the crucifixion.

So there are here two strands of spirituality, each having their own inbuilt tensions. There is the Eucharistic strand and the staurographical strand. The Eucharistic strand always contained within it the danger inherent in all rituals, that it would generate an overblown veneration and awe that cancels out the true intent of all ritual, which is participative. The purpose of the Eucharist was to live again the moment when the new covenant was inaugurated. The Eucharist was relied on as the ritual that could most powerfully bring into the present the saving events that were rapidly disappearing over the horizon of history. The staurographical strand was the strand that took the cross and made it into a symbol invoking powerful beliefs about what it represented. The danger inherent with this was that, as with all symbols, the cross would, through sheer overuse, become no more than a sign. Efforts were needed to reinvent the symbol by means of the arts: carved stations, painted icons, plays, poems. Through the arts, the cross was re-presented to people, stimulating fresh faith.

Chapter 2

———

PASSION MYSTICISM
IN THE MIDDLE AGES

IT SEEMS CERTAIN THAT extreme crucicentrism in Christian spirituality has its true beginnings in the early Middles Ages within the Western, Catholic tradition. In fact, as we move from the relatively meagre pickings of the early church and the Byzantine era, we are confronted with an explosion of devotion to the crucified Christ. The challenge lies not in trying to find some significant portions of text to interact with but in knowing how to bring some kind of order to a vast mass of material and how to select the most significant pieces from the huge number of very interesting poems, meditations, and autobiographical accounts.

The factors that gave rise to passion mysticism in the medieval world would appear to be a shift of emphasis taking place throughout the medieval and Renaissance periods. This was a shift in popular devotion from a kingly exalted Christ in heaven to a very human Jesus, suffering and dying on a cross.[1] After such emphasis on the divinity of Christ as had been seen in late antiquity, perhaps it was inevitable that the pendulum would eventually swing the other way. The trigger for this swing of the pendulum is somewhat mysterious, though we have clearly seen indications of it in the earlier chapter. The growing misery of ordinary people as the Middle Ages reached their height may also have contributed. Until the first bu-

---

1. Medieval spirituality focused, according to Beckwith, on "Christ the incarnate God, and more specifically Christ both as infant and as crucified, the two moments of birth and death, which insist on the claims of the body most emphatically and obviously." Beckwith, *Christ's Body*, 17.

bonic plague of 1349–51, population growth meant that people began to outstrip the natural resources available to sustain them. There was widespread rural poverty and a massive migration to the cities where sanitation was poor and life expectancies short. Sloyan adds to these things the mostly disastrous crusades of 1095–1396, the Hundred Years War of 1337–1453, and the Schism of 1378–1429 as tragedies that contributed to the fear and apprehension of the era.[2] A suffering human Christ could transfigure the deprivations of churchgoers as they beheld the various pictorial sermons of a Christ who suffered, yet overcame death.

This pendulum swing could also be framed in terms of inwardness versus outwardness. In other words, it was a devout reaction against the outwardness of religious rituals that were losing their meaning: "Holy days became holidays, pilgrimages became travel tours, shrines became scenes of bedlam, churches became social meeting places."[3] The new devotion was an endeavor to correct this.

Another possible trigger was the passing of the year 1033, exactly one millennium since the ascension of Christ, and the disappointment surrounding his failure to return. Ideas of judgment appear to have dominated people's minds as they pondered this delayed Parousia, fostering a renewed ardor among the people who all desired to find mercy in the human Christ and his mother.

The Story of Affective Piety

The term affective piety refers precisely to this remarkable shift in devotional mood that begins to be noticeable from the eleventh century and reaches its height during the fourteenth century. It is a shift that happens on a number of different fronts: it coincides with monastic reform and renewal, it coincides with an apparent shift in the dominant form of mysticism from the disembodied "apophatic" type inspired by Pseudo-Dionysius to a very definitely embodied kind, centered around the imitation of Christ. It coincides with a shift in emphasis from the Old Testament to the New, focusing especially upon the Gospel accounts of the crucifixion of Jesus.[4] It also coincides with a broadening out of radical forms of piety

2. Sloyan, "The Popular Passion Piety of the Catholic West," 18.

3. Van Engen (ed.), *Devotio Moderna*, 27.

4. So pronounced is this shift to the New Testament Gospels that medievalists refer to it as the "evangelical revival." Lynch, *The Medieval Church*, 186–92.

from the monasteries to ordinary people, which goes hand-in-hand with the flowering of Franciscan spirituality. Lastly, there is, during this period, a remarkable flourishing of women's spirituality, with some women, such as Catherine of Siena, rising to considerable prominence. Two common threads run through all of these developments: one is an ever-increasing emphasis, already alluded to, on the humanity of Christ, especially his crucifixion (but also his birth and the empathetic sufferings of the Virgin Mary), and the other is an ever-increasing utilization of the emotions in devotion to the crucified Christ, hence the term "affective." The one, in fact, clearly gives rise to the other. Gone is the austerity of the *via negativa* with its ardent pursuit of union with an ineffable, indescribable divine being incapable of feeling our pain. The new mood is visceral, and the new beatific visions are not of glory but of blood and gore.[5] It is also clear that the new mood is extremely popular and produces a form of piety that was embraced by the common people, not just the cloistered. By the time we get to the fourteenth century the dissemination of this new piety is complete. It is a form of spirituality that gripped very large numbers of people with the intense pursuit of an authentic inwardness of faith.[6]

The main methods of crucicentric affective piety had already been developed via the monastic practice of *lectio divina*, which, for centuries had encouraged the slow meditative reading of Scripture.[7] What we see in the Middle Ages is the concentration of this technique on the Gospel accounts of the crucifixion and its elaboration into emotional outpourings and various speculative flights of fancy.

Though there seems to be no singular trigger for the outpouring of affective piety, there are what we could describe as three differing angles on how (and perhaps why) this sudden outpouring of emotion came about. I will briefly review each of these below, before explaining my particular synthesis. We will then have a framework within which to focus on certain key texts, as well as taking a look at phenomena such as the stigmata, the Corpus Christi processions, and the Five Sacred Wounds cult.

The three angles on the origins and development of affective piety are these:

---

5. Camporesi is insightful here: "We all possess an anatomical, physiological sieve, without which it seems that discourse cannot begin. . . . At the origin of mystical language is a sensual alphabet." Camporesi, *Juice of Life*, 70.

6. Tobin (ed.), *Henry Suso*, 14.

7. So Sloyan, "The Popular Passion Piety of the Catholic West," 13.

The Anselm Thesis

The late Sir Richard Southern was one of the most outstanding medievalists of modern times, with his *The Making of the Middle Ages* of 1953 having now been translated into twenty-seven languages.[8] Being a particular expert on Anselm, he tells the story of affective piety from that standpoint. Not only can Anselm be credited, in his view, with beginning to write in the style of emotional tenderness that would characterize the later writings, for instance in his *Prayers and Meditations*, but Anselm also provides the theological framework that made such devotion to the suffering Christ possible: the satisfaction theory of the atonement.[9] This theory of the atonement is rightly considered by historical theologians as game-changing.[10] In contrast to the prevailing view of the atonement, which was all about a face-off between God and the devil with humanity as the hostage and Christ as the ransom payment, Anselm focused on the God-Man himself and tried to answer, using pure logic, the question, why did God become man? Anselm's answer was that man owed an incalculably huge debt to God, a debt so great that only God himself *could* pay it. Yet only man *should* pay it. The perfect solution then is that someone who is fully human and fully divine should pay by freely offering himself. As a human he can genuinely assume man's obligations and as God, the offering of himself would in fact far outweigh what was owed, leading to a surplus of merit that can be shared with humans. Southern believed that this move successfully freed popular understandings of the cross from the impersonal transaction that it had been and brought into focus the human Jesus paying the ultimate price, and the human beneficiaries who, with overflowing gratitude, partake of the merits of his atoning work.

It seems that both Anselm's devotional style and his atonement theology were shared by Bernard of Clairvaux. Bernard's works, in turn, were immensely popular via his influential position within the Cistercian movement. The figure of St. Francis then emerges whose mendicant movement captures the imaginations of the masses and ensures the continued propagation of this style of spirituality long after his death. "With St. Francis and his followers, the fruits of the experiences of St. Anselm and St. Bernard

8. http://www.theguardian.com/news/2001/feb/08/guardianobituaries.highereducation [accessed online 10/07/2015]

9. He explains this in his "theological digression" in Southern, *The Making of the Middle Ages*, 223–25.

10. For the literature see my *Atonement Theories*, 45–62.

were brought to the market place, and became the common property of the lay and clerical alike."[11]

Perhaps one of the biggest problems with the Anselm thesis is the place Southern accords Anselm's satisfaction theory. Firstly, while the *Meditation on Human Redemption* does evoke devotion to the human Jesus, the *Cur Deus Homo* of 1098 totally abstracts the work of Christ into a logical system. After reading the *Cur Deus Homo* we may be inspired by Anselm's comprehensive logical arrangement but we do not find ourselves at the foot of the cross weeping with the forlorn Virgin Mary. Secondly, Burns has pointed out that the wider dissemination of Anselm's view may not have even begun until the mid-thirteenth century, courtesy of Alexander of Hales,[12] twelfth-century scholarship having seemingly "advanced almost without regard for his proposal."[13] It was included in Peter Lombard's monumental *Sentences,* composed between 1223 and 1227, which achieved textbook status into the following two centuries largely thanks to Alexander of Hales.

The Female Spirituality Thesis

In 1982,[14] Caroline Bynum, though not contradicting the Anselm thesis, was the first to point out how neglected the role of women had been in studies of medieval piety. She was followed by a number of feminist medievalists in pointing out that embodied styles of spirituality seem especially to be associated with women. It was mainly women that manifested such physical phenomena as the stigmata, or example. Feminist medievalists often seem at odds with one another due to the very delicate balancing act that is necessary. On the one hand, they want specifically female contributions to be *retrieved* from male-biased retellings of history; on the other hand, they do not want certain styles of spirituality to be *stereotyped* as feminine. Bynam has worked hard on the retrieval, and McNamer has taken this retrieval further to argue that it was women (not Anselm) who were

11. Southern, *Making of the Middle Ages*, 229. Clarissa Atkinson agrees: "adoration of the sacred humanity . . . was adapted by the Franciscans, who transformed it into a popular passion focused on the details of Christ's birth and death and used it to preach penitence to large numbers of lay as well as religious people." *Mystic and Pilgrim*, 154–55.

12. In his *Summa fratris Alexandri* "the Anselmian theory of satisfaction has been assimilated, its complexities reduced, and many of its exaggerations eliminated." Burns, "The Concept of Satisfaction in Medieval Redemption Theory," 293.

13. Burns, "The Concept of Satisfaction in Medieval Redemption Theory," 285.

14. With her book *Jesus as Mother*.

instrumental right from the start,[15] while Beckwith, Bildhauer, Biddick,[16] Aers,[17] and Hollywood[18] have moved against the stereotyping and "essentializing" that they see as implicit in Bynum's work.

The 1033 Thesis

Again not contradicting the essential contours of Southern's version of events, Rachel Fulton[19] has sought to add two things: one is to emphasize that affective piety did not suddenly arise but had many precursors, especially in Anglo-Saxon spirituality. Many other scholars have also sought to draw our attention to Anglo-Saxon examples of lyric that seem to have much in common with post-Anselmian meditations.[20] Byzantine antecedents are also citable.[21] The other contribution of Fulton is to focus not so much on the literary manifestations of this new mood but upon what might have been its main catalyst. She points out that the passing of the year 1033 more or less coincides with the noticeable shift in the mood. Many people, it seems, had been anticipating the Lord's return on or around that year. His delay was interpreted as ominous of his displeasure, and when he did return it was expected that he would return as the Crucified Christ, in accordance with the prediction of Revelation 1:7, "They will look on him whom they pierced." "To understand the development of the devotion to

15. McNamer, *Affective Meditation and the Invention of Medieval Compassion*. Michelle Karnes points out that she has probably overplayed her hand in some respects: *Imagination, Meditation, and Cognition*, 110–15.

16. Biddick, "Genders, Bodies, Borders," 389–418.

17. Aers, "The Humanity of Christ," in Aers and Staley (eds.), *Powers of the Holy*, 35.

18. Hollywood, *The Soul as Virgin Wife*.

19. Fulton, *From Judgment to Passion*.

20. Most recently, a cluster of three essays written for *Essays in Medieval Studies* Vol 22: Frantzen, "Spirituality and Devotion in the Anglo-Saxon Penitentials," 117–28, de Gregorio, "Affective Spirituality: Theory and Practice in Bede and Alfred the Great," 129–39, Heckman, "Imitatio in Early Medieval Spirituality: The Dream of the Rood, Anselm, and Militant Christology," 141–53. Also: Bennet, *Poetry of the Passion* and Huelin, *The Cross in English Life and Devotion*.

21. Shoemaker even claims that it really starts with Maximus the Confessor's *Life of the Virgin* of the seventh century: Shoemaker, "Mary at the Cross, East and West," 570–606. The content is certainly similar to medieval passion piety: "streams of blood came down from his incorruptible wounds, but fountains of tears came down from your eyes." *Life of the Virgin*, 78, Shoemaker's translation: Shoemaker, "Mary at the Cross, East and West," 580. Shoemaker presents a lengthy and strenuous case.

Christ in his suffering humanity . . . we must first understand what was at stake in that devotion: the placation—and repayment—of the all-powerful, all-seeing crucified Judge."[22]

Where Anselm is pivotal is in the new response to the Crucified Judge that he encouraged. Until Anselm, the response was to try to pay for the sufferings of Christ by attempting to "complete" them. Peter Damian (1007–72) became one of many flagellants who felt so sorry and guilty about the pains that humankind had inflicted upon Christ that they tapped into the martyr tradition and took upon themselves the literal physical sufferings of Christ. Devotional literature was designed to arouse shame:

> I fed you with manna in the desert: you felled me with whippings and blows.
> I gave you the water of health to drink from a rock: you gave me bile and vinegar to drink.
> On account of you I smote the kings of the Canaanites: you smote my head with a reed.
> I gave you a royal scepter: you placed a crown of thorns on my head.
> I exalted you with great strength: you suspended me on the gibbet of the Cross.[23]

Humanity had not only been the instrumental cause of the sufferings that were now being itemized in gory detail, but, in return for God's sacrificial love, humanity had been grossly ungrateful. What Anselm successfully pointed to, especially in his *Prayer to Christ*, was that there was no way of paying humanity's debt to God, a thought later enlarged upon in his *Cur Deus Homo* and then his *Meditation on Human Redemption*. No matter how much one was to weep and suffer with Christ, it could *never* outweigh the extent of the debt. Hence the possibility is opened in Anselm for those contemplating the cross to come through sorrow into a place of joyful gratitude for the one all-sufficient sacrifice there offered.

> [I]t was because he was oppressed, quite possibly as much as Peter Damian, by the fear of answering Christ as he came in judgment that Anselm was able to write the prayer he did, with this difference: Anselm, unlike Peter, had convinced himself that there was,

22. Fulton, *From Judgment to Passion*, 64.

23. Schmidt, *Hebdomada Sancta* 1: 105–6, cited in Fulton, *From Judgment to Passion*, 143.

in fact, no debt to be repaid because there was nothing, not even fear, with which he could pay.[24]

If it had not been for Anselm's redirecting of popular feeling then Piero Camporesi's lurid description of the era would be wholly, rather than partly, true: "the torments of Christ, along with the cult of his body and blood, becomes a collective *passio*—all but an epidemic of morbidity, a murky disease of the soul . . . ."[25]

We will now examine the key works of those repeatedly cited as significant to this period: Anselm, Bernard, Bonaventure, Catherine of Siena, Julian of Norwich, and Margery Kempe. By then we will find ourselves on the eve of the Reformation, but will focus on the Catholic Reformation, in particular the Spanish mystics Teresa of Avila and John of the Cross. At appropriate intervals there will be excursions into the developing paraphernalia of passion-piety.

Beginnings: Anselm's *Prayers and Meditations* and Bernard's *Cantica*

Anselm's *Prayers and Meditations*

Whether we consider Anselm's *Prayers and Meditations* to be the true beginning point for affective piety or not, it seems clear that this work was highly significant in the development of passion mysticism. It was nothing less than "a new kind of poetry," claims Richard Southern, "the poetry of intimate, personal devotion."[26] These nineteen prayers and three meditations spanning much of Anselm's life, represent a "leap" towards "a new era of self-disclosure,"[27] an era in which people had new permission to show their feelings, and are noted for their profound beauty.[28] They were mostly written between around 1070 and 1075 (with the *Prayer to the Holy Cross* added in 1082 and the *Meditation on Redemption* added in 1099, and yet further small additions between 1100 and 1104),[29] and they followed

24. In Fulton, *From Judgment to Passion*, 146.

25. Camporesi, *Juice of Life*, 54.

26. Southern, "Foreword," in Benedicta Ward (tr. and ed.), *The Prayers and Meditations of St. Anselm*, 9.

27. Southern, *Saint Anselm*, 100.

28. Hogg, *Anselm of Canterbury*, 5–8.

29. Southern, *Saint Anselm*, 109–11.

a period of silence in his writings. After their dissemination by Countess Mathilda of Tuscany (an example of the highborn, non-monastic readership he appealed to) they were followed by a rash of imitations. The *Prayers and Meditations* were "a huge success."[30]

Attentiveness to passion themes is evident in the second prayer, the *Prayer to Christ:*

> I am like an orphan deprived of the presence of a very kind father,
> Who, weeping and wailing, does not cease to cling to the dear face
> with his whole heart.
> So, as much as I can, though not as much as I ought,
> I am mindful of your passion,
> Your buffeting, your scourging, your cross, your wounds, how you
> were slain for me,
> How prepared for burial and buried;
> And also I remember your glorious Resurrection,
> And wonderful Ascension.[31]

Beginning to articulate themes that would later, in *Cur Deus Homo*, form the heart of his theology of atonement, he is transfixed by the incarnational condescension of God: "the one insulted," who, "willed to die that the sinner might live."[32] This is "a love marvelous and beyond our grasp."[33] In line with the passion meditation that would become so characteristic of the Middle Ages, he dwells on every detail of the crucifixion: the lance, the nails in the hands and feet of the "Creator,"[34] the blood that poured from his side, the gall he was given to drink, and the empathetic sufferings of the Virgin, the "gentle lady,"[35] who must look upon her Son "bound, beaten and hurt,"[36] "stretched on the cross without guilt,"[37] and "cruelly butchered by wicked men."[38]

In the next stanza, he articulates his wish that he could have been there with Joseph of Arimathea taking his Lord from the cross, wrapping

---

30. Ibid., 91.
31. Ward (ed.), *Prayers and Meditations of St. Anselm*, 95.
32. Ibid., 95.
33. Ibid.
34. Ibid.
35. Ibid.
36. Ibid., 96.
37. Ibid.
38. Ibid.

him and laying him in the tomb. His request is that Christ make it up to him for not having seen his flesh, or kissed the place of his wounds or sprinkled his scars with tears, or said goodbye at his ascension. He does not specify in what way this prayer should be answered before taking up the language of the Song of Songs—another familiar feature of passion mysticism from here on: "What shall I say? What shall I do? Whither shall I go? Where shall I seek him? Where and when shall I find him? Whom shall I ask? Who will tell me of my beloved? 'for I am sick with love.'"[39]

His *Prayer to the Holy Cross* may have been prompted by an event in 1082. A boatload of pilgrims were in danger at sea but Anselm held up the skull of St. Honorine and blessed the pilgrims "in the name of the Holy Cross."[40] Whereas, in his *Prayer to Christ,* where the passion of Christ is used as a stimulus to loving devotion and falls very much within what would later be termed Abelardian or "moral influence," in the *Prayer to the Holy Cross* the emphasis is decidedly salvific rather than mimetic. It is this cross that brings us "back from that eternal death to which our misery was leading us, to the eternal life we had lost by sinning."[41] It is a cross "in whom is our salvation, our life, and resurrection."[42] It is wood "by whom we are saved and set free,"[43] and "by which we are sealed for God."[44] He talks to the cross saying that "he [that is, Christ] chose you"[45] so that "through you he might save sinners from death." A chain of paradoxes explores how his killers chose the wood in order to "kill life," while Christ chose this same wood in order to "destroy death." They chose it so as to "condemn the Saviour;" he chose it so as to "save the condemned." They wanted to "bring death to the living" but he acted to "bring life to the dead."[46]

The patristic themes of Christ as victorious conqueror on the cross persist: "hell is despoiled . . . demons are made afraid and restrained, conquered and trampled underfoot,"[47] but hints of the new atonement paradigm are added: "By you sinful humanity is justified, the condemned are

---

39. Ibid., 97.

40. Southern, *Saint Anselm,* 110.

41. Ward (ed.), *Prayers and Meditations of St. Anselm,* 102.

42. Ibid., 102.

43. Ibid.

44. Ibid.

45. Ibid.

46. Ibid., 103.

47. Ibid.

saved, the servants of sin and hell are set free . . . by you the servitude of hell which I inherited is exchanged for the kingdom of heaven. . . . By you my sins are wiped out, by you my soul is dead to its old life."[48] Because of this he is confident of his future in heaven: "I now expect to rejoice in eternity . . . I am sure that if I give thanks, love, and live to your glory, through you I shall at last come to that good."[49]

And it is these new themes that dominate the last of Anselm's cruci-centric meditations, the *Meditation on Human Redemption*. This contrasts with the very first one, the *Prayer to Christ*, which was of the early 1070s. That had been entirely an appeal to a person's moral ambition spurred by the emotions. The second prayer we looked at, the *Prayer to the Holy Cross*, takes us to the early 1080s. This one shows the presence of themes that would soon make up what we now call the satisfaction theory of the atonement. Though the satisfaction theory was distinct from both the triumphalist approach of the fathers and from the moral influence approach of Abelard, it is clear that the three approaches actually coalesced throughout the Middle Ages to the point where the period has recently been described as having but one theory of the atonement.[50] In *Meditation on Human Redemption* we move to a year after the publication of Anselm's magisterial logical exposition of the satisfaction theory of 1098, the *Cur Deus Homo*. This meditation is a devotional supplement to and summary of the *Cur Deus Homo*. It is suffused with the dialectical writing style typical of his other prayers and meditations, which successfully converts the rationalistic subject matter of *Cur Deus Homo* into something more poetic and emotive. He also roundly refutes the patristic ransom-to-Satan theory perhaps even more directly here than in *Cur Deus Homo*: "Or has the devil," he asks, "in justice anything against either God or man, that God had to act in this secret way for man, rather than openly by strength? . . . But clearly God

---

48. Ibid., 103–4.

49. Ibid., 103.

50. Bynum claims this for at least two of the three: "There are not then two redemption theories (Abelardian and Anselmian) in the Middle Ages but one." Bynum, *Wonderful Blood*, 200. She rejects too the notion that the exemplarist approach dominated popular devotion while the satisfaction approach dominated university theology as these two approaches can easily be shown to interweave throughout, even in the case of Bernard, who explicitly apposed Abelard. All writers made full use of both the objective and subjective elements available to them as they contemplated the cross. Bynum, *Wonderful Blood*, 196–200.

owes nothing to the devil except punishment."[51] He also adds something that he seems to have thought of after writing *Cur Deus Homo*: the horrible thought that the blessings of salvation were so cruelly paid for:

> But, Lord, you gave yourself up to death that I might live; how can I be happy about a freedom which is not wrought without your chains? How can I rejoice in my salvation, which would not be without your sorrows? How can I enjoy a life which meant your death?[52]

His answer seems to be twofold, both related: firstly, we should participate in the sufferings of Christ; then we can freely rejoice in what he has done for us. It is, in other words, a move away from ending up in the position of seeing the cross in purely substitutionary terms towards seeing it in more representative and participatory terms,[53] a move probably informed by his Benedictine training:[54] "I must condemn their cruelty, imitate your death and sufferings, and share them with you . . . ."[55] Secondly, Anselm thinks we should take Christ's sacrifice as a pointer to the debt of love that we owe: "Now, little man, leave their cruelties to the justice of God, and think of what you owe your Saviour. Consider what he was to you, what he did for you, and think that for what he did for you he is the more worthy to be loved."[56]

Bernard's Sermons on the Song of Songs

Of the early popularizers of passion mysticism, Bernard of Clairvaux (1090–1153), the highly influential Cistercian monk, was one of the most significant. Bernard was "more overtly affective in his prose," than those

---

51. Ward (ed.), *Prayers and Meditations of St. Anselm*, 231.

52. Ibid., 235.

53. Indeed, there appears to be something deeply rooted in medieval thought that causes parts always to be seen as wholes and wholes as represented in parts such that a purely substitutionary transaction that does not subsume humanity into it would have been inconceivable. According this mode of thinking, "Christ quite literally incorporates all humankind in his death and resurrection." Bynum, *Wonderful Blood*, 202. See her whole argument in 202–4.

54. Sweet, "'Participating in the Passion of Christ,'" 279: "Life in a cenobitic community is a sharing in the sufferings of Christ."

55. Ward (ed.), *Prayers and Meditations of St. Anselm*, 235.

56. Ibid.

who preceded him, more open about his feelings "in a world that was just beginning to express its feelings openly without shame or embarrassment."[57] His influence extended well beyond medieval Catholicism. He was an important formative influence upon the young Luther.[58] In later years, Bernard's bridal mysticism, inspired by the Song of Songs, would be copied by Luther,[59] Zinzendorf,[60] and the Moravians.[61] Though reined in later on, many of the eighteenth- and early-nineteenth-century hymn writers have been noted for similar erotic content, a precedent that seems to have been set by Isaac Watts' use, again, of the Song of Songs.[62] The "sublimated eroticism" of the worship music produced by the Vineyard movement in more recent times has also been noted,[63] but explicit links with the Song of Songs in Charismatic worship are rare. Undoubtedly, the original precedent for all of this Song-of-Songs-inspired erotic content was set by Bernard.[64]

The reason for Bernard's attraction to the Song of Songs as a vehicle for his most dear convictions is probably the central place that union with Christ takes in his theology.[65] First Corinthians 6:17, which speaks of being one spirit with Christ, is referred to fifty-four times within his *Sermons*

57. Sloyan, "Popular Passion Piety," 16.

58. Bernard's works were apparently read out loud at meal times at the Erfurt friary: Tomlin, *The Power of the Cross*, 131.

59. In his *Freedom of the Christian Man*, he depicts the marriage arranged by the Father between the sinner and Christ as one necessarily involving shared possessions: the Bridegroom's "grace, life, and salvation" become the sinner's, while the sinner's "sin's, death, and damnation" become the Bridegroom's: Westerholm, *Perspectives Old and New on Paul*, 31.

60. E.g., Forwell (ed.), *Zinzendorf, Nine Public Lectures on Important Subjects in Religion*, 24–33. This lecture is an exposition of Matt 22:2/Luke 14:17, the Parable of the Marriage Feast.

61. References to "our souls' Bridegroom" survive in English Moravianism until around the end of the eighteenth century when the language that had been used by the English Moravians starts becomes more conventional: Stead and Stead, *The Exotic Plant*, 325.

62. De Jong, "'I Want to be Like Jesus,'" 465–66.

63. Percy, "Sweet Rapture," 71–106.

64. Bernard was by no means the first to use Song of Songs in this way however. He was indebted Origen's efforts centuries earlier. Leclercq, "Introduction to Saint Bernard's Doctrine in the Sermons on the Song of Songs," 311–12.

65. He sees it as a spiritual marriage especially celebrated in *Cantica* 83, where it is stressed that this is a unitive state available even to the most sinful and not the exclusive preserve of a spiritual elite. So Fassetta, "The Christocentric and Nuptial Mysticism of Saint Bernard in the Sermons on the Song of Songs," 358.

on the *Song of Songs*,[66] and it is almost certainly the case that Bernard's crucicentrism is in the service of this central organizing theology.[67] This could also explain his lack of interest in the mechanics of atonement when compared to Anselm, as well as his resistance to a purely exemplarist view of the cross when compared to Abelard, whom he famously opposed.[68] His opposition to Abelard must, however, be nuanced by the obvious attention he pays to the motivating power of love: "For Bernard, the principal motive of the Incarnation consists in this: God became man in order to win men and women over to his love."[69]

This work of Bernard's, hereafter abbreviated as *Cantica*, was designed to be regularly preached to the monks at the monastery of Clairvaux where he was Abbot, with the first twenty-four of them finished by 1137.[70] In the midst of composing them he lost his brother[71] and the entire collection of eighty-six sermons still did not make up a complete exposition of the biblical book by the time he himself died in 1153. Perhaps because of the immense amount of time invested in this text, it is claimed to be "one of the most celebrated and sumptuous religious texts of the Middle Ages."[72]

Parts of his *Cantica* display a form of passion mysticism that combined imagery from the cross with the bridegroom metaphor. The link between the Bridegroom and the passion is Ephesians 5:23–32 in which Christ, the Bridegroom of the church saves her by giving himself up for her, the ultimate demonstration of love.[73] This results in a loving union between the two.

66. Fassetta, "The Christocentric and Nuptial Mysticism of Saint Bernard in the Sermons on the Song of Songs," 347. This union is understood by McGinn to be primarily a union of wills and "not of essence or substance": McGinn, "Love, Knowledge, and Mystical Union in Western Christianity," 9.

67. As is his entire concept of love: "In his *Sermones in Cantica* Bernard insists that the only power by which humans can deal reciprocally with God is love, and that marital love is the highest form, the love that best expresses union." McGinn, "Love, Knowledge, and Mystical Union in Western Christianity," 9.

68. Fassetta, "The Christocentric and Nuptial Mysticism of Saint Bernard," 348.

69. Ibid.

70. Mabillon, Preface to Eales (ed.), *Cantica*, 4.

71. This was 1138. Sermon 26 reflects his profound grief: Harrison, "'Jesus Wept': Mourning as Imitation of Christ in Bernard's Sermon Twenty-Six on the Song of Songs," 437.

72. Ibid., 434.

73. Love, especially divine love, was, unsurprisingly, a preoccupying theme in affective piety and wider medieval culture. A significant influence on Bernard's view of love

Most of Sermons 61–62 of Bernard's *Cantica* are a meditation around the theme of the beloved in the cleft of the rock. The Rock is pictured as Christ, and the cleft, his side wound.[74] It is synonymized as "saving power."

> [W]here is there safe sure rest for the weak except in the Savour's wounds? There the security of my dwelling depends on the greatness of his saving power. The world rages, the body oppresses, the devil lays his snares: I do not fall because I am founded on a rock. I have sinned gravely, my conscience is disturbed but not confounded, because I shall remember the wounds of the Lord. For "he was wounded for our transgressions." What sin is so deadly as not to be forgiven by the death of Christ?[75]

The other four wounds that are venerated by Bernard besides the side wound, were the two holes in Christ's feet and the two holes in his hands:

> there is no lack of clefts by which they [the Lord's mercies] are poured out. They pierced his hands and feet, they gored his side with a lance, and through these fissures I can suck honey from the rock and oil from the flinty stone [a reference to Deut 32:13]; . . . the nail that pierced him has become for me a key unlocking the sight of the Lord's will. Why should I not gaze through the cleft? The nail cries out, the wound cries out that God is truly in Christ. . . . Surely his heart is laid open through his wounds![76]

The bride, usually representing the individual soul courting the gender-neutral "Word" as the lover, but sometimes also the church with the fully gendered Christ as the Lover,[77] is exhorted to dwell in this and other wounds of Christ by continually meditating upon them: "she hears 'My dove in the clefts of the rock,' because all her affections are preoccupied

---

was Cicero's definition of love as disinterested loving for love's sake, finding its reward in itself: Gilson, *The Mystical Theology of St. Bernard*, 8–9. Cf. Bernard of Claivaux, *On Loving God*, 42–44.

74. *Cantica* 61.I.3. Here Bernard acknowledges he is borrowing this interpretation of Song 2:14 from "another writer," probably Gregory the Great or Aponius: Walsh and Edmonds (tr.) *Bernard of Clairvaux on the Song of Songs III*, 142 margin note. The metaphor is extended to include the rock, which Moses struck: ". . . and from the Rock there gushes forth the spring, whence they drink the Cup of the Lord." Bernard, *Cantica*, 196–97.

75. *Cantica* 61.II.3.

76. *Cantica* 61.II.4.

77. E.g., *Cantica* 61.I.1, where he explains: "And when you consider the lovers themselves, think not of a man and a woman but of the Word and the soul." These distinctions are explained philosophically in *Canica* 80–82: Fassetta, "The Christocentric and Nuptial Mysticism of Saint Bernard in the Sermons on the Song of Songs," 356.

with the wounds of Christ; she abides in them by constant meditation."[78] The cleft of the rock is a womb-like, invincible place of safety and child-like abdication.

Throughout the work, Bernard sounds almost Protestant in his insistence on the absolute sufficiency of Christ's mercy[79] and merit[80] over against human meriting. It is likely that this sounds as Protestant as it does simply because Martin Luther was himself so indebted to Bernard in his thoughts about the cross. In this place of trusting identification with the sufficient sacrifice of Christ, the merit of Christ's sacrifice can be shared by the "dove":

> My merit therefore is the mercy of the Lord. Surely I am not devoid of merit as long as he is not of mercy.... A righteousness that is ample and everlasting will amply cover both you and me. In me indeed it covers a multitude of sins.... These are stored up for me in the clefts of the rock.[81]

Visualization will become a common feature within this tradition and its legacy. The crucified Christ must be seen: "If you carry him where your eyes can rest on him you will find that the sight of his afflictions will make your burdens lighter, helped as you will be by him who is the Church's Bridegroom."[82]

Already, then, the practice of visualizing the wounds and blood of Christ as a route to faith and the need for trusting abdication as a route to rest and assurance in the merit of Christ's sufferings are clearly discernible in Bernard.[83] The purpose of this visualization seems to be that we are made to see beyond the appearance of things. One can hear echoes of future Protestantism again in Bernard's Luther-like *theologia crucis* in which the horrors of the crucifixion are juxtaposed with their exact opposite. In his

---

78. *Cantica* 61.III.1. Also 62.IV.7: "What greater cure for the wounds of conscience and for purifying the mind's acuity than to persevere in meditation on the wounds of Christ?"

79. Combined with "mercies" this word occurs thirty-six times in Eales' translation

80. Occurs eighty-four times.

81. *Cantica* 61.II.5.

82. *Cantica* 43.II.5 in Walsh (ed.), *The Works of St. Bernard of Clairvaux. Volume 3: On the Song of Songs II*, 224.

83. Indeed, there was a medieval tradition of "ocular communion," the idea that merely *viewing* the consecrated host on the altar can be a way of receiving the Eucharist: Bynum, "Blood of Christ," 686, 688.

exposition of Song 1:5 the contrast between the outward horrors and inner truths of the cross are explored:

> Beneath the veil of flesh, she recognized God; in death, life; the fullness of glory and honor in the midst of insults; finally, under the black appearance of the Crucified, the whiteness of innocence and the splendor of the virtues; . . . rightly does the bride not disdain the blackness of the pavilions, for she perceives the beauty hidden therein.[84]

The sermons also sometimes face backwards into the patristic era. This is especially the case with Sermon 26 where, as part of his outpouring of personal grief at the death of his brother Gerard, he reverts to *Christus Victor* language:

> You are dead O death, pierced by the hook you have incautiously swallowed, even as the Prophet said: "O Death I will be your death, O Hell I will be your destruction." Pierced by that hook you open a broad and happy exit to life for the faithful who pass through your midst.[85]

Before we continue our survey of some further key devotional writings, it seems fitting to pause for a moment to look at the first of a number of medieval phenomena that form part of the background scenery of medieval passion mysticism.

Excursus 1: The Peculiar Case of the Stigmata

The phenomenon of either the visible wounds or the invisible pain of the wounds of the crucifixion emerging on people's hands, feet, side, and brow is a phenomenon that, though having its officially recognized beginning in St. Francis of Assisi in the year 1224, has continued to this day,[86] attracting

---

84. *Cantica* 28:11.

85. *Cantica* 26.VII.11.

86. The *Catholic Encyclopedia* of 1912 altogether listed 403 documented examples, including many from the nineteenth century. The vast majority of stigmatics were acknowledged to be women: Poulain, "Mystical Stigmata," in *The Catholic Encyclopedia* (New York: Robert Appleton, 1912). Accessed online [03/07/2015]: http://newadvent.org/cathen/14294b.htm The preponderance of women is also noted by Whitlock and Hynes, "Religious Stigmatization," 185–202 and Harrison, *Stigmata*.

a fairly considerable literature.[87] A number of precursors in the centuries running up to the stigmata of St. Francis have also been identified.[88]

According to the received account of St. Francis' life,[89] the saint experienced the stigmata while engaged in a forty-day fast for Lent. During this fast he seems to have fallen into an ecstatic state of pure devotion. A seraph appears to him, which then takes the form of the crucified Christ, and as it does so, the wounds of Christ physically appear on St. Francis' own body. His stigmata uniquely included nails with a rounded head at one end and a sharp point on the other in both his hands and his feet.

Since then, occurrences of the stigmata have been fairly frequent, though almost always within a Southern European Roman Catholic context, with a very marked preponderance within Italy.[90] Only very recently has the phenomenon spread to North America or to non-Caucasians.[91] By 1994, there were estimated to be about twenty living stigmatics in the world, almost all Catholics,[92] and occasionally, as with the famous Padre Pio, attracting huge media attention. Women stigmatics outnumber men by seven to one.[93]

Interpretations of the phenomenon shed far more light on passing fashions in mental health practice or medical science than they do on the stigmata themselves. In the early days of modern medicine, attention was given to attempted cures—which failed—as well as to episodes of round-the-clock observation to ensure that nothing fraudulent was going on.[94] From the 1920s more and more cases came to light of psychosomatic lesions. Through the newfound wonders of hypnosis, it was found that certain psychosomatic phenomena could be suggested to the patient. In

---

87. Lord, "A Note on Stigmata," 299–302; Early and Lifschutz, "A Case of Stigmata," 197–200; Copelan, "Stigmata: Passion and Punishment," 85–90, Whitlock and Hynes, "Religious Stigmatization"; Yarom, *Body, Blood, and Sexuality*; Harrison, *Stigmata*. In a popular journalistic style would be one devout: Freze, *They Bore the Wounds of Christ*, and one deeply skeptical: Nickell, *Looking for a Miracle*.

88. Muessig, "Signs of Salvation."

89. The account of Bonaventure soon acquired quasi-canonical status, with all other accounts deliberately sidelined.

90. In 1908 this was 229 out of 321 worldwide cases according to one count up courtesy of a French medic, Dr. Imbert-Gourbeyre: Harrison, *Stigmata*, 9.

91. Harrison, *Stigmata*, viii.

92. Ibid., 2.

93. Ibid., 10.

94. Poulain, "Mystical Stigmata."

one experiment of 1928, a patient who was already very troubled in mind, was induced under hypnosis to produce the stigmata. Her forehead obligingly began, over several hours, to produce bleeding pin pricks. Similar experiments, though none involving suggesting crucifixion wounds to the patient, continued into the 1960s.[95] Others, ignoring the medical evidence for "psychogenic purpura," as these psychosomatic lesions are called, also argued for suggestion, but of a different kind. They reckoned that history itself provided all the suggestion needed for those already prone to suggestion. They appealed to the historical fact that there seem to be no definite occurrences until Francis, yet after Francis the stigmatics are positively queueing up to have their seeping lacerations, weeping pin pricks, and dripping hands admired by all.[96] More recently, as we enter the age of neuroscience, one study seizes on the fact that occurrences of the stigmata almost always coincide with periods of fasting.[97] Due to evolutionary factors, Fessler argues, periods of severe dietary constriction lead to "indifference to harm."[98] This is due to the fact that, in times of scarcity it was the adrenaline-junky cavemen that went out and hunted for the most nutritious food while the risk averse stuck with their watered-down cabbage soup and withered away. And it is starvation, accompanied by the resultant low serotonin levels, that stimulates this high level of risk taking. These irrational behaviors can include self-mutilation: "The removal of normal motivational barriers to harm thus facilitates injurious behavior which may result in rewarding endorphin releases."[99] In St. Francis and other stigmatics of the time, "The salience of open wounds in depictions of Christ beginning in the 13th century," according to Fessler, "provided a ready meaning system that likely shaped the experiences, actions, and accounts of devout Catholics having a psychological disposition to dietary constriction and

95. Harrison, *Stigmata*, 12–13. By 1989, there were seventy-one recorded cases of spontaneous psychogenic purpura: Harrison, *Stigmata*, 14.

96. "[W]e have the striking fact that not a single case of stigmatization was heard of before the beginning of the thirteenth century. No sooner, however, was the extraordinary phenomenon which marked the last days of St. Francis published throughout the world, than other unquestionable cases of stigmata began to occur . . . and have continued to occur without intermission ever since." Thurston, *The Physical Phenomena of Mysticism*, 122.

97. Fessler, "Starvation, Seratonin, and Symbolism," 81–96.

98. Ibid., 81.

99. Ibid., 88.

attendant dissociation and self-mutilation."[100] On this reckoning, Francis and subsequent stigmatics can all point to the true cause of their miracle: a knife. Sheer hunger apparently drove them to gouge away at themselves while being abetted by the proliferation of crucifixion portrayals everywhere they looked.

Are these phenomena of divine origin? No scientific research can tell us that, but the restricted provenance of the stigmata: still flourishing mainly within Roman Catholicism, especially Italian, would seem to point to human suggestion, albeit of an extraordinary kind.

Bonaventure's Crucicentrism

A browse through *Francis and Clare: The Complete Works*[101] does not yield any obvious evidences of crucicentrism. The cross was pivotal at two moments in St. Francis' life, the first being when he received a command, which emanated from the crucified Christ while he prayed at the foot of a crucifix, to rebuild Christ's ruined house. This resulted in the very short *Prayer before the Crucifix*, which, despite its name, is a prayer mainly for clear guidance and does not mention the cross.[102] The second moment was towards the end of his life, in 1224, when he received the stigmata. It was this latter event which Bonaventure developed in his *Life of St. Francis*. But, beyond this, the life of St. Francis seems to be given a crucicentric cast by Bonaventure, his fervent admirer, that does not seem justified from what little has come down to us from the writings of Francis himself.

In Clare of Assisi, however, there is more evidence of passion piety. Ingrid Peterson describes how "the crucified Christ, the mirror of the invisible God" was "the center of her spirituality."[103] In a letter to Agnes of Prague, who was just about to enter the cloisters, she writes: "Be strengthened in the holy service which you have undertaken out of an ardent desire for the Poor Crucified, who for the sake of all of us took upon himself the passion of the cross."[104] In Clare's fourth letter to Agnes, inspired by Wisdom 7:26,

---

100. Ibid., 90, citing Yarom, *Body, Blood, and Sexuality*.

101. Armstrong and Brady (eds.), *Francis and Clare*.

102. Ibid., 103.

103. Peterson, *Clare of Assisi*, 290.

104. *First Letter to the Blessed Agnes of Prague* 13–14, in Armstrong and Brady (eds), *Francis and Clare*, 191.

she describes Christ as a mirror reflecting the glory of God, maintaining this image through a greater portion of the letter:

> Look at the parameters of this mirror, that is, the poverty of Him who was placed in a manger and wrapped in swaddling clothes. O marvelous humility, O astonishing poverty! The King of the angels, the Lord of heaven and earth, is laid in a manger! Then, at the surface of the mirror, dwell on the holy humility, the blessed poverty, the untold labors and burdens which He endured for the redemption of all mankind. Then, in the depths of this same mirror, contemplate the ineffable charity which led him to suffer on the wood of the Cross and die thereon the most shameful kind of death. . . . From this moment, then, O queen of our heavenly King, let yourself be inflamed more strongly with the fervor of charity.[105]

Clare brought out the central point of Francis' spirituality: identifying with Christ through poverty, and used the cross in addition to the humanity of Christ as a way of driving home this central truth.

In the main, however, Franciscan spirituality is cross-centered largely because of Bonaventure's writings and not because of its founder, there being a puzzling lack of emphasis on the humanity or crucifixion of Christ in Francis' own writings.[106] From the feast of St. Francis in October 1259, when Bonaventure visited Mount Alverna for himself, the crucified Christ seems to become the center of Bonaventure's entire theology.[107] And this theology was expressed in the by now familiar affective fashion, he being noted by Bestul for his "intimate, affective, apostrophic style, marked by familiar address to Christ."[108] In *The Mystical Vine* Bonaventure asks, "Who would not be filled with sorrow at the sight? Who could keep back sobs and tears? As it is a devout act to rejoice for Jesus, so it is devout to weep for him."[109]

He also continued in the tradition of dwelling on the details of Christ being spat at, pushed around, stretched out upon the cross, and left with open wounds.[110] The work of the atonement is understood in a way that

---

105. *Fourth Letter to Blessed Agnes of Prague* 19–24, 27 in Armstrong and Brady (eds.), *Francis and Clare*, 205.

106. Delio, *Crucified Love*, 3.

107. Delio, *Simply Bonaventure*, 32.

108. Bestul, *Texts of the Passion*, 44.

109. Bonaventure, *Mystical Vine* IV.3–4.

110. Dreyer, "Bonaventure's Spirituality of the Cross," in Dreyer (ed.), *The Cross in Christian Tradition*, 215.

echoes Anselm: Christ's death is the only sacrifice that could have been sufficient:

> The age in which grace is revealed demanded that no oblation be offered except a pure, acceptable, and all-sufficient one. But no such sacrifice exists but the one offered on the cross, namely the body and blood of Christ.[111]

As is clear from his *The Soul's Ascent to God*, he is also heir to the rich tradition of meditations on the mystical union with God that Bernard had explored so masterfully in the *Cantica*.[112] The passion themes discernible in Bonaventure's works may be quite readily divisible into crucifixion themes and blood of Christ themes.

Crucifixion Themes

Theologically, it is clear that Bonaventure takes his lead from the satisfaction theory as found in Peter Lombard's *Sentences*.[113] The strong *Deus-Homo* element in satisfaction theory is present: "Nor could humans," says Bonaventure, "have recovered the friendship of God except through a fitting Mediator, who could touch God with one hand and human beings with the other, who would be the likeness and the friend of both . . . ."[114]

Exemplarism also is strong, though the satisfaction theme does not disappear: "Now, nothing could show humans the way to virtue more clearly than the example of an agonizing death endured for the sake of divine justice."[115] And the reason that this example is so compelling for Bonaventure is that it expresses an astonishing condescension on the part of God. Bonaventure is captivated by "God's overwhelmingly generous love

---

111. *Breviloquium* VI, 9.3. Discussed in Daniel Horan, "Christcentricity, Unity and Ethics in Bonaventure's Theology of the Eucharist," 512.

112. McGinn, "Love, Knowledge, and Mystical Union in Western Christianity, 10.

113. Burns lists the places in Bonaventure's commentary on the *Sentences* where this view is expounded: Burns, "The Concept of Satisfaction in Medieval Redemption Theory," 297. This, together with the emphasis on incarnation and moral example, is one of the three central facets of Bonaventure's soteriology, according to Zachary Hayes, *The Hidden Center*, 94.

114. Bonaventure, *Breviloquium* IV.4.

115. Ibid., IV.9.2.

and willingness, as Creator of the universe, to enter that creation in a most complete way."[116]

> The Just One fell in love with the iniquitous, the Beautiful One with the vile, the only God and the Holy One with the sinful and unholy. Oh tremendous condescension! See how much he loved us. Who could explain it well enough![117]

For Bonaventure, the supreme example of someone who took up his own cross was St. Francis, who, "paid great attention to the mortification of the flesh so that he might carry externally in his body the cross of Christ which he carried internally in his heart."[118] Following a vision of Christ crucified, St. Francis, Bonaventure claims, became scarcely able to bring to mind the passion of Christ without "tears and sighs,"[119] a fact that, for Bonaventure, further reinforced St. Francis' status as a disciple of Christ who truly understood what it meant to deny himself, take up his cross, and follow Jesus.[120] Bonaventure himself declared, with the apostle Paul, "With Christ I am nailed to the Cross,"[121] yet a big part of St. Francis' self-denying emulation of Christ was his poverty, often described in terms of being naked: "Thus the servant of the Most High King was left naked so that he might follow his naked, crucified Lord, whom he loved."[122] The receiving of the stigmata is similarly understood as having to do with St. Francis' transformation "into the likeness of Christ crucified."[123] St. Francis' experience of the crucified Christ forms the starting point for Bonaventure's *The Soul's Journey into God*: "Let us, then, die and enter into darkness. Let us silence our cares, our desires, our imaginings. With Christ crucified let us pass out of this world to the Father . . . ."[124]

---

116. Dreyer, "Bonaventure's Theology of the Cross," 195.

117. Bonaventure, *The Mystical Vine*, XVI.1.

118. Bonaventure, *The Life of St. Francis* I.6.

119. Ibid., I.5.

120. Ibid.

121. Bonaventure, *The Tree of Life*, Prologue.

122. Bonaventure, *The Life of St. Francis* II.4. Also *Life of St. Francis* XIV.4: "In all things he wished to be conformed to Christ crucified, who hung on the cross poor, suffering, and naked." See also Dreyer's helpful survey of this theme in Bonaventure: Dryer, "Bonaventure's Spirituality of the Cross," 223–26.

123. *Life of St. Francis* XIII. 3.

124. Bonaventure, *Soul's Journey into God* 7.6.

Blood of Christ Themes

The theme of redemption predominates when the blood of Christ is invoked. For example, Bonaventure's St. Francis was attracted "to souls redeemed by the precious blood of Jesus Christ,"[125] and was "more than a brother to those who are stamped with the image of their Creator and redeemed with the blood of their Maker,"[126] and the world and its salvation can only be redeemed, "With the price of his sacred blood."[127] There is also a cleansing theme. Through Christ's blood, "We are cleansed from the filth of vice . . . ."[128] But more than this, the blood is noted also for its plenteous and warming qualities, overcoming human meanness and hardness: "O heart diamond-hard, immerse yourself in the plenteous blood of our kid and lamb; rest in it and become warm; once warm, be softened; once softened, let flow a fountain tears."[129] The blood of Christ is also implied in the Lamb's victory over Satan: "Now that the combat of the passion was over, and the bloody dragon and raging lion thought that he had secured a victory by killing the Lamb, the power of divinity began to shine forth . . . ."[130]

Excursus 2: The Feast of Corpus Christi

From 1264 in Liège, present day Belgium, the Feast of Corpus Christi became official via papal edict. It had been the brainchild of a beguine by the name of Juliana who claimed to have been shown by Christ via two dreams of the moon with a piece missing from it that there was an annual feast that was missing from the church. This new feast was to be a solemn public celebration of the institution of the Eucharist. It took place by way of a procession through the streets with the Blessed Sacrament held aloft by a priest in an elaborate housing called a "monstrance." By the late 1300s, Corpus Christi processions had become woven into the fabric of medieval culture, taking on elaborations not only of a religious but also of a commercial nature. Besides the almost inevitable use of the processions as

---

125. Bonaventure, *Life of St. Francis* VIII.1.

126. Ibid., IX.4.

127. Ibid., XII.1.

128. Bonaventure, *The Soul's Journey into God*, 4.

129. Bonaventure, *Mystical Vine*, XV.3.

130. Bonaventure, *The Tree of Life*, 33.

displays of "urban status, rank, and wealth,"[131] (the most privileged walked nearest to the consecrated host; a fifth of adult males and all unmarried females were excluded[132]) there was the added complexity of the need to go via the magnificent churches that had been built by the wealthy donors in the procession. They became principally the concern of the Guilds, lay fraternities that came to prominence as a result of the Black Death and the sheer numbers of people needing to receive their last rites.[133]

Later Medieval Mystics

Julian of Norwich's *Shewings*

Julian of Norwich (1342—c. 1416), named after the church of St. Julian in Norwich where her anchoress's cell was built, is an original in many ways. Not only is her *Shewings* or *Revelations of Divine Love* the first book in English that we know of that was written by a woman, but the content of this work shows uncommon theological acumen, which makes it stand out from the common fare of fourteenth-century devotional literature. She tackles the problem of evil in a sophisticated and subtle theodicy in the form of her allegory of the servant, though in many ways, the whole of her Long Text might be seen as a "meditation on the problem of evil and its remedy."[134]

The sixteen visions that constitute the *Shewings* were given to her in 1373, and her Long Text, which describes these visions, was written in the 1390s. Its message is aimed at people who already have a strong faith commitment and who hate sin but who "find themselves tempted by feelings of impatience and despair,"[135] a purpose that reaches its climax in the most famous saying of the *Shewings*: "Sin is necessary, but all will be well, and all will be well, and every kind of thing will be well."[136] And this making of all things well is, according to the Lord's revelation to her, centered on

---

131. Beckwith, *Christ's Body*, 33.

132. Ibid., 34.

133. Ibid., 102–3.

134. Jantzen, *Julian of Norwich*, 167.

135. Gatta, "Julian of Norwich,"175.

136. Colledge and Walsh (eds.), *Julian of Norwich, Showings* 27, 224.

his passion. It is in Christ's terrible suffering that the only thing about sin that has a real existence in Julian's view, namely the pain that results from it, was taken up. We are consoled by this while our questions about why God allowed sin to enter in the first place receive no direct answer in this life. Interestingly, Julian does not allow for the existence of wrath in God towards her readers[137] and insists that God apportions no blame for sin.[138] The cross has no role in satisfying the justice of God, therefore. Despite this, there is a strong Reformed-esque doctrine of imputed righteousness.[139]

She shares with her contemporaries a fascination with the gruesome details of the Lord's crucifixion, a fascination so graphic as to have been compared to Quentin Tarantino's *Reservoir Dogs* in one quite recent study.[140] Julian's *Shewings* shares with the film the use of brutality against the male body as a beginning point for contrastingly tender ethical entreaties, *Reservoir Dogs* itself having a surprisingly tender *pieta* scene of a man cradling a dying man. In Julian's writing, the brutal details of the sufferings of Christ are, "the foundational inspiration . . . ."[141]

> After this as I watched, I saw the body bleeding copiously in representation of the scourging, and it was thus. The fair skin was deeply broken into the tender flesh through the vicious blows delivered all over the lovely body. The hot blood ran out so plentifully that neither skin nor wounds could be seen, but everything seemed to be blood.[142]

Strikingly, the author of the Tarantino study asks, not what is gained by dwelling on such brutality but what is lost by not doing so, what is lost by attending only to sanitized versions of brutality that never summon an ethical response.[143]

Julian's descriptions are not only bloody, however, but contain descriptions of the body turning black or blue, descriptions that mark her out as a survivor of the bubonic plague and a witness of its horrors. The Black Death had struck in 1348–49, during which time Julian, then aged

---

137. "[F]or in him is found no wrath." Colledge and Walsh (eds.) *Julian of Norwich, Showings*, 49, 265, and all of that chapter.

138. Colledge and Walsh (eds.), *Julian of Norwich, Showings*, 45, 257.

139. See discussion of her soteriology in Turner, *Julian of Norwich*.

140. Brintnall, "Tarantino's Incarnational Theology," 66–75.

141. Ibid., 68.

142. Colledge and Walsh (eds.), *Julian of Norwich, Showings*, 12, 199.

143. Brintnall, "Tarantino's Incarnational Theology," 72.

six, would have seen the population of Norwich decimated. Then, at the age of twenty-seven, the plague struck again. It was in the wake of this that she asked God to send her an illness, which would strike at age thirty and be near fatal enough to afford her a real encounter with death. Watkins quite plausibly puts such a strange request down to her state of mind as a plague survivor.[144]

In apparent contrast to this tendency to dwell upon the brutalized body of Jesus is Julian's use of the tender nurturing love of motherhood as a key metaphor in her theology. Importantly, Julian never says that Christ is *like* a mother or that God has qualities that are *like* those of a mother. Rather, she is convinced that the human qualities that we see in earthly mothers are themselves divine qualities. In the Godhead we find archetypal motherhood rather than a similitude to motherhood: "she is saying that our relationship to Christ can be understood most fully only if we regard him as a child would her mother. Or, to put it differently, to know Christ as mother is to know 'the very nature of God.'"[145] For this reason, Julian can talk freely of Christ as "our Mother" while retaining the masculine pronoun throughout. She never loses grip of the fact that Jesus is the male itinerant teacher from Galilee.[146]

Above all, it is in the passion that the Lord shows his motherhood: "for in our Mother, Christ, we profit and increase, and in mercy he reforms and restores us, and by the power of his Passion, his death and his resurrection, he unites us to our substance."[147]

If there is a theory of atonement that Julian is assuming, commentators seem to recognize in her the recapitulation theory of Irenaeus in which Christ as Second Adam "unites us to our substance" or reconnects us to our essential humanity, having renewed it and restored it in himself.[148] A distinctive feature is the feminizing of the progenitor of the new human race: in Irenaeus it is the new Adam, decidedly male. In Julian it is the motherly Christ birthing the church from his side wound,[149] the agonies

144. Watkins, "Two Women Visionaries," 177.

145. Reinhard, "Joy to the Father, Bliss to the Son," 632.

146. Ibid., 638.

147. Colledge and Walsh (eds.), *Julian of Norwich, Showings*, 58, 294. This is one of the few times the resurrection is mentioned.

148. Dearborn, "The Crucified Christ as the Motherly God," 290.

149. Reinhard, "Joy to the Father, Bliss to the Son," 633 n. 14. Julian describes Christ's side-wound as a womb: "With a kindly countenance our good Lord looked into his side, and he gazed with joy, and with sweet regard he drew his creature's understanding

of crucifixion being paralleled with birth pangs,[150] and the elements of the sacrament compared to breast milk.[151] But, in line with the patristic recapitulation model more generally, Julian's approach is true to type in that it concerns itself with healing and restoration. Salvation is "the healing of human nature itself."[152]

> When Adam fell, God's Son fell; because of the true union which was made in heaven, God's Son could not be separated from Adam, for by Adam I understand all mankind. Adam fell from life to death. . . . God's Son fell, into the valley of the womb of the maiden . . . and powerfully he brought him out of hell.[153]

While the atonement is understood to deal with sin, even to the point of Christ absorbing the blame for it,[154] yet sin is not understood to be the main problem, but the wounding of human nature that results from it. Sin and evil have no actual substance for Julian.[155] For Bynum, Julian's work is an example of only a few similar works of the time that did not go with the flow of the "guilt-tripping and scapegoating implicit in the late medieval obsession with human responsibility for the death of Christ."[156] Julian avoids this tendency by always insisting on the death of Christ as representative of fallen humanity. Christ's wounded humanity thus speaks to us not of our guilt but of our redemption: "If it is the *humanitas* that suffers," observes Bynum, "then *all* are in the suffering body lifted to God . . . ."[157] Julian's understanding of Christ's blood is everywhere more subtle than a straight-

---

into his side by the same wound; and there he revealed a fair and delectable place, large enough for all mankind that will be saved and will rest in peace and in love." Colledge and Walsh (eds.), *Julian of Norwich, Showings* 24, 220. The receptivity of this womb is a notable feature, it draws people in where they find salvation, unlike a normal womb that expels a newborn: Reinhard, "Joy to the Father, Bliss to the Son," 637.

150. Colledge and Walsh (eds.), *Julian of Norwich, Showings*, 60, 297–99.

151. Ibid.

152. Pelphrey, *Christ Our Mother*, 160.

153. Colledge and Walsh (eds.), *Julian of Norwich, Showings*, 51, 274–75.

154. "And so has our good Lord Jesus taken upon him all our blame; and therefore our Father may not, does not wish to assign more blame to us than to his own beloved Son Jesus Christ." Colledge and Walsh (eds.), *Julian of Norwich, Showings*, 51, 275.

155. "But I did not see sin, for I believe that it has no kind of substance, no share in being, nor can be recognized except by the pain caused by it." Colledge and Walsh (eds.), *Julian of Norwich, Showings*, 27, 225.

156. Bynum, *Wonderful Blood*, 206.

157. Ibid.

forward notion of satisfaction or substitution might allow.[158] And neither is her attachment to it fully explained by reference to the exemplary power of Christ's sacrifice.[159] Rather, for Julian, the abundantly flowing blood of Christ, which she so vividly describes in her opening vision, is "the locus of life and joy"[160] and the ultimate revelation of divine love. Hence the blood of Christ so readily lends itself in Julian to the unconventional metaphors of mothering and birthing.

Excursus 3: The Five Sacred Wounds Tradition

Before we come to Catherine of Siena, who shows a particular interest in the side-wound or side-hole of the crucified Christ, it is well to note the already growing and widespread devotion to all five of the wounds associated directly with the crucifixion of Jesus. The wounds incurred from the flagellation and the crown of thorns are thus excluded and the attention is fixed on the four nail wounds and the side-wound from the lance, which tradition held to have been used by Longinus, sometimes equated with the centurion described in the Gospel accounts.

Earlier descriptions than Catherine of Siena's of the church being born out of the side-hole like Eve came out Adam can be found as far back as Augustine,[161] and we have just now encountered that same image in Julian of Norwich too. In the early twelfth century, William of St. Thierry compared the side-hole to the door of Noah's ark through which all who enter could be saved.[162] Such devotion to the side-hole would eventually give rise to devotion to the Sacred Heart, which was deemed to have been pierced by the lance, though it would not be until the seventeenth century visions of Margaret Mary Alacoque that the feast of the Sacred Heart would be established.

Devotion to the five wounds has disparate origins but can be seen as an emerging trait within Bernard of Clairvaux's writings and in the devotions of the Franciscans, not least of whom was Clare of Assisi herself and her "Litany of the Sacred Wounds."[163] Later, devotion to the wounds, but

158. Bynum, *Wonderful Blood*, 207.

159. Ibid.

160. Ibid.

161. *Tractate 120 on John 2* according to Sloyan, *Crucifixion of Jesus*, 173.

162. *Meditatio 6*, cited in Sloyan, *Crucifixion of Jesus*, 173.

163. It concludes: "O Almighty and Eternal God, Who hast ransomed the human

especially the wound of the lance, is notable in the late medieval English adaptation of the Franciscan Latin text *Stimulus Amoris*, which, in the modern version is called, *The Goad of Love*:[164]

> Ah blessed be that spear and blessed be those nails that made this opening. O that I had been there instead of that spear. Then I would never have gone out from Christ's side but I should have said, "This is my rest and here shall I remain."[165]

The origins of an official Feast of the Five Wounds date back to the founding of the Kingdom of Portugal in 1139 following a crusade against the Moors. In an echo of the Battle of Milvian Bridge, Alfonso Henriquez had been commanded by Christ to blazon an emblem of the five wounds across the shields of his soldiers if he was to be sure of victory.[166] This feast spread across Europe being especially well established in Germany by the sixteenth century.[167] As we will note in the next chapter, this persisted into the seventeenth century Habsburg dynasty.

However, the purer form of this devotion seems to be found in the unofficial use of it. It appears to be an important symbol of the unitive state in which, "The boundaries of Christ's body and the body of the devotee are made so soft and so continuous with each other that where one ends and where the other begins becomes indeterminable."[168] Here is the *Goad of Love* again:

> Ah certainly this is a lovely and venerable passion that so accords contraries and so joins dissimilarities and so fastens two sheer kinds with the bond of blessed love, and joins them inseparably in the bliss of endless joy.[169]

---

race by the five wounds of Thy Son, Our Lord and Saviour Jesus Christ: we beseech Thee, by the merits of His precious blood, to grant unto us, who, each day, venerate these same adorable wounds, to be delivered from a sudden and unprovided death." Musser (ed.), *Kyrie Eleison*.

164. Kirchberger (ed.), *The Goad of Love*.

165. Author's translation from: Kane (ed.), *The Prickynge of Love*, 12. I am indebted to Beckwith, *Christ's Body*, 56–60 for drawing my attention to these passages.

166. Holweck, "Five Sacred Wounds, The," *The Catholic Encyclopedia* (New York: Robert Appleton, 1912). Accessed online 10/11/2015: http://www.catholic.com/encyclopedia/five-sacred-wounds-the.

167. Gougaud, *Devotional and Ascetic Practices in the Middle Ages*, 82, cited in Sloyan, *Crucifixion of Jesus*, 170.

168. Beckwith, *Christ's Body*, 59.

169. From Kane, *Prickynge of Love*, 33.

Such phenomena are well described by Beckwith as a piety that is "obsessed with belonging, with the fantasy of fusion . . . and so with the entrances to Christ's body."[170] It is a clear example of the ongoing quest for participation in the crucified Christ.

Catherine of Siena's Letters and Dialogue

Catherine of Siena (c. 1340–80) was a contemporary of Julian of Norwich, though it is certain that the two had no knowledge of each other. She was number twenty-four out of twenty-five children and was a visionary from a young age. As a teenager she joined a group of other lay women of Dominican tradition called the Mentellate. At the age of twenty-one she received a vision that resulted in her mystical espousal to Christ.[171] It is notable that while both were ardent ascetics, Catherine's life was cut considerably shorter than Julian's owing to her uncontrolled fastings. Having become what might today be termed anorexic,[172] she starved herself to death.[173] On the way to so untimely a death her other ascetic practices involved sleeping for only thirty minutes out of every forty-eight hours and the wearing of a chain around her waist, which kept pinching her skin.[174]

Both women were dealt a hand by society that condemned them to complete obscurity unless they could furnish a raft of astonishing visionary experiences with which they could lend weight to the things they had to say. This narrow opening for women, that of taking up the role of the ascetic, the mystic, became so important during the fourteenth century that most of the more prolific mystical writers of the period were women.[175] It is described as a "societal demand for visions and asceticism,"[176] and is the

---

170. Beckwith, *Christ's Body*, 42.

171. Gutgsell, "The Gift of Tears," 243.

172. Though see Bynum's discussion of food asceticism in medieval women and the comparisons that are drawn with eating disorders: Bynum, *Holy Feast and Holy Fast*, 194–207. She concedes that, while Catherine of Siena could certainly be described as anorexic and even bulimic (she often resorted to vomiting), the classification does not help explain the behavior, only the social context does, a context in which women used food in a variety of ways because "food was the basic resource over which they [medieval women] had most control." 208.

173. Watkins, "Two Women Visionaries and Death," 184–85, 187–88.

174. Flynn, "The Spiritual Uses of Pain in Spanish Mysticism," 257.

175. Bynum, *Jesus as Mother*, 172.

176. Watkins, "Two Women Visionaries and Death," 174.

demand that almost certainly brought about Catherine's premature death. Towards the end of her life, after writing many letters, she wrote her only book, the *Dialogue*. Her dying words were, "Blood! Blood! Blood!"[177]

Her 382 letters are replete with references to the passion of Christ and it occupies a central place also in the *Dialogue*. She repeatedly affirms that it was love that kept Jesus fixed to the cross,[178] a love that made the Son rush "to give himself to the shame of the cross."[179] It was a "burning love" with which the Son poured out his blood.[180] As such, the cross seems to be supremely a revelation of love: "she develops the idea that God *reveals* himself on the cross with a persistence all her own."[181] Because of this dominant revelatory significance, the cross and blood of Jesus take on the role of deciphering the whole meaning of God and his relationship to humans:[182] "This blood gives you knowledge of the truth when knowledge of yourself leads you to shed the cloud of selfish love."[183] The converse of this enlightenment is also true for Catherine, namely, that sin is mainly ascribed to ignorance.[184] Yet, to remain enamored with the passion purely as a clue to the loving purpose of God might incline her towards an examplarist view of the cross. This is especially the case when we consider her evident regard for the need to suffer with Christ if we are to be his true disciples. This suffering, if flowing out of love for Christ and hatred for one's sin, even has the power to atone for oneself.[185] However, she does not stop here, but sees a grander plan that involves the renewal of the image of God in all humanity, its restoration to creational brilliance. Christ's blood was poured out to renew the image of God in us. The theology of incarnation is also drawn upon to describe

177. Ibid., 195.

178. E.g., Letters 3, 5, 16, 26, 42. Foster and Ronayne (eds.), *I, Catherine*.

179. Letter 2, Foster and Ronayne (eds.), *I, Catherine*.

180. *Dialogue* 4.

181. Foster and Ronayne (eds.), *I, Catherine*, 36.

182. Ibid.

183. *Dialogue* 4.

184. Foster and Ronayne (eds.), *I, Catherine*, 37. Letters 5, 17, 34.

185. *Dialogue* 4: "Those who have heartfelt contrition, love for true patience, and that true humility which considers oneself worthy of punishment and unworthy of reward suffer with patience and so make atonement. . . . Behave, then, you and my other servants, with true patience, with sorrow for sin and love of virtue. . . . If you do, I will be appeased for your sins. . . . The sufferings you endure will, through the power of charity, suffice to win both atonement and reward for you and for others." Hoffke (ed.), *Catherine of Siena: The Dialogue* .

this purpose of God to renew humanity, for which she uses the image of grafting:

> Life is grafted onto death, so that we mortals have gained life through this union. And because God has been grafted onto the human being, this God-and-human-being has plunged, love-smitten, to the opprobrious death of the cross. Onto this, the tree of the human being, that incarnate Word willed to be grafted.[186]

Until that restoration is complete, it appears we can repose in an imputed status that at once clothes our continuing nakedness and rouses us from indifference. It is at once justifying and sanctifying:

> The blood has covered our nakedness, since it has clothed us with grace. In the heat of the blood the ice has melted, and our lukewarmness has caught fire; in the blood the darkness has been lifted, and light has been given to us; in the blood self-love has been consumed.[187]

She shares very much in the widespread interest in the side-wound of Christ:

> Up, then, my dear child, let us no longer be sleeping the sleep of negligence, but let us enter into the open workshop of the side of Christ crucified (where we find the blood), with anguished sorrow and lamentation for the offense to God.[188]

> At the end of this grand stairway of the opened side you shall find an entire shop of scented spices. There you shall find the God who is a human being; there the soul is sated and made altogether drunk, provided she see not herself. . . . I would, then, and thus do I pray you on the part of Christ crucified, that you should warm and bathe yourselves in the blood of Christ crucified. And that you may be made one thing with him . . . .[189]

> Hide in the wounds of Christ crucified, and bathe in his precious blood![190]

186. *Letters* 2:120, cited in Camporesi, *Juice of Life*, 75.

187. *Letters* 2:72, cited in ibid., 67.

188. *Letters* 2:73, cited in ibid., 69.

189. *Letters* 2:7, cited in ibid., 72.

190. *Letters* 2:85, cited in ibid., 73.

Excursus 4: The Passion Play

It was during the Corpus Christi processions mentioned earlier that another tradition began to proliferate, that of the passion play. These plays became as common an Easter phenomenon in the Middle Ages as Nativity plays are at Christmas today. The main literary inspiration behind the scripting of the plays was Bonaventure's *Meditationes*. This was translated and adapted in England by Nicholas Love as *Mirror of the Blessed Life of Christ*. The Corpus Christi processions were differentiated from the passion plays in that the Corpus Christi processions involved the presence of Christ himself in the Eucharist held in the Monstrance.[191] This instilled a certain reverence and a participative element in that, whenever the procession stopped, some of the procession would become actors portraying the events of Calvary, and the rest would be the audience. Then, as the procession carried on, the actors would merge with the crowd. These two factors: the presence of Christ himself as the main actor and the eliding of stage with audience seemed to preserve the Corpus Christi processions from excesses. The passion plays, by contrast, had none of these constraints and were prone to comic portrayals of devils and other characters that were purely to raise a laugh rather than illustrate the Scriptures.[192] And it was this bawdy portrayal rather than any objection to drama per se that aroused Luther's censure and the eventual banning of passion plays and Corpus Christi processions by 1525.[193]

Another factor contributing to the notoriety of passion plays was the anti-Semitic feelings often aroused by them. Arriving relatively late on the scene was the Oberammergau passion play, which started in 1634 following a miraculous deliverance of the village from a plague outbreak. The play has been performed in every year ending in zero, plus special anniversary years such as 1934. This passion play is singled out in Jewish literature as a particularly heinous example of anti-Semitic portrayals of Jews as Christ-killers. It was this kind of play that would arouse audiences to go on the rampage attacking Jews. Hitler even praised the Oberammergau play for its portrayal of Jews. It helped him get his message across. Indeed, the very name of Oberammergau has been so tainted by its history that by 1980 it became necessary to include a lengthy disclaimer as well as some adjustments to the portrayal itself so that the Jewishness of Jesus himself is

191. Loewe, "Proclaiming the Passion," 244.

192. Ibid., 248.

193. Ibid., 247.

made clearer and the advocacies of Nicodemus and Joseph of Arimathea are brought out more fully.[194] It remains, however, a remarkable theatrical feat that, despite its huge cast, continues to make use only of people who are genuinely native to the village.[195]

Margery Kempe's *The Book of Margery Kempe*

Margery Kempe (c. 1373–c. 1438)[196] of Bishop's Lynn (present day King's Lynn), England, is the quintessential weeping passionist. She was known to break into spontaneous crying up to twelve times a day. Her dictated account of her life is the first ever autobiography in the English language. She was from a fairly privileged background, her father John Burnham (or Brunham) being the mayor of the town and a member of parliament. She was married to John Kempe, who was a prominent person in the town, by whom she became the mother of fourteen children.[197]

It was just after the harrowing birth of her first child that she received her first vision. During this vision, and in the wake of a time of deep spiritual crisis over an unconfessed sin,[198] Christ came and sat on her bed and was clothed in purple silk. However, after this she returned to enjoying the things of the world, especially fashion but also tried to run a brewery and a mill for a while.[199] It was not until a much later experience that her life changed dramatically. This latter experience involved hearing a melody while lying in bed that was "so sweet and delectable that she thought she had been in paradise."[200] This turned her life around to such an extent that, in 1373, despite a sex life with her husband, John, that had been passionate

194. Kille, "More Reel Than Real: Mel Gibson's *The Passion of the Christ*," 347, referencing Cohn-Sherbok, *The Crucified Jew: Twenty Centuries of Christian Anti-Semitism*.

195. The web page for the 2010 performance is here: http://www.oberammergau-passion.com/en-gb/the-passion-play/passionplay-2010.html [accessed online 15/03/2016].

196. Key sources include: Atkinson, *Mystic and Pilgrim*; Staley, *Margery Kempe's Dissenting Fictions*; Petroff, *Body and Soul*; Gallyon, *Margery Kempe of Lynn and Medieval England*; Castagna, *Re-Reading Margery Kempe in the 21st Century*. A good translation of the text from Middle English is Windeatt (ed.), *The Book of Margery Kempe*.

197. It is her role not merely as a lay person but also a wife and mother that Atkinson sees as marking her out from anything that had gone before: Atkinson, *Mystic and Pilgrim*, 219.

198. The events are told in chapter 1 of her *Book of Margery Kempe*.

199. *Book of Margery Kempe*, chapter 1.

200. Ibid., chapter 3.

and enjoyable, she finally persuaded him to agree to a life of chastity so that she could be wedded to Christ alone. Following this she went on a number of pilgrimages to holy sites in Britain, Continental Europe, and the Holy Land, while her husband doubtless took to having very cold baths. They lived apart to avoid the possibility of unchastity, but it was in his separate house in later life that John, sadly, fell down the stairs and nearly died. She cared for him in the last year of his life while he became childish and incontinent.[201]

Not long after her experience of hearing music, she found herself extraordinarily prone to tears. She was influenced by Brigit of Sweden and by Walter Hilton,[202] both of whom set a precedent in sacralizing weeping as an important part of the spiritual pilgrimage, yet her own crying seems to have arisen quite of itself. She went to Julian of Norwich for advice, and Julian assured her that, however troubling this seemingly uncontrollable gift of tears was, it could not be a devil that had given such a thing.[203]

In common with Julian of Norwich she was "intelligent" and "articulate,"[204] but added a certain amount of self-confidence, being variously described as "self-advertising," "eccentric and self-centered,"[205] demonstrative to the point of being "a case for a psychiatrist rather than a theologian,"[206] and even a "feminist." Bradford deems her to be too self-centered to be interested in teaching other Christians,[207] while Ellen Ross sees her public ministry of tears as a distinctive intercessory and perhaps prophetic ministry to others.[208] This latter perspective would seem borne out by the Lord's words to her that she records:

> I have ordained you to be a mirror amongst them, to have great sorrow, so that they take example from you to have some little sorrow in their hearts for their sins, so that they might through that

201. Ibid., chapter 76.

202. There is evidence that she followed the instructions suggested in Hilton's *Ladder of Perfection*: Gutgsell, "The Gift of Tears," 249, citing Bhattacharji, "Tears and Screaming," in Patton and Hawley (eds.), *Holy Tears*, 233.

203. She apparently spent many days with her in "holy dalliance, communing in the love of our Lord Jesus Christ." *Book of Margery Kempe*, chapter 18.

204. Bradford, "Julian of Norwich and Margery Kempe," 153.

205. Knowles, *The English Mystical Tradition*, 149.

206. Vandenbroucke, "New Milieux, New Problems" in Leclercq, Vandenbroucke, and Bouyer (eds.), *The Spirituality of the Middle Ages*, 426.

207. Bradford, "Julian of Norwich and Margery Kempe," 158.

208. Ross, *The Grief of God*, 122–25.

be saved; yet they have no love to hear of sorrow or of contrition. But, good daughter, do your duty and pray for them while you are in this world.[209]

A notable feature of her spirituality is the fact that, despite being illiterate, she was remarkably conversant in Scripture, a fact that aroused not admiration but suspicion, partly on account of the fact that she was a woman and partly because of the strength of John Wycliff's Lollard movement in her area. She was made to stand trial on accusations of Lollardy three times, but was able to successfully defend herself by affirming transubstantiation.

Kempe became especially emotional during Corpus Christi processions through the town:

> And most of all, when she saw the precious sacrament borne about town with lights and reverence, the people kneeling on their knees, then she had many holy thoughts and meditations, and then she would cry and roar, as though she would have burst, for the faith and the trust she had in the precious sacrament.[210]

Palm Sunday likewise was an emotional occasion:

> Then had she so much sweetness and devotion that she could not bear it, but cried, wept and sobbed very violently. She had many a holy thought of our Lord's Passion, and beheld him in her spiritual sight, as truly as if he had been before her in her bodily sight.[211]

She understood her Savior's suffering to have been "for her love,"[212] that is, to win it, and was once deeply moved by a sermon that was seemingly full of recurrences of the phrase: "Our Lord Jesus languishes for love."[213] And, sure enough, love came forth from her as she listened: "she could no longer keep the fire of love enclosed within her breast, but, whether she would or no, what was enclosed within would insist on appearing without."[214]

Kempe's pilgrimage to the Holy Land afforded her the chance of actually visiting the place believed to be Golgotha. This stimulated a very strong outpouring of emotion: "she had such great compassion and such great

---

209. *Book of Margery Kempe*, chapter 78.

210. Ibid., chapter 72.

211. Ibid., chapter 78.

212. Ibid., chapter 28.

213. Ibid., chapter 78.

214. Ibid.

pain to see our Lord's pain, that she could not keep herself from crying and roaring though she should have died for it."[215]

For modern readers her spirituality tends to seem "profoundly other,"[216] as does the spirituality of a great many of the medieval mystics. And even within the otherness of her contemporaries, she seems to have an otherness that marks her out even from them: "Nowhere in Christian literature is there a character quite like Margery Kempe," says Margaret Gallyon, "and nowhere is there a book of mystical devotion quite like hers."[217]

Her aim seems to have been very simple, especially in the light of the abandoning of her conjugal debts to her husband in deference to quasi-nuptial relations with Christ. Owen Cummings describes it as "communion."[218] Chapter 36 of Margery Kempe's *Book* includes some fairly explicitly nuptial conversations between herself and Christ now that she could, quite literally it seems, share her bed with him instead of her husband. Similarly, Bhattacharji, insists that Kempe's tears should be understood not as expressions of loss or of penitence: they do not mourn the death of Christ, rather they are "tears over the closeness of Christ to human beings in his ever-present humanity."[219] And as we saw from her Palm Sunday experience, the love of Christ towards humanity, climaxing in his passion, was intended to bring forth the responding "fire of love," in true Abelardian fashion.

Margery Kempe is a fitting point at which to conclude the Middle Ages and move on to the Catholic Reformation. Kempe represents the high water mark in the affective piety tradition, a truly "embodied piety"[220]

---

215. Ibid., chapter 28. She speaks for herself in the third person throughout.

216. Petroff, *Body and Soul*, x.

217. Gallyon, *Margery Kempe of Lynn*, 14.

218. Cummings, "The Liturgical Margery Kempe," 350, 355: "Margery knows experientially, even though she may not be able to put it into theological terms, that all the spiritual apparatus of the church exists to bring about further communion with God. Like other women mystical writers before her, she reaches into nuptial images to express this communion. . . . The tears are an expression of a deep spirituality of communion." See also Cummings, *Eucharist and Ecumenism*, 57–67, though the point is not made so strongly in the book than in the article.

219. Bhattacharji, "Tears and Screaming," in Patton and Hawley (eds.), *Holy Tears*, 239.

220. Gutgsell, "The Gift of Tears, 243.

The Spanish Mystics

Strictly speaking, the following two mystics belong to the Counter or Catholic Reformation, typically judged to have begun with the Council of Trent in 1545 and to have ended with the Peace of Westphalia in 1648. The Discalced (or bare-footed) Carmelites, of which Teresa of Avila was the founder, represented one of many monastic reforms that took place. However, in terms of telling the story of devotion to the passion, the continuities with medieval passion meditation seem sufficiently strong as to include the Spanish Mystics within the same chapter as the medieval mystics.[221]

Teresa of Avila (1515–82)

Teresa of Avila, also known as Teresa of Jesus, espoused a theology of the cross that has been likened to Martin Luther's,[222] with a personality that could also be matched to Luther's in that it was "individuated, passionate, uncompromising, indomitable."[223] Whether Teresa should be "canonized or exorcised," has, as with many an extreme ascetic, been a point of discussion.[224] As with Count Zinzendorf, whom we will encounter in the next chapter, Teresa's spiritual breakthrough appears to have been stimulated by an *Ecce Homo* painting.[225] She remained resolutely devoted to the earthly, human Christ all her life.[226] The cross was central even in her highest raptures of spiritual ecstasy. In her *Interior Castle* she describes how even in the seventh mansion those who are truly spiritual are those who are "branded with His sign, which is the sign of the cross."[227] Nugent's claim that Teresa "knew neither the name of Plato nor the idea of Platonism," and that "[s]he did not, like Plotinus, apologize for having a body,"[228] is perhaps a little mis-

221. Flynn, likewise, keeps "medieval" and "early modern" together: "Perhaps no other major world religion endows pain with greater spiritual significance than Christianity, and among Christians none spoke so directly to the issue of suffering as the mystics of late medieval and early modern Europe." Flynn, "The Spiritual Uses of Pain in Spanish Mysticism," 257.

222. Nugent, "What has Wittenberg to Do with Avila?" 650.

223. Ibid., 651.

224. Ibid., 652.

225. Ibid.

226. Ibid., 653.

227. Peers (ed.), *Teresa of Avila: Interior Castle*, 229.

228. Nugent, "What has Wittenberg to Do with Avila?" 656.

leading as the indebtedness of her and the whole Spanish mystical tradition to Pseudo-Dionysius is very clear,[229] Pseudo-Dionysius' *Mystical Theology* being the main prism for Neoplatonism into this tradition.

John of the Cross (1542–91)

Also known as San Juan (and specialists who study him are called sanjuanists) there has been surprisingly little attention given to John's atonement theology.[230] Deep at the heart of his whole understanding of the atonement is that it is "a romance—a marriage."[231] It is an act of self-sacrificial love and service on the part of the Trinity towards fallen humanity, even to the point of the Son attaching himself to and, in some sense, subjecting himself to the creature.[232] This emphasis on love brings him into a very similar thought world to that of Julian of Norwich and, like her, he finds the patristic recapitulation theory to be highly amenable. The influence of Irenaeus is suggested from his poetic references to the two trees: the tree in paradise and the tree of the cross. Here, Christ is speaking:

> Your mother, human nature, was corrupted in her first parents beneath the forbidden tree, and you were redeemed beneath the Cross. If your mother at that tree sentenced you to die, I from the Cross have given you life.[233]

However, John adds his own unique twist to his use of this model. In a way evocative of Möltmann's ideas many centuries later about the godforsakenness of the Son on the cross, John pictures Christ as undergoing

229. "Dionysius' name is reverently invoked by Spanish religious authors in the sixteenth century as the leading patristic authority on mystical theology." Girón-Negrón, "Dionysian Thought in Sixteenth-Century Spanish Mystical Theology," 694.

230. Johnson, "The Crucified Bridegroom," 393–94.

231. Ibid., 395.

232. "Anyone who loves a creature, then, is as low as that creature and in some way even lower because love not only equates but even subjects the lover to the loved creature." *The Ascent of Mount Carmel* I, IV:3. This is balanced by John's belief in the divinization of the soul so that God gets some benefit, as it were; the benefit being that he, through union with and divinization of the soul, can bring to fulfillment his original purposes for it. *The Living Flame of Love*, III, 8. Johnson, "The Crucified Bridegroom," 402.

233. *Spiritual Canticle* (Second Redaction) XXIII, 3. This is an exposition of Song of Songs 8:5, though Johnson rightly observes a parallel with Irenaeus *Against Heresies* V, 29.1. Johnson, "The Crucified Bridegroom," 395.

his own Dark Night of the Soul while enduring the agony of the cross, stating that God "forsook Him, that He might pay the whole of man's debt and unite him with God, being thus annihilated and reduced as it were to nothing."[234] Johnson points out that where, for believers, the Dark Night of the Soul is an experience of advance purgatory, for Christ, the experience was of hell.[235] Christ thus spares the devout the dark night of hell by enduring it for them so that the dark nights they experience are the dark night only of purgatory, a purifying rather than punishing experience.

Conclusion

So, to return to our original question: what has the church done with the atonement? One of the first things that struck me as I got into the subject matter of this book straight after writing *Atonement Theories* is how little the church has made use of what the theologians have said about the atonement. The devotional outpourings of the faithful often bear almost no relation to the deliberations of theologians who, in fairness, are in most cases no less faithful, and, as in the case of Anselm, often hold passports from both places. For the most part, the disconnect seems not to arise from any want of deep spirituality on the part of the theologians or from any lack of intellectual power on the part of ordinary Christians and those who lead them, but from the fact that we are looking at two different quests. Theologians are on a quest to be able to understand and explain things while the people we have been looking at here are not at all concerned with understanding or explaining the atonement. Their quest is a sacramental one.

We saw in the first chapter that first-millennium Christians had developed a twofold crucicentric faith that centered on the elements of the Eucharist and the symbol of the cross. The ritual of the Mass was always in danger of sliding away from its all-important re-living, participative dynamic into a spectacle. It would surely have sounded absurd to the ears of the earliest church that we now commonly use the phrase "hearing the Mass." The idea of fully participating was lost during this period. Meanwhile the symbol

---

234. *The Ascent of Mount Carmel* II, VIII:11. This annihilation consists in an annihilation of his reputation, of his physical body and of the help available to him from the Father: *The Ascent of Mount Carmel* II, VIII:11. See also Johnson, "The Crucified Bridegroom," 398.

235. Johnson, "The Crucified Bridegroom," 395, 399. See also Stein, *The Science of the Cross*, 30.

of the cross was always in danger of sliding into a mere sign, an over-used and consequently dead symbol devoid of the power to re-present redemption to the faithful. In other words, the sacramental power of both points of contact was imperiled by the very success of them: vast un-catechized hoards hearing the Mass and surrounded by crosses.

The answer was to introduce something sensual that could make the central redeeming moment in the life of the Redeemer more immediate. And so steps were taken to rescue the elements of the Eucharist from their encasement in priestly performance. The cult of martyrdom was early on a very obvious way of moving beyond the rituals into real participation but, later on, pilgrimages to martyr graves and the martyr relics held by various churches took the place of actually being a martyr. Even the shift to an interest in biblical holy sites and New Testament relics was only a development of this same instinct to supplement a performed Mass with the act of physically going somewhere and making contact with something.

Other steps were taken to reinvigorate the symbol of the cross by converting it from a dying symbol into a fully living metaphor. The shocking paradoxes of the *Dream of the Rood* in which the tree is the narrator is a prize example, but even the everyday act of crossing oneself would have re-presented and re-appropriated the power of the symbol.

In the more sacramental traditions there has always been, right at the center of the worship of the gathered church, an element of drama,[236] of non-verbal communication, of sign and symbol: a liturgical art form that retells an ancient story. In the sacramental worldview there is a general assumption that the material can be a vehicle for the spiritual.[237] This is described by von Balthasar as "the sacramental principle."[238] And it seems that it is as we take seriously this gaping need in us all to engage with divine things using material things and symbolic actions, that much of what we have looked at can be made sense of.[239] By deploying these strategies, the church was reclaiming the sacramental power of the atonement. The church thus gives the work of redemption something by which it can touch us, often literally. Only then does atonement theology start to prove useful. The theology

---

236. Baillie describes the *"dramatic* symbolism" of the Eucharist, referring to the actions of the priest. It is an "acted parable." Baillie, *Theology of the Sacraments*, 94. See also Graham, "Liturgy as Drama," 77: Communion is "a dramatic enactment of the gospel in which all present participate in a variety of roles."

237. Sherry, *Spirit and Beauty*, 139.

238. Balthasar, *Prayer*, Part 3, chapter 2.

239. Baillie, *Theology of the Sacraments*, 54.

comes into play only as participants in atonement try to describe what it has just imparted to them through this sacramental retrieval. It might be a sense of triumph over evil, of the gracious forgiving of sin, or of a debt of service that is now owed. But this theologizable result is secondary to the more primal and often wordless sacramental connection that has been made in each case.

In this chapter we see these strategies deployed with an increased urgency that seems almost frenzied. People seem desperate to be there, weeping with Mary, grieving with John, and attending to the lifeless corpse with Joseph and Nicodemus. They want to see his blood flowing plenteously; they want to live inside the Savior's wounds like the dove in the cleft of the rock. What seems already to be very clear is that an atonement that does not involve deep participation by the adoring believer in the crucified (and, we assume, risen) Jesus is not an atonement that is of interest to faith. If this element is lacking then we are left only with an historical miscarriage of justice or a bare creedal statement. It is the imperative of participation that explains why Bynum's statement is so very true: "There are not then two redemption theories (Abelardian and Anselmian) in the Middle Ages but one."[240] The loving response emphasized by Abelard was assumed by all. It also explains why, even when Anselm found that there was no way to pay our debt to God by participating in the sufferings of Christ, that he still affirmed a different kind of participation: one of glad gratitude.

It seems that I might be able to build on what emerged from my first volume, which was something I could call the Incarnation Criterion: that the strongest atonement theories are those that best express the incarnation of the God-Man and take their cues from it. We add to that now the Participation Imperative: that the atonement theories that the people of God are likely to find the most fit for purpose are those that best facilitate a redemptive participation in the cross.

With these loose ends only lightly tied for now, we will proceed to our next great concentration of crucicentric piety, that of Zinzendorf and the Moravians.

---

240. Bynum, *Wonderful Blood*, 200.

Chapter 3

ZINZENDORF, THE MORAVIANS, AND THE WESLEYS

The Reformation Transition

WHAT MAKES POSSIBLE OUR next concentration of crucicentric piety is the continuity of passion devotion across the new confessional divide that was created by the Reformation. The Protestants, of course, were keen to remove certain elements such as crucifixion iconography and any reference to purgatory and acquiring merits through indulgences or self-effort. But a recent paper by Lucy Busfield[1] has shown that there was otherwise a very high degree of continuity, at least as far as the English Reformation is concerned, between Catholic and Protestant passion pieties.[2] The strong associations between passion-centered piety and female expressions of faith is another point of continuity with the Middle Ages and is something that continues into early Methodism. It has been suggested that the link, in this regard, is between the agonies of childbirth and the sufferings of the crucified Christ,[3] an observation that possibly finds support in the examples

1. Busfield, "Women, Men and Christ Crucified," 217–36.

2. Busfield also cites Henrksen, *Milton and the Reformation Aesthetics of the Passion*, 40, 51–63 for support.

3. Busfield, "Women, Men and Christ Crucified," 219, citing Mak, *Heart Religion in the British Enlightenment*, 171–218.

we saw in the last chapter of women likening the side-wound of Christ to a womb out of which the church was born.

Just one example of early Reformation passion piety is Katherine Parr (1512–48), Henry VIII's last wife who, mercifully, survived him.[4] In her case, one of the main sources of continuity is her liking for Thomas à Kempis' *The Imitation of Christ*,[5] a work that was also significant for John Wesley and has retained a strong place in evangelical devotion. Parr's *Prayers and Meditations* of 1545[6] is indebted to Book III of Kempis' work. In her writings she dwells upon the pierced heart, the torn skin, and broken sinews and veins and desires to be bathed in "that blessed blood."[7]

The theology of the Reformation, likewise, secured an ongoing basis for continued crucicentric piety. Into the eighteenth century, evangelicals were using the word "gospel" very considerably,[8] and always the content intended was the Reformation heritage of the free offer of justification through the sacrificial death of Christ. Hindmarsh observes that the eighteenth-century evangelical concept of "gospel" was actually even more narrowly focused on atonement and justification than the original Reformation concept had been.[9]

Hymn Break

Before we move into Pietism, however, we have good reason to pause at an outstanding hymn dating from the late Reformation: Samuel Crossman's *My Song Is Love Unknown* of 1664. It is rooted in the Puritan tradition and reflects the newfound individualism of the age, but in a way that is profoundly engaging. It draws us in to the indignation and amazement, the self-searching and gratitude that gather around the central paradox of the hymn: the joys of Palm Sunday and the horrors of Good Friday[10]:

---

4. Busfield also mentions Lady Jane Grey, the Nine-Day Queen (1536–54. Reigned: 10–19 July 1553), and a number of other examples.

5. Busfield, "Women, Men and Christ Crucified," 220.

6. Available in Mueller (ed.), *Katherine Parr: Complete Works*.

7. Busfield, "Women, Men and Christ Crucified," 221 citing Mueller (ed.), *Katherine Parr: Complete Works*, 558–59.

8. Hindmarsh, *Evangelical Conversion Narrative*, 14–15.

9. Ibid., 14.

10. Watson, *The English Hymn*, 88.

My song is love unknown,
My Saviour's love to me;
Love to the loveless shown,
That they might lovely be.
O who am I,
That for my sake
My Lord should take
Frail flesh and die?

He came from His blest throne
Salvation to bestow;
But men made strange, and none
The longed-for Christ would know:
But O! my Friend,
My Friend indeed,
Who at my need
His life did spend.

Sometimes they strew His way,
And His sweet praises sing;
Resounding all the day
Hosannas to their King:
Then "Crucify!"
is all their breath,
And for His death
they thirst and cry.

Why, what hath my Lord done?
What makes this rage and spite?
He made the lame to run,
He gave the blind their sight,
Sweet injuries!
Yet they at these
Themselves displease,
and 'gainst Him rise.

They rise and needs will have
My dear Lord made away;
A murderer they save,
The Prince of life they slay,
Yet cheerful He
to suffering goes,
That He His foes
from thence might free.

In life no house, no home,
Here might I stay and sing,
No story so divine;
Never was love, dear King!
Never was grief like Thine.
This is my Friend,
in Whose sweet praise
I all my days
could gladly spend.[11]

Also active in the very late seventeenth and early eighteenth century would be Isaac Watts, the godfather of the English hymn. His *When I Survey*, published in 1707, draws from a similar Puritan background to Crossman's and may be likened to the spiritual autobiographies that were the product English Puritanism.[12] There is some profound content here. It moves from the rather self-assured "survey" into a succession of "autodestructive acts."[13] The viewer of Christ on the cross is deeply humbled and radically reoriented by the experience until, in the end, only a total self-offering will suffice:

When I survey the wondrous cross
On which the Prince of glory died,
My richest gain I count but loss,
And pour contempt on all my pride.
Forbid it, Lord, that I should boast,
Save in the death of Christ my God!
All the vain things that charm me most,
I sacrifice them to His blood.

See from His head, His hands, His feet,
Sorrow and love flow mingled down!
Did e'er such love and sorrow meet,
Or thorns compose so rich a crown?
Were the whole realm of nature mine,
That were a present far too small;
Love so amazing, so divine,
Demands my soul, my life, my all.[14]

11. *Hymns and Psalms*, No. 173.

12. Watson, *The English Hymn*, 163.

13. Ibid., 161.

14. *Hymns and Psalms*, No. 180.

Introducing Pietism

Though the term can be used more loosely to refer to any kind of fervent evangelical piety, Pietism, strictly speaking, is the name we give to a movement that began at the very end of the Reformation and that extended far enough into the lifetime of Friedrich Schleiermacher (1738–1834) for him to have had plenty of contact with it. It was a reaction to dry Protestant scholasticism, especially of the Lutheran variety.

The period in which Pietism emerged was a time of "a revival of moral and religious earnestness."[15] Emerging within this earnestness, Pietism had an originating genius that made it the beginning point of much that is now taken for granted in evangelical Protestantism, such as the need to be born again and undergo a definite, punctiliar conversion experience, rather than signing up to one of the great Protestant confessions of faith and then living a life of cold religious formality.[16] Pietism exhibited a strong desire to move away from lifeless Lutheran orthodoxy and placed the doctrine of regeneration uppermost in its soteriology.[17] This brought about the desired focus upon the subjective state of the believer as opposed to his or her objectively justified status.[18] Such spiritual rebirth would lead to a pious and holy life, the longed-for result. Indeed, Halle Pietism, its earliest form, initiated by Philip Jakob Spener with his book *Pia Desideria* in 1675, was so concerned with the imperative of reformation of character that it dramatically underplayed the Lutheran doctrine of justification. Halle Pietism was thus blamed for *de*forming rather than *re*forming.[19]

---

15. Tappert (ed.), *Pia Desideria by Philip Jacob Spener*, 1.

16. Stoeffler cites the holiness orientation of Protestant preaching, the "vastly expanded hymnody," and Pietism's vision of "a world in need of the Gospel of Christ" as Protestant "firsts." For him, "Pietism was the most important development in Protestant spirituality." Stoeffler, "Preface," in Erb (ed.), *Pietists: Selected Writings*, ix.

17. "[B]oth in Spener and in Francke we read more about regeneration than about justification." Stoeffler, *German Pietism During the Eighteenth Century*, 10.

18. Erb (ed.), *Pietists: Selected Writings*, 6. It also brought the sharp division between "head" and "heart" that became so characteristic of Pietism and its more modern counterparts: "Let us remember that in the last judgment we shall not be asked how learned we were . . . ." Tappert (ed.), *Pia Desideria by Philip Jacob Spener*, 36. This approach would be especially influential upon Pietism's North American descendants, according to Erb (ed.), *Pietists: Selected Writings*, 25.

19 Erb (ed.), *Pietists: Selected Writings*, 6. The conflict with Lutheran orthodoxy that this new outlook brought about is covered in detail in Stoeffler, *Pietism: Selected Writings*, 8–23, 57–71.

However, it seems that before long even Pietism fell fowl of legalistic tendencies, the unintended result, no doubt, of its sincere moral rigorism.

Enter Zinzendorf

From 1727 a recognizably new form of Pietism began to emerge, whose leader, Count Nicolaus Ludwig von Zinzendorf (1700–1760)[20] actually came to reject the increasingly legalistic Halle Pietism that he had been brought up with. Zinzendorf's group, who would become known in England as the Moravians,[21] drew much of its leadership from Bohemia and Moravia in the present day Czech Republic. Its membership, a complex mixture of Protestants,[22] was one small part of a widespread emigration

20. Among the general works on Zinzendorf's life and theology are Beyreuther, *Zinzendorf und die Christenheit*; Beyreuther, *Studien zur Theologie Zinzendorfs*; Lewis, *Zinzendorf*; Aalen, *Die Theologie des jungen Zinzendorf*; Weinlick, *Count Zinzendorf*; Freeman, *An Ecumenical Theology of the Heart*; Meyer and Peuker (eds.), *Graf Ohne Grenzen*.

21. Throughout this piece of work, the term most familiar to the non-specialist English-speaking reader—Moravians—will be used, though, on the Continent the Moravians would have referred to themselves as the *Brüdergemeine*, the "Brethren's Congregation." Even in Britain, the Moravians of the eighteenth century would normally have referred to themselves not as Moravian but rather as the "United Brethren," or "Brethren." The term "Moravian Church" only became official in the British Province in 1908: Stead and Stead, *Exotic Plant*, 3–4.

22. A significant body of research has thrown into serious doubt the traditional historical account of origins that claims direct continuity with the original *Unitas Fratrum*. This was a community of proto-Protestants that broke with Rome in 1457 and was almost destroyed by the Thirty Years' War (1618–48). It survived, so the story goes, as an underground church called the Hidden Seed from 1627 until 1722 when the first Czech refugees arrived on Zinzendorf's estate. Then began the time of the Renewed Brethren. Atwood finds it questionable whether any of the two thousand Czech refugees who came to Zinzendorf were ever members of the old *Unitas Fratrum*. He helpfully cites three significant contributions to the debate that also argue against this traditional understanding: Molnár, "The Pious Fraud of Count Zinzendorf," 29–38; Ward, "The Renewed Unity of the Brethren, ixvii–xcii; and Sterrick, "Mährische Brüder, böhemische Brüder, und die Brüdergemeine," 106–14. Atwood, *Community of the Cross*, 21. Zeman makes clear how complex was the makeup of Czech Protestantism both before and after the influence of Luther and Calvin swept through the region. Distinguishing between Moravian Anabaptists, Hutterite Brethren, and the *Unitas Fratrum*, he devotes four pages to explaining the terminology alone. Zeman, *The Anabaptists and the Czech Brethren in Moravia 1526–1628*, 55–58. Substantial books continue to appear in English, however, that adhere, at least in part, to the traditional account of Moravian origins, most notably Podmore, *Moravian Church in England*, 5–6, who claims descent from the *Unitas*

from the Protestant heartlands of central Europe in the wake of Counter Reformation repression. Now, these refugees were safe to practice their religion on Zinzendorf's estate in Saxony.

Moravian Pietism displayed all the characteristic marks of evangelicalism. Among these evangelical identity markers was a strong theology of the cross.[23] From the Moravians onwards, the subjective dimension in the Christian life, already recovered by Halle Pietism, was no longer centered upon the new birth; now it was centered on the personal appropriation of the merits of Christ's death. This cross-centered spirituality went on to form a central component of what is now recognized as an essential part of the "vital orthodoxy" that underlay all the great eighteenth-century revivals.[24] Because of its essentially subjective nature, the use of the word "blood" became more appropriate than "cross," since "blood," both symbolically speaking and biblically speaking, is the aspect of a sacrifice that can be most readily manipulated and applied to the worshipper. It is fluid and distributable. Harking back to Bernard, the side-wound of Christ would become another point of subjective contact, this time requiring the worshipper, like Thomas, to approach in faith and touch the wound of the Savior.

Zinzendorf's spiritual roots ran deeply into Halle Pietism. Both parents were Pietists. His schooling from the ages of ten to sixteen was Pietist and when, finally, his widowed mother left him in the care of his grandmother, it was his grandmother's Pietist devotion that would influence him most of all. One incident during his Grand Tour at the age of eighteen is hailed by Lewis[25] as especially significant. This moment was his viewing of Dominico Feti's *Ecce Homo* in Düsseldorf Art Gallery on the 22 May

---

Fratrum for the Moravians but that they had, until Töltschig and the Nitschmanns revived them, "little knowledge of the traditions of their ancestors." He is clear, however, that, by April 1727 about a third of the adult population of Herrnhut (220 in total) was German. The Steads, after an impressive literature review, arrive at a nuanced position that allows *Unitas Fratrum* descent for a significant portion of the group, but emphasizes its mixed complexion: Stead and Stead, *Exotic Plant*, 13–29.

23 Bebbington identifies the theology of the cross as one component in his now well-used "quadrilateral" of distinctives that has characterized all forms of evangelicalism, the other three components being biblicentricity, activism, and conversionism: Bebbington, *Holiness in Nineteenth-Century England*, 36–41, 53–57, 77–78.

24. Piggin, *Firestorm of the Lord*, 45–49.

25. "There and then the young Count asked the crucified Christ to draw him into 'the fellowship of his sufferings' and to open up a life of service to him." Lewis, *Zinzendorf*, 28–29. This was not, however, the moment of Zinzendorf's conversion: Hutton, *A History of the Moravian Church*, 186. So Atwood, *Community of the Cross*, 98.

1719. It portrays Jesus wearing a crown of thorns. Beneath the painting is a caption saying:

> *"Ego pro te haec passus sum; tu vero, quid fecisti pro me?"*
> I for you have suffered this; truly, what have you done for me?[26]

This, however is unlikely to be the main origin of Zinzendorf's peculiar *theologia crucis* and is more likely to have been the catalyst that reacted with elements already present in Zinzendorf's spirituality. Two other influences would have impacted Zinzendorf from a much younger age. The aristocracy into which Zinzendorf was born was itself steeped in passion mysticism, particularly the Five Sacred Wounds cult. Ferdinand II (1619–37) had significantly influenced the German aristocracy in this direction. Ferdinand II himself would kneel and, with arms extended, kiss the floor five times each day in memory of the five wounds of Christ.[27] Secondly, Zinzendorf's childhood was already steeped in Luther and his theology of the cross thanks to his grandmother. Behind his devout grandmother lay the voice of Martin Luther. She would read aloud from his works so frequently that Zinzendorf claimed in adult life that he could still expound Luther on any given topic.[28]

In 1734, Zinzendorf underwent a "conversion" to Luther (as if that were needed), becoming especially fond of the Augsburg Confession. Thus it was with the Moravians that Luther's emphasis on pure grace merited by Christ's blood alone combined with Zinzendorf's background and experiences to form a particular brand of Protestantism characterized by devotional warmth, an emphasis on subjective religious experience, and ecumenism,[29] the religion of the heart.

The *Nine Public Lectures* of 1746[30] are significant in that they capture Zinzendorf's theology at the height of the so-called Sifting Period. This was

26. Translation by Freeman, *An Ecumenical Theology of the Heart*, 63.

27. Saunders, *Cross, Sword and Lyre*, 203–4.

28. Freeman, *Theology of the Heart*, 53.

29. "One may say that the theological views which are particular to the Moravian Church were formed by an awareness that Christianity at its heart is relational and devotional, not conceptual." Freeman, *Theology of the Heart*, 5.

30. These were given during Zinzendorf's residency in England (1746–55) and attended by the Bishop of Lincoln, John Thomas. Despite the highly unorthodox tone of these lectures, the Bishop went onto become highly influential in persuading Parliament, and hence the Church of England, to recognize the Moravians as an "Ancient Episcopal Church," and accept them into communion with the Church of England. This formally took place with the passing of the Moravian Act in 1749: Podmore, *Moravian Church in*

a period from 1743 to 1750 during which Moravian "blood and wounds theology," which we will encounter more of shortly, was at its height. In these lectures Zinzendorf's listeners are encouraged to visualize the wounds of Jesus: "Thus if you have serious thoughts about the Savior, conclude that the bleeding Savior stands before your hearts, that he is there in person, He longs to have you glance at His wounds."[31]

The reason why Jesus apparently wants his wounds to be so much the focus of the worshipping mind is the morally transformative power that they hold. In the following extract, Zinzendorf has added Bernard's Bridegroom metaphor, which is mixed with Zinzendorf's particular fondness for John 20:24–29 (the risen yet still wounded Jesus appearing to Thomas):

> For the Saviour is never in all eternity without His sign, without His wounds: the public showing has His holy wounds as its ground. . . . If we, therefore, want to invite people to the marriage, if we want to describe the Bridegroom, it must be said like this: "I decided to know nothing among you except Jesus as He hung upon the cross" (1 Cor. 2:2), as He was wounded. I point you to His nail prints, to the side, to the hole which the spear pierced open in His side. . . . As soon as this look strikes your heart, you run to the marriage feast.[32]

Yet, as with so many similar cases we have already looked at, this moral influence factor does not mean a mere exemplarist function for the cross,[33] since all true believers are believers because they have participated in the wounded Savior; they have dealt with their doubts, like Thomas, and committed their hearts to the wounded Christ. They are, henceforth, *ein Christ,* in vital eternal union with him:

> He who in this moment, in this instant, when the Saviour appears to him and when he says to him, as to Peter, "Do you love me in this figure?"—he who can say, "You know all things; you know that I love you"; he who in this minute, in this instant loses himself

---

England, 247.

31. Zinzendorf, *Nine Public Lectures,* 67.

32. Ibid., 28. Cf. Atwood: "Zinzendorf was obviously influenced by the marriage mysticism of late medieval Europe, but he connects this imagery with the Atonement in a unique fashion. . . . Zinzendorf connects his marriage mysticism closely to a Lutheran cross theology." Atwood, *Community of the Cross,* 91.

33. There is, as Atwood has pointed out, little direct reference to "morality or purity," in Moravian hymns: "The tone is that those who love Jesus are moral and chaste but there is no need to stress moral behavior." Atwood, *Community of the Cross,* 147.

in his tormented form and suffering figure—he remains in him eternally, without interruption . . . .[34]

In fact, the regenerating Holy Spirit himself, flows from the wounds of Christ:

> And as for the Holy Spirit who constructs himself as it were out of the matrix of his holy Side's Wound, . . . He then first, when the spear penetrated the dear Lamb, gushed out along with the incorruptible blood and life of the Lamb and with the Source of all, during this time, into human individuals to restore their little spirit (John 7) and has taken along the whole host of souls in his πληρώμα.[35]

In a way that anticipates the Pentecostals, devotion to the Holy Spirit was a central aspect of the life of the Moravian community. The famous communion service of 13 August 1727, when the Holy Spirit was said to fall upon all those present (about 220 people by that time[36]), melded them into a unity that had previously been difficult to sustain. Besides the better-known *Litany of the Wounds*,[37] two litanies to the Holy Spirit—the *Te Matrem* and *The Church's Prayer to the Holy Spirit*—were used every week.[38] Until Zinzendorf's death and the subsequent revision of much Moravian doctrine, the Holy Spirit was revered as Mother,[39] a simple, accessible

---

34. Erb (ed.), *Pietists: Selected Writings*, 320, citing *Nine Public Lectures* 25 September 1746. The text was John 21:6.

35. Zinzendorf, *Ein und zwanzig Discurse* 16 December 1747 (parentheses original), cited in Freeman, *Theology of the Heart*, 192.

36. Randall, "Recovering Evangelical Spirituality," 36.

37. Many Moravians felt considerable attachment to this litany. Zinzendorf himself recommended that if any outsider wished to understand Moravianism truly, it is to "our hymns, our *Litany of the Wounds*, and the homilies upon the same" that he or she must go: Atwood, *Community of the Cross*, 141, translating from *Helpers Conference Minutes* of the Moravian Archives, 8 November 1748, chapter 6. A complete translation of the Litany appears in Atwood, *Community of the Cross*, 233–37. See also Atwood, "Zinzendorf's Litany of the Wounds of the Husband," 189–214.

38. Atwood, "The Mother of God's People," 900.

39. Devotion to the Holy Spirit as Mother was, according to Zinzendorf, "an extremely important and essential point . . . and all our *Gemeine* and praxis hangs on this point." Atwood, "The Mother of God's People," 887, translating from Zinzendorf's *Eine Rede, vom Mutter-Amte des heiligen Geistes. Gehalten in London den 19 Oct. 1746*. Also: Kinkel, *Our Dear Mother the Spirit*. Having said this, Atwood's own survey, in a later piece of research, of a wide range of eighteenth-century Moravian hymnody yielded a total of only sixty-three references to "Holy Spirit" and sixty-four to "Mother." This

concept that fitted well alongside concepts of Christ as Husband[40] and God as Father—the three most intimate relations that humans know.[41] The *Te Matrem* also shows a clear vision of the relationship between the work of the Son and the work of the Spirit: "Divine majesty, who proceeds from the Father, who praises the Son as the creator and points to his suffering . . . ."[42]

With regards to the atonement, the note of forgiveness is only sounded in the midst of extolling the profound moral transformation awakened in the heart by a vision of the wounded, suffering Christ:

> Then I think: Good-bye,
> You self-empowered repenting.
> Like wax before the fire, I
> Want to melt in Jesus' suffering.
> My heart shall see the wrath
> In this suffering, pain
> And see the cleansing bath
> For all my transgressions' stain.[43]

The moral influence factor is never far away from Zinzendorf's thinking: "If only the power of his blood/Would master my hard heart/Push into every part!"[44] To balance this, the note of Christ's merit is sounded with equal strength: "May He let you share in His bloody atonement . . . may He let His penance for all the world bless you with grace and pardon of sins; may our Lord bless you with His merits . . . ."[45] There is merit inherent in the wounds themselves: "the bleeding Husband forms Himself in the innermost part of the soul. Then the heart stands full of Jesus, full of His wounds and His sores, full of the Merits of the Lamb"[46] "Blood" also

---

compares, according to a total of his figures, with 295 references to "Lamb," 273 references to "wounds," and 225 references to "blood." Atwood, *Community of the Cross*, 144–45. This somewhat undermines his own claim that the Moravian emphasis on the Spirit is "one of the best kept secrets in the history of Christianity," Atwood, "The Mother of God's People," 908.

40. E.g., this extract from Zinzendorf: "I believe that my Husband, by His own blood, by His real death on the tree of the cross, has placed me in a privileged position." *Nine Public Lectures*, 70.

41. Atwood, "The Mother of God's People," 890–91.

42. Translation by Atwood, "The Mother of God's People," 886.

43. Erb (ed.), *Pietists: Selected Writings*, 309.

44. Zinzendorf, *Nine Public Lectures*, 56.

45. Ibid., 64 and 94.

46. Ibid., 94.

appears alongside "righteousness" to convey the same idea.[47] The classic example of this would be Zinzendorf's most famous hymn, translated by John Wesley:

> Jesus, Thy blood and righteousness
> My beauty are, my glorious dress.
> Midst flaming worlds in these arrayed
> With joy shall I lift up my head.

Related to this (and included in verse 3 of the above hymn[48]) there is the note of pleading the blood:

> [W]e must come to Him entirely natural, in the most wretched form in which we happen to find ourselves, pleading His blood, His faithfulness, and His merits, and reminding Him that we men are the reward of His suffering . . . .[49]

For Zinzendorf, to plead the blood is to surrender all attempts at the acquisition of merit before God on one's own account, to boldly approach God on the basis of Christ's merit and to remind God of one's status as blood-bought.

In all of this, Zinzendorf, like any good Lutheran, was doubtless assuming the atoning significance of the blood[50] but wanted to move beyond there and use the blood to shore up the faith of his followers against the onslaughts of the age. Previous to the *Nine Public Lectures* there had been an emphasis on the blood of Christ as a ransom,[51] but now the blood and wounds of Christ were being recruited by Zinzendorf to speak a message of anti-intellectual fideism to prevailing Enlightenment ideas.[52] The genius of

---

47. Ibid., 73, 76.

48. "When from the dust of death I rise / To claim my mansion in the skies / E'en then shall this be all my plea / 'Jesus hath lived, and died, for me.'"

49. Zinzendorf, *Nine Public Lectures*, 101.

50. His orthodoxy as a Lutheran won him his ordination as a Lutheran minister in 1735: Freeman, *Theology of the Heart*, 6.

51. Hamilton and Hamilton, *History of the Moravian Church*, 155. As early as 1734, Zinzendorf had been especially taken with the biblical uses of the word *lutron*. This was, apparently, owing to the influence of the hymnody of the "Bohemian Brethren" on him: Atwood, *Community of the Cross*, 98.

52. Freeman provides an incisive overview of Zinzendorf's engagement with the Enlightenment as its ideas steadily spread, summing up Zinzendorf's reaction to it in the words of Pascal: "The heart has its reasons, which reason does not know." Freeman, *Theology of the Heart*, 43 (citing Pascal, *Pensees*, Section iv). Zinzendorf anticipated many of the replies of Schleiermacher: feeling instead of rationalism, religious experience instead

Zinzendorf was in the highly audacious and sensuous language with which he enthralled a generation, providing it with "an anatomical, physiological sieve"[53] through which spiritual truths could pass. Through liturgy, hymnody, and sermon he made mystical longings expressible and union with the Godhead conceivable.

The Moravians

Interest in the Moravians shows no sign of abating. There is a wealth of published research about the Moravians from an American, British, and German perspective.[54] And their place in the history of devotion to the atonement is assured. The study of the devotion of this fascinating group shows that their devotion to the atonement was sincere and white-hot. This clearly brought dividends in terms of an extraordinary personal assurance of faith, even when facing death, and an equally dauntless missionary urge. Yet, alongside this strength of feeling are elements of the truly bizarre. Thankfully, though, some of the medieval outpourings have already prepared us for some of this.

The use of references to the blood and wounds of Jesus, around which much that was characteristic of Moravian spirituality was organized, soon became excessive. This excess reached its peak during the aforementioned Sifting Period. At this time, Zinzendorf had been absent for some time and the Herrnhaag[55] community, a plant of the original Herrnhut, had become

---

of religious hatred and dogma, the difference being that Zinzendorf drew these answers from the cross rather than the person of Christ. The wounds of Christ gave Zinzendorf a strong theodicy at a time, especially following the 1755 Lisbon earthquake, when many were asking the "why suffering?" question. Cf. Freeman, *Theology of the Heart*, 45–46, Faull, "Faith and Imagination," in Faull (ed.), *Anthropology and the German Enlightenment*, 23–56.

53. Camporesi, *Juice of Life*, 70.

54. The following are among the more recent general works. From an American perspective: Hamilton and Hamilton, *History of the Moravian Church*; Atwood, *Community of the Cross*; Peucker, *A Time of Sifting*. From a British Perspective: Towlson, *Moravian and Methodist*; Lewis, *Zinzendorf* (which, despite the title, is mostly about the Moravians); Podmore, *Moravian Church in England*; Mason, *Missionary Awakening* and Stead and Stead, *Exotic Plant*. From an American and German perspective: Gollin, *Moravians in Two Worlds*. For works in German to 1987, see Meyer, *Bibliographisches Handbuch zur Zinzendorf-Forschung*.

55. Developments here, leading to its eventual closure, are described in Stead and Stead, *Exotic Plant*, 70–74.

dominated by the vibrant spirituality of some of its younger members. These young people, striving for true intimacy with Jesus, took some of Zinzendorf's teachings to extremes. There appear to have been three main components to this. Firstly, they became enamored with the teaching of Jesus, mediated by Zinzendorf, on the importance of becoming like little children. Secondly, they were steeped in Christ-erotic ways of expressing their love for Jesus as their souls' Bridegroom. Thirdly, they displayed an extreme and highly gruesome emphasis on the wounds of Jesus.

It is in the hymns and liturgies of the Moravians that their doctrine comes to full and vivid expression.[56] Communion took on a dimension of spiritual fervor unknown even among the most passionate of medieval sacramentalists:

> Afterwards we sat us down to the Agape with our Spirits watching every Bloody Drop flowing from our incomparable Friend in Agony, and at last enjoyed that which words cannot utter without a Holy Shuddering of the Fraim. The Body and Blood of Christ.[57]

According to the Steads a strong influence on the Moravians, mediated via Zinzendorf, was the sacred music of the imperial court of Habsburg alluded to earlier, as well as some extreme examples of the hymns of Johann Scheffler (1624–77), seventy-nine of which found their way into an early Moravian collection.[58] Worshippers must visualize, must look upon the wounds: "Here let me dwell, and view those wounds/Which life for me procures."[59]

Lutheran ideas of merit are also prominent:

> Jesus, Thee I view in spirit,
> Covered o'er with blood and wounds:
> Now salvation through Thy merit
> For my sin-sick soul abounds . . . .[60]

---

56. Zinzendorf himself said, "Liturgists are more important than preachers and teachers." Atwood, *Community of the Cross*, 141, translating *jüngerhaus Diarium* 1 September 1759. Cf. "There is more dogma in our canticles than in our prose." Moravian saying quoted in Linyard and Tovey, *Moravian Worship*, 10.

57. Extract from the diaries of the English Moravian community at Fulneck, cited in Stead, *Exotic Plant*, 305. Cf. Stead, "Moravian Spirituality and its Propagation in West Yorkshire during the Eighteenth-Century Evangelical Revival," 242–43.

58. Stead and Stead, *Exotic Plant*, 331–33.

59. *Moravian Hymn Book*, No. 104.

60. Ibid., No. 97.

Through Thy sufferings, death and merit,
I eternal life inherit.[61]

Related to the idea of merit is the picture of Christ as the ascended High Priest pleading before the Father on the basis of his sacrifice:

All heavenly host adore Thee,
Seated at Thy Father's side:
There for sinners Thou art pleading . . .
Help us to sing our Saviour's merits.[62]

This is our only plea,
That Thou for us hast died.[63]

These themes of merit and pleading will re-occur frequently in the hymns of Charles Wesley. There is also the theme of childlike abdication. It is here that the terminology can seem, to an outsider, to be strange and perverse, though, in the light of some medieval devotion, it is nothing new:

Now rests my whole mind on
In one nook of the Side-hole,
And dreams of Blood alone:
Sometimes it is as a wide Hall,
Sometimes so close and Deep
As if each Heart in it
Alone did lie and sleep.[64]

Lovely Side-hole, take in me:
Let me ever be in Thee
O Side-hole's Wound, My Heart and Soul,
Does pant for thy so lovely Hole.[65]

For both Zinzendorf and the Moravians, the religion of the heart was a religion in which the sincere heart would gaze upon the wounds of the risen Christ and, like Thomas, have its doubts removed. In supra-rational faith, the Moravian soul then lives for him who died for her. The hearts of the devout are knit to the Savior in rapturous love. This devout love,

---

61. Ibid., No. 101.
62. Ibid., No. 108.
63. Ibid., No. 273.
64. *Moravian Hymnal* 1748 Part III, No. 67, cited in Stead, *Exotic Plant*, 310.
65. Ibid., No. 59, in Stead, *Exotic Plant*, 309.

which never forgets the blood and wounds that supply the merit of every true believer, is expressed in language that seems strange and extreme. Such language is deliberately irrational. It is the language of revolt against the sterility of Enlightenment thought and scholastic religion.

In the process of this revolt something similar is going on that we have seen already: the revitalization of metaphor. And, again, the key strategy is to use paradox:

> The doctrine of justification by grace through faith, which in Lutheran Orthodoxy had become sterile academic debate, was recast in terms of the ever-present paradox of the both beautiful and horrible wounds of Christ. . . . It was in the light of this primal paradox that the paradox of being a justified sinner was to be understood and experienced.[66]

For the Moravians the primary way of experiencing now the historical event of the atonement was via a wholehearted abandonment of the self to it in worship. The adoring heart then discovers that the object of worship is not a crucified Jesus hanging limp and helpless but a glorified Lamb still bearing his wounds and still appearing to his disciples. It is at this central point, according to the Moravian understanding, that feeling runs deep enough for sin to be cast out. The Moravians entertained no self-righteous asceticism. Their ideal was a devoted heart.

There is much about Moravian spirituality that has a contemporary significance. Firstly, the cultural context of the Moravians was one characterized by the Post-Reformation collapse of religious consensus. This collapse of consensus opened the way for essentially nonreligious definitions of reality, such as empiricism and rationalism, to fight it out on the bourgeois academic stage. The way the Moravians dealt with this was by taking an anti-intellectual turn back to a medieval style of mysticism invested with strongly emotive and intuitive avenues to knowing. Via the ex-Moravian Schleiermacher, with his emphasis on religious feeling, the spirituality of Moravianism was prophetic of and contributory towards the onset of the Romantic era. Both of the above: the collapse of epistemological consensus and the rush towards non-cognitive ways of knowing are also characteristic of the postmodern age. What a Moravian style of passion piety achieves in such a context might be described as the expulsive power of a higher affection. Its fostering of religious affection is the key to its success. Spiritual indebtedness is its sole sanctifying power.

---

66. Atwood, "Understanding Zinzendorf's Blood and Wounds Theology," 46.

The Wesleys

There is much competition over who or what should take pride of place as the most influential factor in the formation of John Wesley's theology.[67] A lot seems to depend on what particular church tradition those studying him represent. Hempton concludes that rather than any one influence being pre-eminent in Wesley's theology, it is "Wesley's eclecticism" itself that is "pre-eminent."[68] Cracknell and White list Wesley's mother, Thomas á Kempis, and Jeremy Taylor as his most important early influences during the period when he was preoccupied with the concept of "purity of intention."[69] Here, my one intention is to identify from whence his emphasis on the blood of Christ most likely came. His journals would appear to reflect a Moravian point of origin, there being almost no references to the blood of Christ in Wesley's journals until after he had made the acquaintance of Peter Böhler in February 1738,[70] a little over three months before his Aldersgate experience (May 24), which sealed for him the truth of Böhler's theology. Hence, although Wesley's atonement devotion went on to become very different to that of the Moravians, its point of origin is almost certainly Moravian.[71]

---

67. Hempton, *Empire of the Spirit*, 56–57.

68. Ibid.

69. Cracknell and White, *Introduction to World Methodism*, 7–9.

70. The first mention of the blood of Christ in John Wesley's journals is on Sunday 14 April 1738 when he describes preaching, in the wake of prolonged discussions with Böhler, a sermon on the theme of "free salvation through faith in the blood of Christ," at St. Ann's, Aldersgate. However, in his sermons, there are a number of references to the blood of Christ prior to his exposure to the Moravians. In one, he even proclaims that, "It is his daily care, by the grace of God in Christ, and through the blood of the covenant, to purge the inmost recesses of his soul . . . ." His first obviously Böhler-influenced sermon was delivered at St. Mary's, Oxford entitled, *Salvation by Faith*. According to Outler's chronology, this was delivered 11 June 1738, according to Smith's dates, this was 7 June 1738. In this he speaks for the first time of "a full reliance on the blood of Christ; a trust in the merits of his life, death, and resurrection; a recumbency upon him as our atonement and our life . . . ." All his sermons that make mention of the blood of Christ are as follows (Where Smith's dating differs from Outler's, Smith's is given after the forward-slash): sermons 101 (1732), 17 (1733), 127 (1735), 1 (1738: *Salvation by Faith*), 9 (1739/46), 21 (1739/48), 22 (1739/48), 23 (1739/48), 24 (1740/48), 25 (1740/48), 26 (1740/48). In his letters there is only one reference to the blood of Jesus prior to May 1738. From then onwards, for the next couple of years, the subject of faith in the blood of Christ becomes an urgent and recurrent one.

71. Other much earlier influences need not be excluded, however. Böhler's role appears to have been to open Wesley's eyes to the possibilities of repose by faith alone in the blood of Christ instead of good works.

With the arrival of Moravian Peter Böhler in London, on 7 February 1738, the influence of the Moravian Church on English Christianity began.[72] Böhler apparently looked up John Wesley on the very day he disembarked.[73] John Wesley was later to become enamored with the spirituality of Böhler, who displayed "dominion over sin and a constant peace from a sense of forgiveness," which Wesley saw as "a new gospel."[74] John and Charles Wesley's first contact with the Moravians had been in October 1735 on their perilous voyage across the Atlantic to Savannah. This encounter was to lead to John Wesley becoming aware of his own lack of faith.[75]

Wesley soon became a close companion of Zinzendorf himself. The split between the two leaders came in 1741 when Wesley and Zinzendorf could not agree on the issue of sanctification.[76] Zinzendorf's view of the blood was strictly forensic and firmly Lutheran: "All Christian Perfection is, Faith in the blood of Christ. Our whole Christian Perfection is imputed, not inherent."[77] At this time Zinzendorf was breaking all allegiance to Halle Pietism and declaring that Moravians were not Pietists. His objection to the Hallensians was the same as his objection to the Methodists: both believed in a soul-searching preliminary experience in which the claims of the law become frightening. Zinzendorf and his followers came to describe this as the "legal" approach, while the Moravian approach, castigated by Wesley as antinomian, emphasized surrender to God's grace through the atonement.[78]

By August 1742, John Wesley's connections with the Moravians had become weak enough for him to overtly castigate them for their beliefs about the blood and wounds of Jesus, in a sermon described as "very furious."[79] The English reaction to Moravian blood and wounds theology widened in 1749 with the publication of the first English-language Moravian hymnal. The English found the references to the blood and wounds as well as the

72. Wood, *The Inextinguishable Blaze*, 85.

73. Hamilton, *A History of the Church Known as the Moravian Church*, 85.

74. Heitzenrater (ed.), *Works of John Wesley* 18, 247–48: 24 May 1738.

75. Heitzenrater (ed.), *Works of John Wesley* 18, 142–43: 18–30 January 1735.

76. The Fetter Lane Society had already split over the issue of quietism, the setting up of a new society at the Foundry on 23 July 1740 marking the beginning of the first Methodist Society.

77. The full conversation is available in English in Freeman, *Theology of the Heart*, 188.

78. Hindmarsh helpfully highlights this difference with the support of archival records of conversions: *Evangelical Conversion Narrative*, 162–92, especially 165–67.

79. Podmore, *Moravian Church in England*, 76.

overt eroticism of the hymns deeply offensive.[80] By 1754, much of the outlandish blood and wounds language had been edited out of the Moravian Hymn Book of the British Province.[81] There is, however, evidence of a strong magnetic power to Moravian spirituality, even in its extreme forms, which was felt among an increasing number of English Christians.[82] There is also evidence that John Wesley's soteriology, in the latter half of his years in ministry, became more Lutheran in its emphasis on the imputed righteousness of Christ.[83] Much of his distaste for Moravian beliefs appears originally to have been rooted in their love of Luther. Wesley linked Luther with the dreaded spectre of antinomianism, which he saw too often in his converts. Wesley's passion for holiness of life made him suspicious of Luther and therefore of Moravian theology.

From the early 1740s onwards, John Wesley's attitude to the Moravians oscillated between bitterness over their beliefs and an irresistible admiration for their spirituality. Charles Wesley, however, maintained a consistently charitable spirit towards them, even momentarily falling under the spell of their quietist fad.[84] His hymns also contain some overtly Moravian phraseology:

80. Stead and Stead, *Exotic Plant*, 266.

81. Ibid., 323. See also a fascinating study of how the original content of *O Sacred Head Once Wounded*, was toned down via its translation into English from Gerhardt's own adaptation of a medieval original (called *Membra Jesu Nostri*): Faithful, "A More Brotherly Song, a Less Passionate Passion," 779–811.

82. Podmore, *Moravian Church in England*, 134: "That the spirituality of the Sifting Time provoked opposition in England is well documented; what has not been accepted is that to many who joined the Moravians it was deeply attractive and an important reason for their doing so." Podmore lists "Identity" (as the truest, best, and most favored church), "Refuge" (allowing an anti-Enlightenment abdication of both will and reason), "Pastoral Care" (through small groups, home visits, and marriage guidance), "Spirituality" (which among the English Moravians became increasingly focused on the Eucharist), "Community Life" (most notably at Fulneck in Yorkshire), "Worship" (solemn, liturgical, powerful experiences for many), and "Style and Celebration" (highly visual, much use of baroque art), as the main reasons for the appeal of Moravianism in eighteenth-century England: Podmore, *Moravian Church in England*, 120–58. Cf. Stead, "Moravian Spirituality," 233–59.

83. Piper discusses this, citing strong evidence from the primary literature as well as two recent studies of Wesley: Piper, *Counted Righteous in Christ*, 38.

84. So Podmore: "Charles Wesley was drawn to the Moravians and their teaching much more than John." Podmore, *Moravian Church in England*, 76. Moravian quietism or "stillness" doctrine seems to be rooted in the strong influence that Madam Guyon's writings had begun to have over Zinzendorf: Hindmarsh, *Evangelical Conversion Narrative*, 175. This will not be the last time we note the influence of Guyon. Keswick teachings

Thy Offering still continues new,
The vesture keeps its bloody hue,
Thou stand'st the ever-Slaughtered Lamb
Thy Priesthood still remains the same . . . .[85]

Charles Wesley, like the Moravians, also valued the subjective appropriation of Christ's blood and wounds: "I feel the life his wounds impart;/ I feel my Saviour in my heart."[86] And again: "Come feel with me His blood applied:/ My Lord, my Love, is crucified."[87] However, Charles Wesley's hymns display a much more soteriological, and arguably more biblical, emphasis than those of the Moravians, Charles Wesley being especially interested in the theme of cleansing. This theme, of course, is best expressed in his *O For a Thousand Tongues*:

He breaks the power of cancelled sin,
He sets the pris'ner free;
His blood can make the foulest clean,
His blood availed for me.[88]

Equally famous and even more full of atonement theology is *And Can It Be*. One reader of my first volume corresponded with me by email[89] and reminded me how this hymn deviates quite strikingly from standard penal substitution speak. It uses racial and federal categories:

He left his father's throne above –
So free, so infinite his grace –
Emptied himself of all but love,
And bled for Adam's helpless race . . . .

No condemnation now I dread
Jesus and all in him is mine!
Alive in him my living Head
And clothed in righteousness divine.[90]

---

also owe a great deal to her.

85. Charles Wesley cited in Davie, *Christian Verse*, 159.

86. Davie, *Christian Verse*, 159.

87. *Redemption Hymnal*, No. 173.

88. Ibid., No. 8.

89. Email from Joel Kidwell, Pastor of Zion United Methodist Church, Gordonville, dated 18 February 2016.

90. *Methodist Hymnbook*, No. 371.

John Wesley too, as well as Charles, clearly set a precedent for crucicentrism in his followers. He describes his own preaching: "At first we
preached almost wholly to unbelievers. To those therefore we spake almost
continually of the remission of sins through the death of Christ, and the
nature of faith in his blood."[91] This emphasis appears to have lastingly influenced his followers. His entry for 6 September 1742 describes a meeting
with a number of ladies who all reported some remarkable spiritual experiences, not all of which he was comfortable with:

> [T]hus far I approved of their experience (because agreeable to
> the written word), as to their feeling the working of the Spirit of
> God, in peace, and joy, and love. But as to what some of them said
> farther, concerning feeling the blood of Christ running upon their
> arms, or going down their throat, or poured like warm water upon
> their breast or heart, I plainly told them the utmost I could allow,
> without renouncing both Scripture and reason, was, that some of
> these circumstance might be from God (though I could not affirm
> they were) working in an unusual manner, no way essential either
> to justification or sanctification; but that all the rest I must believe
> to be the mere empty dreams of an heated imagination.[92]

Wesley and Christian Perfection

Synan describes John Wesley' *Plain Account of Christian Perfection* as a
"veritable manifesto"[93] for all the holiness groups that would later come
into being in the nineteenth century. It is without doubt, however, that
the writing of this book, Wesley's most sustained treatment of the theme,
would not have taken place were it not for a series of events that together
make up the Perfectionist Revival or Otley Revival of the 1760s. Of the year
1760, Wesley himself records:

> Here began that glorious work of sanctification which had been
> nearly at a stand for twenty years. From time to time it spread, first

91. Heitzenrater (ed.), *Works of John Wesley 10: Minutes of Conference*, 2 August
1745, 152.

92. Heitzenrater (ed.), *Works of John Wesley 19: Journal and Diaries* II, 295–96: 6
September 1742. I am indebted to my colleague and Wesley scholar Dr. George Bailey
for alerting me to this.

93. "This eighty-one page document has served as a veritable manifesto for all the
holiness and perfectionist groups that have separated from Methodism during the past
two centuries." Synan, *The Pentecostal-Holiness Tradition*, 6.

through parts of Yorkshire, afterward in London, then through parts of England, next to Dublin, Limerick, and through the south and west of Ireland. And wherever the work of sanctification increased, the whole work of God increased in all its branches.[94]

A characteristic of this revival, which was clearly by no means restricted to the Yorkshire village of Otley, was that it affected "long-established believers."[95] The beginning point appears to have been a meeting held in Otley on 13 February 1760,[96] but soon Wesley is able to collect hundreds of personal testimonies of people who, following a struggle with a strong sense of sin and failure, came through to a point of liberty.[97]

One of these testimonies was noteworthy enough for Wesley to include it in chapter 24 of his *Plain Account*. It is that of Jane Cooper, who heard Wesley speak on Galatians 5:5: "For we, through the Spirit, eagerly wait for the righteousness of faith." This awakened in her the desire to be "truly happy." She goes on:

> I was kept watching unto prayer, sometimes in much distress, at other times in patient expectation of the blessing. The Tuesday after you went, I thought I could not sleep, unless he fulfilled his word that night. I never knew as I did then the force of these words: "Be still and know that I am God." I became nothing before Him, and enjoyed perfect calmness in my soul. I knew not whether he had destroyed my sin; but I desired to know, that I might praise Him. I soon found the return of unbelief, and groaned, being burdened.

Her struggles continue until she is prayed for by a Mrs. G., who was a Calvinist. Jane Cooper recalls:

> I was in a moment enabled to lay hold on Jesus Christ. And found salvation by simple faith. He assured me the Lord, the King, was in the midst of me, and that I should see evil no more. . . . I saw Jesus altogether lovely; and knew he was mine in all his offices. And, glory be to him, He now reigns my heart without a rival. I find no will but his. I feel no pride; nor any affection but what is placed on Him. I know it is by faith I stand; and that watching unto prayer

---

94. Heitzenrater (ed.), *Works of John Wesley* 9: *Methodist Societies*, 473–74.

95. Staniforth, *Methodist Pentecost*, 7.

96. Heitzenrater (ed.), *Works of John Wesley* 9: *Methodist Societies*, 473.

97. These numbered around four hundred by 1762: Staniforth, *Methodist Pentecost*, 12.

must be the guard of faith. I am happy in God this moment, and I believe for the next.[98]

In the *Plain Account* it is clear that Wesley held that a process of sanctification was begun in the heart at regeneration but that a second experience was needed to bring "full salvation," or, "entire sanctification." This second blessing involved the cleansing away of all sin followed by an influx of love towards God and people taking its place in the believing heart. Hence, entire sanctification was referred to as "perfect love." The blood of Christ eradicated the negative, creating space for the inundation of the positive: the continual inclination to do the will of God. All failings from this point onwards were considered by Wesley to be unintentional. He preferred to call all subsequent sins "infirmities," which the atoning blood continually covered. In this way, it was necessary for even the fully sanctified believer to continually lean upon the merits of Christ, just as a branch must draw sustenance from the tree, even though the believer is now, technically, perfect. The ambiguity of all this teaching, utilizing multiple terms such as Christian perfection, perfect love, entire sanctification, and full salvation, did not go unnoticed by Wesley's critics.

Despite the confusion in the detail, it is important not to miss the very strong proposal that Wesley makes. At one point in the *Plain Account* he also reminisces about the crucial insight given him by the Moravians concerning justifying faith in Christ's blood.[99] The insight that justification was by faith alone was crucial. This principle of faith could then be applied to sanctification in just the same way, wresting perfection from beyond death to make it attainable in the present. Gone would be the defeated gradualism of the Reformed doctrine. Faith rarefied his Christian perfection into something that could happen to anyone if they were expectant, whereas his earlier doctrine of Christian perfection had been decidedly semi-Pelagian, as expressed in his 1733 sermon *The Circumcision of the Heart*, focusing as it did on the human means of attaining it.[100] Now it was clearer than ever

98. Heitzenrater (ed.), *Works of John Wesley* 13: *Treatises* II, 183–84.

99. "In August following, I had a long conversation with Arvid Gradin, in Germany. After he had given me an account of his experience, I desired him to give me, in writing, a definition of "the full assurance of faith," which he did in the following words . . . 'Repose in the blood of Christ; a firm confidence in God, and persuasion of His favour; the highest tranquillity, serenity, and peace of mind; with a deliverance from every fleshly desire, and a cessation of all, even inward sins.'" Heitzenrater (ed.), *Works of John Wesley* 13: *Treatises* II, 140–41.

100. McGonigle, *Sufficient Saving Grace*, 243–44.

that sanctification, like justification, could happen simply by faith, and to anyone who was expectant, and this possibility had been proved by what was happening in Otley.

The most notable feature of the references to the blood of Jesus in Wesley's *Plain Account* is the total dominance of the cleansing motif. This is in large measure due to the fact that he takes 1 John 1:7 as one of a number of proof texts for his doctrine of Christian perfection, claiming that the cleansing described is complete and final in this life:

> A Christian is so far perfect as not to commit sin. . . . For he sayeth not, The blood of Christ *will* cleanse (at the hour of death, or in the day of judgment), but it "cleanseth," at the present time, us living Christians "from all sin." And it is equally evident, that if any sin remain, we are not cleansed from all sin.[101]

To illustrate the cleansing dynamic of the blood, he quotes freely from his brother's extravagant imagery:

> Come, thou dear Lamb, for sinners slain,
> Bring in the cleansing flood:
> Apply, to wash out every stain,
> Thine efficacious blood.
> O let it sink into our soul
> Deep as the inbred sin;
> Make every wounded spirit whole,
> And every leper clean![102]

Hymn Break

Before we leave the eighteenth century, it seems wrong not to mention William Cowper, though he does not exactly fit within the movements we have just been looking at. There is a link to the Evangelical Revival in that Wesley's contemporary George Whitefield mentored John Newton, and John Newton in turn nurtured the newfound faith of the anxious and sensitive William Cowper. The theology was Calvinistic, though the church which Newton and Cowper attended and wrote poems and hymns for was an Anglican parish church in Olney, Bedfordshire. He was inspired by reading Zechariah 13:1, and here seems to enjoy a rare and hard-won personal

---

101. Heitzenrater (ed.), *Works of John Wesley* 13: *Treatises* II, 149–50.

102. Ibid., 165.

assurance of salvation after a lifetime of battling depression. The words shock the reader into seeing again the power of being cleansed. He does this by pushing the tired metaphor in a direction that is almost too concrete and literal for us to cope with: bathing in blood that has come from Christ's actual veins. It is "evangelical baroque."[103]

There is a fountain filled with blood
Drawn from Emmanuel's veins;
And sinners plunged beneath that flood
Lose all their guilty stains,

The dying thief rejoic'd to see
That Fountain in his day;
And there have I, as vile as he,
Wash'd all my sins away.

Dear dying Lamb, thy precious blood
shall never lose its power
till all the ransomed church of God
be saved, to sin no more.

E'er since, by faith, I saw the stream
thy flowing wounds supply,
redeeming love has been my theme,
and shall be till I die.[104]

Also belonging to the same era would be Augustus Toplady's *Rock of Ages* of 1763. A reference to Exodus 17:6 (water from the rock) and Exodus 33:22 (Moses hiding in the cleft of the rock) could be inferred from the song. The occasion of its first writing, however, is thought to be Toplady getting caught in a thunder storm in Burrington Combe in Somerset, and hiding in a cleft of one of the sheer cliff faces that line the gorge on both sides.[105] Apparently he wrote the words on the back of a discarded playing card. The opening line is especially lovely, moving us from hardness and permanence to refuge and softness.[106] We have, in extreme brevity, "the majesty of God and the frailty of humanity."[107] There is almost certainly also

103. Watson, *The English Hymn*, 295.

104. *The United Methodist Hymnal*: http://www.hymnary.org/hymn/UMH/622 [accessed online 18/03/2016].

105. Hodges, *The Story of Hymns*, 114–15.

106. Watson, *The English Hymn*, 274.

107. Ibid.

a nodding reference, surprising in a devout Calvinist, to the Five Sacred Wounds tradition that we have seen.

> Rock of Ages, cleft for me,
> Let me hide myself in Thee;
> Let the water and the blood,
> From Thy riven side which flowed,
> Be of sin the double cure,
> Cleanse me from its guilt and power.
>
> Not the labours of my hands
> Can fulfill Thy law's demands;
> Could my zeal no respite know,
> Could my tears forever flow,
> All for sin could not atone;
> Thou must save, and Thou alone.
>
> Nothing in my hand I bring,
> Simply to Thy cross I cling;
> Naked, come to Thee for dress;
> Helpless, look to Thee for grace;
> Foul, I to the fountain fly;
> Wash me, Saviour, or I die.[108]

Conclusion

I have here attempted to trace a scarlet thread of passion piety that, in both England and Germany, ran uninterrupted through the transition from a Roman Catholic to a Reformed faith. Through Lutheran Pietism the line is traceable to Zinzendorf and his followers and then on to the Wesleys. Amongst the Moravians there was a fervent desire for intellectual and emotional abdication to Jesus. Moravian spirituality was a spirituality of unqualified devotion to Christ in the tradition of the medieval mystics. It was a radically anti-Enlightenment movement. Further, they reckoned that if they were devoted enough to the all-conquering Lamb, there would be no need for self-denial, mortification, or asceticism. Indeed, their paintings showed a certain opulence that was entirely in keeping with certain aspects of the German aristocracy of which Zinzendorf was a part. Like the baroque of Zinzendorf's home, their language was flowery, extravagant, and hyperbolic. When this extreme devotional language was applied to

108. *Hymns and Psalms*, No. 273.

the blood and wounds of Jesus, the result was shocking. Charles Wesley was able to soften the vulgarities and present evangelical passion piety to a wider public, and bequeath it to subsequent generations. In spite of John Wesley's repudiation of Moravian blood mysticism, the theological system he created made the blood of Jesus logically essential to his whole doctrine of the second blessing. Being permanently and completely cleansed by the blood was an essential preliminary to receiving the sanctifying grace of the Spirit.

Two legacies of spirituality appear to have been bequeathed to Christianity from this period. Firstly, the tendency towards visualization as a stimulant to faith causes the physical symbols of the medieval sacrament to live on just as vividly in the minds of the rather less sacramental evangelicals—though the Moravians clearly revered the Eucharist and the Wesleys too were not exactly low church. Yet there does begin here a growing expectation that God now infuses the mental image of the crucified Christ—rather than the physical elements—with his real presence. Faith in a visualized blood and wounds melts the heart and inspires repentance, like a mental icon. Secondly, the cleansing theme, so central to Wesley's theological system, would prove to be a powerful motif, dominating the hymnody and preaching of the holiness movements of the nineteenth century. To these we now turn.

Chapter 4

———

THE HOLINESS MOVEMENTS

The First American Methodists

IT IS IMPORTANT NOT to miss the continued growth and vibrancy of Methodism in Britain after the death of Wesley,[1] as well as the constant trans-Atlantic borrowing that took place within English-speaking evangelicalism throughout the nineteenth century.[2] The key difference between British and American evangelicalism in the nineteenth century was the extent to which revivalism was embraced. In America, a crisis-orientated revivalistic approach, both inside and outside Methodism, became widely accepted, while in Britain, under the watchful eye of an established church, revivalism never became mainstream.[3] And it was the revivalistic atmosphere that allowed Methodism and the holiness message to especially

---

1. "[W]e may speak of Wesleyan Methodism at the turn of the nineteenth century as a community with well-functioning institutional bases, considerable spiritual strength and vitality, and with many of the elements of a full church order." Cracknell and White, *World Methodism*, 31. By the time of the *Census of Religious Worship* of 1851, 3 percent of the adult population of England and Wales was Methodist: Cracknell and White, *World Methodism*, 34. At the jubilee of the Methodist New Connexion in 1848, the movement described itself as having "an active, fervid, and joyous piety." Bebbington, *Holiness*, 53, citing *The Jubilee of the Methodist New Connexion*, 398. Only later in that century did the Methodist insistence on conversion and the centrality of the atonement begin to be played down: Bebbington, *Holiness*, 54–55.

2. See Carwardine, *Transatlantic Revivalism* and Kent, *Holding the Fort*.

3. Carwardine, *Transatlantic Revivalism*, xiv.

thrive in America. The first Methodist sermon ever to be preached in America came from the mouth of Capt. Thomas Webb in New York City in 1766.[4] During 1773–76, Methodism took firm hold in Virginia by means of a significant revival.[5] The founding of the Methodist Episcopal Church in 1784[6] was followed in 1787 by the founding of the African Methodist Episcopal Church, which of all the Methodist groups in North America would prove to be the most consistently loyal to Wesleyan perfectionism.[7] By 1800, Methodism, with its attendant doctrine of Christian perfection, was a major denominational block and began tipping the theological scales of popular religion away from the Calvinism of the Puritan settlers. In 1801, the hysterical Cane Ridge camp meeting revival in Bourbon County, Kentucky, was a significant event attracting tens of thousands of people[8] of partly Baptist and partly Methodist complexion. By 1812, the Methodists were holding at least four hundred camp meetings annually throughout the United States.[9] By mid-century, Methodism was the dominant religion of North America.

Dayton[10] has observed that the early preaching of the Methodists in America was inevitably salvation orientated, the vast majority of people attending the camp meetings being unchurched. The renewed emphasis on Christian perfection that took hold during the 1830s coincided with a change in the makeup of Methodist churches from first to second generation Christians. People no longer needed to know how to be saved but how to become better Christians, and this in the face of the advances of German liberalism, deism, Unitarianism, and many other challenges to evangelical faith.

The style of spirituality underwent a change also. Those attending the early camp meetings, as well as those preaching to them, were still mostly

---

4. Synan, *Holiness-Pentecostal Tradition*, 7.

5. Ibid., 9.

6. Cracknell and White, *World Methodism*, 32. Baker cites this early denominationalization of the movement in America as the main reason for its strength relative to British Methodism that was slow to make the break with Anglicanism complete and final: Baker, *From Wesley to Asbury*, 18.

7. Synan, *Holiness-Pentecostal Tradition*, 28.

8. Murray cites eye-witness estimates of between 10,000 and 21,000 at any one time: Murray, *Revival and Revivalism*, 152–53.

9. Ibid., 183.

10. Dayton, *Theological Roots of Pentecostalism*, 65.

of a Calvinist spirituality, exemplified by this eye-witness description of the 1801 revival from a Presbyterian:

> [T]here appears to be in the subjects of this work a deep heart-humbling sense of the great unreasonableness, abominable nature, pernicious effects and deadly consequences of sin; and the absolute unworthiness in the sinful creature of the smallest crumb of mercy from the hand of a holy God.[11]

However, the Calvinist mindset of throwing oneself utterly upon the mercy of a sovereign and holy God was set to change dramatically as the century unfolded. This change involved the democratization of Christianity and its reduction to the individual's response to the call of the gospel. In Calvinist Christianity, the atonement was of great value in easing the sting of a stricken conscience before an Almighty God who, in the manner of Jonathan Edwards, holds sinners by a mere thread over the flames of hell.[12] To the Calvinists, the death of Christ propitiated an angry God. To the Arminians of the generation following, the blood cleansed the responsive and consecrated heart. To the Calvinists, the blood was something that God chose, over against the penitent sinner's eternal damnation. To the Arminians, the blood was something that the sinner chose in his decision to renounce the world and all its allurements and follow God with all his heart.

The Rebirth of Methodist Perfectionism: Phoebe Palmer.

Dayton[13] agrees with Dieter[14] that by around 1830 American Methodism had begun to neglect its own cardinal doctrine, that of Christian perfection, but that throughout the 1830s, movements were afoot to revive the doctrine. Phoebe Palmer and her sister, Sarah Lankford, represented the first major thrust in the direction of reviving perfectionism within American Methodism.[15] Their Tuesday Meeting for the Promotion of Holiness, held

11. Murray, citing the Presbyterian David Rice, in *Revival and Revivalism*, 157.

12. Edwards, *Sinners in the Hands of an Angry God*, 19.

13. Dayton, "From 'Christian Perfection' to the 'Baptism in the Holy Ghost,'" in Synan (ed.), *Aspects of Pentecostal-Charismatic Origins*, 42.

14. Dieter, *The Holiness Revival of the Nineteenth Century*, 22.

15. In the last thirty years, there has been some interesting research on Phoebe Palmer. In particular, a strong link has been made between her pneumatology and her role as a female preacher. Her doctrine of the Spirit was to base itself increasingly on Acts

at the Palmers' home, was soon to be augmented by the magazine *Guide to Holiness*, which reached a readership of up to 30,000.[16] These meetings plus the magazine revived perfectionism within the Methodist fold. By the end of the decade, the movement became two-pronged as there was also a growing interest in the doctrine amongst the Presbyterians and Congregationalists instigated by Charles Finney and Asa Mahan at Oberlin.

Palmer's experience of sanctification began with "an enlarged appreciation of the Atonement"[17] in the light of her own inability to be holy. Once her experience of sanctification was complete, she appears to have drawn two principal lessons from it that would go on to dominate her preaching on the subject. Firstly, she came to understand the importance of testimony. She felt that her side of her "covenant" with the Lord would be that she would agree to tell others of her experience, "perhaps before hundreds."[18] Failure to do this would lead to the dreaded loss of sanctification, such as that experienced famously by Wesley's successor John Fletcher, who lost the blessing five times due to a reluctance to testify.[19] From here onwards she would always preach "the binding nature of the obligation to profess the blessing."[20] Secondly, Palmer's experience appears to have taught her to live in a continual experience of cleansing as she offered herself as a continual sacrifice.[21] She thus recovers, quite correctly, the present tense of 1 John 1:7 (*katharizei*) that Wesley, by claiming a once-and-for-all cleansing, had effectively turned into an aorist. From these insights came her altar theology:

> This, I was given to see, was in verity placing all upon the altar that sanctifieth the gift, and I felt that, so long as my heart assured me that I did thus offer all, that it was a solemn duty as well as a high and holy privilege, to believe that the blood of Jesus cleanseth at

---

2:17–21 (Peter's quotation of the LXX of Joel 2:28–32 on the Day of Pentecost). This passage makes an explicit link between Spirit reception and the power (and implicit right) as a "maidservant" to "prophecy." This shift from a Pauline to a Lukan pneumatology was widespread in evangelicalism by mid-century and "opened up new possibilities for women": McFadden, "The Ironies of Pentecost," 63.

16. Synan, *Pentecostal-Holiness Tradition*, 18.

17. White, *The Beauty of Holiness*, 19–20, citing Phoebe Palmer's diary of 27 July 1837.

18. White, *The Beauty of Holiness*, 20–21.

19. Ibid., 139.

20. Ibid., citing Palmer's *Faith and its Effects*.

21. White, *The Beauty of Holiness*, 23.

the present and each succeeding moment so long as the offering is continued.[22]

Her altar theology was an adaptation of Wesley's system that made the experience of the second blessing more readily accessible via a threefold process of consecration, faith, and testimony.[23] If her listeners followed these three steps, they could assure themselves that they possessed this blessing, regardless of any evidence to the contrary. The whole process was thus becoming fairly mechanized. The agony and soul-searching was removed and holiness was now a blessing that was simply there for the taking: "When the Savior said, 'It is finished!' then this full salvation was wrought out for you. All that remains is for you to come complying with the conditions and claim it . . . [;] it is already yours.[24]

The immediacy of the experience is celebrated in her hymn *The Cleansing Wave*:

> Oh, now I see the cleansing wave,
> The fountain deep and wide!
> Jesus, my Lord, mighty to save,
> Points to His wounded side.
>
> *The cleansing stream I see, I see!*
> *I plunge, and oh, it cleanseth me!*
> *Oh, praise the Lord: it cleanseth me;*
> *It cleanseth me, yes, it cleanseth me.*
>
> I see the new creation rise;
> I hear the speaking blood!
> It speaks polluted nature dies!
> Sinks 'neath the cleansing flood.
>
> I rise to walk in heaven's own light,
> Above the world and sin,
> With heart made pure and garment white,
> And Christ enthroned within.[25]

As can be seen from this hymn, the switch from a once-and-for-all cleansing to a continuous cleansing is, in practice, fairly academic. She clearly has the same eradicationist view of sanctification as Wesley, so that

22. Palmer, *Guide to Holiness*, 210.

23. White, *The Beauty of Holiness*, 136.

24. Palmer, *Faith and its Effects*, 39–40.

25. *Redemption Hymnal*, No. 342.

even if the cleansing is not final, as Wesley understood it to be, it is so over-whelmingly effective that it "speaks polluted nature dies," and enables the believer to live "above the world and sin." The mode of appropriation was faith. The new object of faith was not simply a distant cross, it was now the blood applied. The language of loving response had now become the language of personal hygiene and sanitation: "It cleanseth me." This thought of a powerful, personal cleansing, available to anyone willing to follow the necessary steps, captured the imaginations of a generation of revivalists. It served to feed the idealism of a generation that thought they would see the world utterly cleansed of evil and the millennial dawn appear.

Hymn Break

Before we leave the early nineteenth century, it behooves us to make room for a hymn that proved to be among the best loved hymns of evangelicalism in the decades to come: Charlotte Elliot's *Just as I Am* of 1835. Though not emerging from within the holiness movements, it shares similar concerns and is part of a wider body of hymnody produced by Elliot that was focused around her tender compassion for the suffering of individuals.[26] She herself was incapacitated with an illness at the time of writing this. There is almost certainly also a reference in the refrain of this hymn to her conversion experience in which she was assured by a Dr. Malan with the words: "Come to Him just as you are."[27] The hymn is notable for the way that longings build in the first three lines of every stanza, culminating in the third line, which leaves the singer "poised"[28] for the joy that then comes with the fourth. Here is the original poem upon which the hymn was based:

> Just as I am—without one plea,
> But that Thy blood was shed for me,
> And that Thou bidst me come to Thee,
> —O Lamb of God, I come!
>
> Just as I am—and waiting not
> To rid my soul of one dark blot,
> To Thee, whose blood can cleanse each spot,
> —O Lamb of God, I come!

26. Watson, *The English Hymn*, 428.

27. Sheppard, *Great Hymns and Their Stories*, 115.

28. Watson, *The English Hymn*, 429.

Just as I am—though toss'd about
With many a conflict, many a doubt,
Fightings and fears within, without,
—O Lamb of God, I come!

Just as I am—poor, wretched, blind;
Sight, riches, healing of the mind,
Yea, all I need, in Thee to find,
—O Lamb of God, I come!

Just as I am—Thou wilt receive,
Wilt welcome, pardon, cleanse, relieve;
Because Thy promise I believe,
—O Lamb of God, I come![29]

Back across the Atlantic

The crusade across Britain in 1841–47 of the Irish-American Methodist Preacher James Caughey was historically significant. It followed the efforts of the outlandish camp meeting revivalist Lorenzo Dow in 1805–7 and 1818–19, and preceded the campaign of D. L. Moody that would sweep the British Isles thirty-two years later. As Carwardine has pointed out, however, the overshadowing of Caughey by those who came after him in history is unfortunate.[30] In his day, Caughey was enormously popular and highly influential, particularly upon William Booth, then a fiery young evangelist. During his tour, which included Finney-style new measures revivals, most of the urban centers of the Midlands and North were included: Liverpool, Birmingham, Leeds, Hull, Sheffield, Huddersfield, York, Nottingham, Lincoln, Sunderland, and Chesterfield. Caughey could boast at least twenty thousand new converts and nine thousand cases of entire sanctification during his first British crusade.[31]

Christian perfection, as well as salvation was urged upon his hearers and readers. Perfection is construed as a victory: "Go on to perfection; and may you all at last be enabled to shout, 'Victory, victory, in the blood of the

---

29. Babington, *Selections from the Poems of Charlotte Elliot*, iv.

30. Carwardine, *Transatlantic Revivalism*, 102. Along with Charles Finney, Caughey was a household name among British nonconformists of the mid-nineteenth century: ibid., xiv.

31. Ibid., 111.

Lamb!"[32] The "master sin" for Caughey was "the sin of trampling on the precious blood of Christ."[33]

Thanks to Caughey, a precedent was set in Britain that allowed further American itinerants to visit and bring the effusions of their holiness ideals to British evangelicalism. The challenge remained, however, which would not be overcome until Moody came, of the general disdain of the middle and upper classes for republican America,[34] reeking as it did of hated and much feared French republicanism. Both Dow and Caughey had appealed mostly to working class nonconformists, a success that must have seemed somewhat incendiary in the revolutionary climate of the times.

The Salvation Army[35]

The theology of William and Catherine Booth was profoundly influenced by Phoebe Palmer's altar theology.[36] The Booths went on to extend their eradicationist theology of Christian perfection into the social sphere, engaging in a widening campaign against all the social evils of working class Britain. As opposition mounted against the Booths and their followers, this holiness crusade was seen increasingly as a spiritual warfare. An article in the *Sunday Telegraph* written in commemoration of the Salvation Army's centenary puts it aptly: "To the Booths, and especially to Catherine Booth, the Devil was a personal opponent and as real as one's next door neighbor."[37] In the face of this enemy, the Booths were utterly defiant and completely confident of the power of Christ to defeat sin and Satan. And, more particularly, this strong faith was faith in the power of Christ's blood. As the Christian Mission took on the name of the Salvation Army, and William Booth took the title of general, the cleansing of the blood would be

---

32. Caughey, *Sermons*, 41.

33. Ibid., 103.

34. Kent, *Holding the Fort*, 50, 63.

35. Besides Merritt (ed.), *Historical Dictionary of the Salvation Army*, see Coutts, *The History of the Salvation Army*, 7 vols.; Murdoch, "Evangelical Sources of Salvation Army Doctrine"; Murdoch, *Origins of the Salvation Army*; Walker, *Pulling the Devil's Kingdom Down*, as reliable sources.

36. Catherine Booth said of Palmer's books that they "have done me more good than anything else I have ever met with." Walker, *Pulling the Devil's Kingdom Down*, 23, citing a letter to her mother dated 21 January 1861.

37. "History of the Salvation Army," *Sunday Telegraph* (30 May 1965), cutting, Nottingham City Archives.

coupled with his belief in baptism in the Spirit to produce the now famous piece of branding: Blood and Fire. Through Blood and Fire all the forces of "Darkest England" would be overcome.

William Booth's theology has been described as the theology of Wesley, Whitefield, and George Fox.[38] Of these, Wesley[39] would have to be singled out as the greatest influence upon his theology,[40] albeit mediated via Caughey, with whom he was often compared. One of Booth's earliest letters reveals something of the nature of his spirituality: "I want to be a devoted, simple, and sincere follower of the Bleeding Lamb."[41]

The formative contribution of Catherine Booth as co-founder of the Salvation Army has received due attention in recent years.[42] Her role, along with a number of other evangelical women in the nineteenth century is rightly celebrated.[43] As early as the 1850s, the conviction grew within her of the legitimacy of female ministry[44] and she was a powerful speaker in her own right. The *Wesleyan Times* of March 1865, compared Catherine's preaching to "Finney and the revivalists."[45] This would be a reference to her insistence on preaching for a verdict, an immediate decision for Christ, a conviction that she and William shared.

38. Begbie, *Life of William Booth*, 1, 79.

39. Amongst his words of advice to his future wife were these: "Read one or two of John Wesley's sermons now and then." Letter to Catherine, 17 November 1852. Begbie, *Life of William Booth*, 1: 159.

40. "He was emphatic from those early days to the end of his life on this doctrine of persistent faith, on this doctrine of Entire Sanctification. He never changed his mind in this respect." Begbie, *Life of William Booth*, 1: 86–87.

41. Extract from a letter written from London to a friend in Nottingham, dated 1850. Begbie, *Life of William Booth*, 1: 115. See also this resolution made by the struggling young Booth in London, dated 9 December 1849: "3rd That I will endeavour in my conduct and deportment before the world and my fellow servants especially to conduct myself as a humble, meek, and zealous follower of the bleeding Lamb . . . ." He goes on: "I feel my own weakness and without God's help I shall not keep these resolutions a day. The Lord have mercy upon my soul. I claim the Blood. Yes, oh Yes, Jesus died for me." Begbie, *Life of William Booth*, 1: 105–6.

42. The most substantial study of this kind is Walker, *Pulling the Devil's Kingdom Down*.

43. McFadden, "Ironies of Pentecost," 66, 72; Murdoch, "Female Ministry," passim, Walker, *Pulling the Devil's Kingdom Down*, 243. Also Hattersley, *Blood and Fire*, 106–7, who surmises, in line with some recent scholarship, that "[i]t was Phoebe Palmer's gender as much as her ideology which attracted Catherine Booth."

44. Murdoch, "Female Ministry," 349.

45. *Wesleyan Times*, 13 March 1865, quoted in Hattersley, *Blood and Fire*, 147.

During the 1870s, while the first Keswick Conventions were taking place among the middle classes, the Salvation Army were on the streets, bravely singing and testifying their way into the hearts of the poor and wretched. This decade was the time of their stiffest opposition. Until the police took a firmer stand, the mocking Skeleton Army represented a fairly organized attempt at disrupting the Salvation Army wherever they went. They were assisted by members of the public, especially publicans, who felt that their trade was threatened by the way that drunkards were being overtly targeted by the Army's evangelistic efforts. The Salvation Army's message was atonement-centered:

> After one or two had spoken, the publican on the left opened his window and pitched a pail of water on to the crowd below. Immediately the people moved; but though the sisters were principally upon that side, and the water fell upon their Sunday hats plentifully, the ring was not broken for a moment, and every one heard the hearty Amen that burst from all as the dear sister who was speaking wiped the water from her face, and cried, "May the Lord save that dear man." In the meantime the crowd had tremendously increased, and God came into our midst. Then the publican gave us another pail of water; but still we kept believing and the ring was unbroken. There was a solemn influence; no one spoke a word while we sang—
>> But till washed in the Blood of a crucified Lord
>> We can never be ready to die.[46]

Surprisingly, as will be seen from my survey of the *Salvation Army Song Book*, the victory theme is not prominent in the hymn singing of the Salvationists. Rather it was the cleansing that mattered. It was by that cleansing that the devil would be overcome and victory over sin and evil achieved. There appeared to be something emotive for the singers in the mere mention of the word "blood," especially when coupled with "fire":

> Hark, hark, my soul, what warlike songs are swelling,
> Through Britain's streets and on from door to door;
> How grand the truths those burning strains are telling
> Of that great war till sin shall be no more!
> Salvation Army, Army of God!
> Onward to conquer the world with Fire and Blood . . . .[47]

---

46. Report from Chatham, 1877. Begbie, *Life of William Booth*, 1: 424.
47. Begbie, *Life of William Booth*, 1: 451–52.

Begbie comments: "the phrase 'with Fire and Blood' was sung, or rather roared, again and again, until perspiration ran down the faces of the soldiery as they clasped one another's hands and beamed.[48]

When not witnessing on the streets, the style of spirituality that the Salvationists exhibited was even more extravagant. Holiness meetings were frequent and were clearly very powerful experiences for many. Once again, it was the blood that appeared to take theological pride of place. The following is an extract from *The Salvationist*:

> Good times all day on Sunday. Saints jumping, dancing, crying, shouting, and rolling on the ground. We disgusted some people. . . . Then came the power. All got down after Mr Ballington said a few words; then came the glory. . . . A young man who rushed out of his seat, fell at the penitent-form and cried for mercy—which he soon obtained as soon as he ventured his all on the Blood—being so overpowered with the glory, for we had it down and no mistake, got up, and looking in my face with his hands on his breast, said, "I think I am going to die, but the Blood cleanseth me." . . . After this, over twenty more rushed forward, while those who had obtained the blissful peace stood round singing, with faces of rapture and tears of joy, "I am sure, I am sure Jesus saves, Jesus saves, and His Blood makes me whiter than snow."[49]

The religious context of high Victorian Britain, with its propensities towards formalism and ritualism exacerbated by the Tractarian movement, partly explains the outlandish revivalism of these meetings. Other factors may be the class of people attending. These were mostly lower middle and working class people for whom decorum and respectability never had been of such a high priority as it was for the middle and upper classes. Thirdly, the influence of American revivalism, mediated via Caughey and Palmer, ran deeply into the religious complexion of the Army's leadership. Booth himself defended sensationalism by reference to the thunder and lightning of Sinai and the tabernacle regalia, concluding that: *"The only religion God cared about was one that continually moved the worshippers in the most sensational manner conceivable."*[50]

In the Salvation Army then, the cleansing motif reaches a climax. In an extreme movement, this motif is used to an extreme. It is a defiant cry

---

48. Ibid.

49. Begbie, *Life of William Booth*, 1: 454–56.

50. Ervine, *God's Solder*, 1: 535 (italics original).

of victory over all forms of sin and evil, whether addictions, deprivations, religiosity, or worldliness. All of these are rendered powerless by the eradication of inbred sin. The agents of this eradication are blood and fire: the touch of the atonement upon all who believe and the life of the Spirit within all who believe.

Holiness Hymns

Three considerable collections of hymns emerged out of the holiness movement that had a significant impact upon British Christianity. These all drew from the same eighteenth-century Watts-Wesley dominated pool of hymns and each added new hymns of their own, often imitating the phraseology and imagery of eighteenth-century hymnody. All three collections represented spiritualities that matured contemporaneously with each other during the 1860s to 1880s. The theology appears similar. The main discernible difference, where their treatment of the atonement is concerned, is in the degree of evangelistic focus. Keswick's *Hymns of Consecration and Faith* is the most introspective hymnbook. It has no "warning and entreaty" section and only a fairly small "Missionary Hymns" section comprising thirty-three hymns (hymns 420–53, 5.4 percent of the total collection). The *Salvation Army Song Book*, by contrast, with its "Salvation" section comprising 22 percent of its hymns (hymns 1–198), the majority of which are addressed to sinners,[51] is the most overtly evangelistic. In the middle there is Ira Sankey's *Sacred Songs and Solos*, which, like the *Salvation Army Song Book*, was compiled with inquirers in mind. Its section of hymns on "The Gospel," all addressed to unbelievers and backsliders,[52] comprises 12 percent of the total compilation.

Here I will focus my statistics on the occurrences of the word "blood" in association with Jesus as a fairly fail-safe (and easy-to-spot) indicator of the presence of atonement. Keswick's *Hymns of Consecration and Faith*, for example, is one of the most atonement-dominated hymnals ever to have been produced, with almost one in three of its hymns referring to the blood of Jesus at least once. The *Salvation Army Song Book* is similar, with an average of one in four of its songs carrying at least one mention of the

---

51. E.g., No. 76: "Come, sinners, to the Gospel feast; Oh, come without delay, For there is room on Jesus' breast, For all who will obey."

52. E.g., No. 429: "Where will you spend Eternity? This question comes to you and me! Tell me, what shall your answer be—Where will you spend Eternity?"

blood of Christ. In Ira Sankey's *Sacred Songs and Solos* one in six of its songs touch on the theme. The arguably more mainstream *Hymns Ancient and Modern* was first published in 1861. The ratio of hymns containing at least one reference to the blood in this hymnal is one in eight, and in its successor, the *English Hymnal* of 1906, the figure is down to one in nine. In these broad church hymnals, most of the references to the blood are restricted to the Eucharistic hymns, the hymns for the seasons of Lent and Passiontide and the section for "Mission Services." It is clear that the blood theme was generally much more important to worshippers with some level of holiness background than to worshippers who were outside the movement.

Just to add a little color to my statistics, in *Hymns of Consecration and Faith* almost every hymn revels in some aspect of the cross and drains it dry of every drop of blessing it might yield for the holiness and consecration cause. Worshippers are "Clinging, clinging, clinging to the Cross,"[53] harking back to the medieval mystics and the Moravians, they shelter in the "wounded side" of Jesus,[54] and they take their stand "Beneath the Cross of Jesus."[55] It is a "wounded hand" that knocks on the door of their hearts[56] as they sing "Glory to the bleeding Lamb!"[57] They long to reach out to the straying lambs "for whom the Shepherd bled"[58] and sing for the lost who "die in darkness," as they themselves have "the life which has been purchased with the Saviour's precious blood"[59] and must share it with the heathen so that they too might know the "balm that's found at Calvary."[60] The white harvest fields themselves have already been purchased by "the precious blood" of God's beloved Son.[61] They begin to see a relationship between the Holy Spirit and the cross when they sing: "By Thy Holy Spirit's teaching, Calvary's healing stream we know,"[62] and "His Spirit and His blood make my cleansing complete."[63] They ask the Holy Spirit to "Con-

53. No. 84.

54. No. 33.

55. No. 100.

56. No. 159.

57. No. 216.

58. No. 333.

59. No. 428.

60. No. 449.

61. No. 451.

62. No. 411.

63. No. 204.

vince us of our sin, then lead to Jesu's blood."[64] They thus learn to "bathe in the crimson tide."[65]

In the 1930 edition of the *Salvation Army Song Book,* not only does the word "Blood" always receive capitalization, but all adjectives and metaphors associated with it do too: Precious,[66] Purple,[67] Flood,[68] Fountain,[69] River,[70] and so on. Of the total references to Christ's Blood, 191 (42 percent) express the idea of cleansing and washing. In order to aid the worshippers as they appropriate this cleansing, every imaginable liquid image is employed. The worshipper lives in the "Cleansing Fountain" and dwells in the "Saviour's side."[71] He or she plunges beneath the "Precious Blood," beneath that "cleansing Flood," while the hand takes hold of Jesus.[72] Alternatively, they may prefer to "dip"[73] in the blood or to fling themselves at the cross "For the Blood is flowing there."[74] All sorrows[75] and doubts[76] are swept away in the River that is "streaming"[77] and "flows."[78] It is a "sin-cleansing wave,"[79] a "Crimson Tide,"[80] a "Blood-current."[81] It is construed either as flowing from the cross[82] or flowing or gushing from the riven side of Jesus.[83] It is

64. No. 170.

65. No. 534.

66. No. 293.

67. No. 831.

68. No. 831.

69. No. 552.

70. No. 239.

71. No. 552.

72. No. 421.

73. No. 293.

74. No. 356.

75. No. 222.

76. No. 417.

77. No. 34.

78. No. 75.

79. Chorus No. 298.

80. No. 62.

81. No. 379.

82. No. 356.

83. No. 377; 275.

a "Purple Flood,"[84] a sin-cleansing wave,[85] a "cleansing Fountain" in which garments may be washed,[86] sin destroyed,[87] guilt removed[88] and souls cured[89] as the "Precious Blood" is applied.[90] That blood may now "Flood and cleanse" the heart itself.[91]

The Keswick Convention

The very first Keswick Convention was held in 1875 in Keswick, surrounded by beautiful scenery in the heart of North West England's Lake District. The numbers attending the first Keswick Conventions were modest. The total seating capacity of the tent used for the first two years was only six hundred.[92] Most of those attending the first Conventions were "middle-aged or elderly"[93] and those attending did so with the feeling that they were losing their reputations in the process,[94] there being still a deeply held suspicion of "enthusiasm" in the Church of England.

The influence of even of the first Keswick Convention, however, was considerable. As early as August 1875, a convention modelled on Keswick was held in Melbourne, Australia. Many others followed throughout the English speaking world, perhaps most notably at Wellington, South Africa from 1889 under Andrew Murray and at Llandrindod Wells from 1903 under Jessie Penn-Lewis. By 1879, the seating capacity at the original Keswick was about a thousand.[95] By 1885, the Keswick Convention was attracting crowds of one-and-a-half thousand. By 1907, there were six thousand in

84. No. 831.

85. No. 298.

86. No. 409.

87. No. 590.

88. No. 538.

89. No. 325.

90. No. 32.

91. No. 410.

92. Sloan, *These Sixty Years*, 22. Pollock prefers a seating capacity of "nearly a thousand," Pollock, *Keswick Story*, 11.

93. Pollock, *Keswick Story*, 45.

94. Ibid., 49. The first conventions attracted widespread suspicion of wrong doctrine, allegations of Christian perfection being the most common.

95. Based on the eye-witness account of Australian Keswick speaker H. B. Macartney: Pollock, *Keswick Story*, 51.

attendance. During the 1920s, numbers averaged at around the five thousand mark, a very large proportion of whom were now under thirty years of age.[96] Young people had begun flocking to Keswick from the 1880s onwards, leading eventually to the formation of the Inter-Varsity Fellowship by Norman Grubb in 1919. Bebbington holds that the Keswick doctrine of sanctification—its most distinctive teaching in the early days—held normative power amongst conservative evangelicals until the 1950s and 60s.[97]

The main thing that brought about the Keswick Conventions was an underlying dissatisfaction which was felt by the leaders who instigated the many conferences that preceded the first Keswick Convention: London and Chamonix, 1873, Hampton-on-Thames, Mildmay, Broadlands, and Oxford, 1874, and Brighton, May 1875. At the Oxford Convention for the Promotion of Scriptural Holiness, William Boardman, an influential American teacher of the "Higher"[98] Christian life struck a chord with many by saying: "Forgiveness did not satisfy me, I wanted the dominion of sin destroyed. Purification, not less than pardon, I saw to be required."[99] The conviction that mere salvation, mere justification, mere forgiveness was not enough and that there had to be more to the Christian life than persistent defeat was pivotal for many attendees. The dissatisfaction was widespread, as the wording of the invitation to the Oxford Convention indicates: "In every part of the country, the God of all grace has given many of His children a feeling of deep dissatisfaction with their spiritual state."[100] They therefore sought "practical victory over all known sin, and of maintained communion with their Lord."[101] Dayton also highlights the powerlessness that people increasingly felt during the nineteenth century as they struggled to cope with the "growing social complexity" of the age.[102] Though this may seem surprising to us whose lives are even more complex and busy, the Victorian era was one in which many felt that they were living . . .

---

96. Randall, *Evangelical Experiences*, 14, 16.

97. Bebbington, "Holiness in the Evangelical Tradition," in Barton (ed.), *Holiness Past and Present*, 309.

98. His book *The Higher Christian Life* was first published in Britain in 1860 as an attempt at making an essentially Wesleyan doctrine of sanctification intelligible to those who were, like himself, outside the Methodist tradition.

99. Boardman, *The Higher Christian Life*, 140.

100. Cited in Pollock, *Keswick Story*, 22.

101. Sloan, *These Sixty Years*, 10.

102. Dayton, *Theological Roots of Pentecostalism*, 77.

without leisure and without pause—a life of haste—above all a life of excitement, such as haste inevitably involves—a life filled so full . . . that we have no time to reflect where we have been and whither we intend to go . . . still less what is the value and the purpose and the price of what we have seen, done and visited.[103]

Many of the women who attended Keswick came "burdened with domestic demands and many other pressures,"[104] and struggled with such things as "enslavement to anger and harsh language."[105] They longed for Keswick's rest, and often went home transformed by powerful spiritual experiences.[106] Freedom from addictions to tobacco, alcohol, and gambling were also commonly reported.[107]

In the face of the kinds of pressures evangelicals were struggling with, the doctrine birthed by the Reformation was, arguably, beginning to be seen as deficient, though there would have been few outside of the liberal Protestant tradition that would have been willing to put it quite that way. It is strongly implied though, in the kinds of dissatisfaction that we have already seen described by Boardman and others. Part of that deficiency was the result of a gulf opened up from the Lutheran Reformation onwards between a justification that must not sanctify and a sanctification that must not be complete or final. Sanctification within Protestant doctrine had then fallen increasingly under the spell of the gradualism that was part and parcel of Enlightenment thought. This helped to fuel the impatience of all holiness advocates as they sought a real and lasting victory over sin, not a protracted struggle. Boardman insisted upon a "present Saviour" who "does actually deliver the trusting soul from the cruel bondage of its chains under sin, now in this present time."[108]

The Anglican middle classes who attended the early Conventions were keen to distance themselves from fanatical perfectionist teaching,[109] yet it

103. A comment from W. R. Greg made in 1875, cited in Houghton, *The Victorian Frame of Mind, 1830–1870*, 7. I am indebted to Dr. Neil Hudson who tracked down this priceless snapshot of Victorian life.

104. Haddad, "The Mystical Theology of Jessie Penn-Lewis," 61.

105. Ibid.

106. Ibid.

107. Ibid., 62.

108. Boardman, *The Higher Christian Life*, 266.

109. See especially Cumming, "What We Teach," in Stevenson (ed.), *Keswick's Triumphant Voice*, 19–20. Having said this, Keswick was never dogmatic about its theologies and Bebbington sees Keswick as a synthesis of the Calvinistic and Wesleyan approaches.

is clear that American Methodist views of sanctification, re-interpreted by the Pearsall Smiths and by William Boardman, played their part in the formation of early Keswick expectations of its own kind of second blessing. Their slogan was "Holiness by faith in Jesus, not by effort of my own."[110] It was a holiness performed by the risen Christ himself in response to the believer's full surrender and identification with Christ in death and resurrection. The expectation of an identifiable divine response was the logical corollary of the act of perfect surrender once the rest of faith had been entered. This element of resting was imported into the movement from the seventeenth-century French quietist tradition,[111] which had also, you may recall, enthralled Zinzendorf and the Moravians for a time. An important non-Catholic filter was provided in the form of Thomas Upham and his very evangelical account of the life and beliefs of Madam Guyon.[112] The French mystical tradition had largely done away with the self-mortifications of the older mystical traditions, its main selling point having been that anyone could follow this path. Its techniques centered on the Prayer of Simple Regard, which was combined with an insistence (everywhere present in Guyon's *Experiencing the Depths of Jesus Christ*) that one need only look within to find Christ.

Hannah Whittall Smith and her husband Robert Pearsall Smith were significant during the very earliest days of Keswick before a scandal involving Robert Pearsall Smith abruptly ended the English ministry of the couple.[113] Both Robert and Hannah were from a Quaker background. Robert testified to having been "a 'religious man' for ten long and toilsome years," before discovering from the Bible in a railway carriage what the blood of Christ had done for him.[114] Hannah had gone through a period of religious doubt earlier in her life that caused her to question, in particular, the doctrine of the atonement.[115] By the time of her extremely popular and highly influential book, *The Christian's Secret of a Happy Life*, published in 1888,[116]

Bebbington, *Holiness*, 73.

110. Aldis, *The Message of Keswick and its Meaning*, 39.

111. Chiefly Madam Guyon, Brother Lawrence, and François Fenelon.

112. Upham, *Life, Religious Opinions and Experience of Madam De La Mothe Guyon*.

113. The reasons for this were made known for the first time in Pollock's *Keswick Story*, 35.

114. Smith, *Account of the Union Meeting*, in Warfield, *Perfectionism*, 253.

115. Dieter, *Holiness Revival*, 132.

116. Smith, *The Christian's Secret of a Happy Life*. By 1941, it had sold a hundred

this low view of the atonement had clearly been corrected, probably thanks to her exposure to the Plymouth Brethren, which began in 1858.[117] Most of her first chapter is devoted to proving that the purpose of the cross was to set people free not just from the guilt of sin but also from its power. This she does very convincingly: "Is He called a Redeemer? So, then, I do expect the benefit of my redemption, and that I shall go out of my captivity."[118] Specifically, both Hannah and Robert had come to a strong conviction about the importance of Romans 6:6 (about the old man being crucified with Christ and there being no more slavery to sin) in making the cross effective in the life of a believer. She describes their discovery of this passage as the "secret of victory."[119] Specifically it meant the realization that they were not forced to yield to the mastery of sin,[120] though such victory could be lost if instead of letting the Lord win the battle over temptation they took matters into their own hands.[121]

> [T]he Cross of Christ which has effectually separated us from the penalty or consequence of our sins is also the means by which we become separated from their power[;] . . . the only true way of overcoming the evil within us is by recognizing our position as those that have crucified the flesh with the affections and lusts[;] . . . the reckoning of ourselves to be dead indeed unto sin is the great duty of faith, and the secret of a life of abiding communion with God.[122]

Jessie Penn-Lewis

Speakers at Keswick included Canon Harford-Battersby, the vicar of St. John's, Keswick, and the organiser of the first Keswick conventions, H. W.

---

thousand copies according to the publisher. The American publisher, Fleming H. Revel, claim two million for their "authorized edition."

117. Whittal Smith, *The Unselfishness of God and How I Discovered It*, 110. See also her reflections on Isaiah 53:11, sparked by her concerns about the Calvinism of the Plymouth Brethren: ibid., 125–28.

118. Smith, *The Christian's Secret of a Happy Life*, 23.

119. Ibid., 37. See also: Whittal Smith, *The Unselfishness of God and How I Discovered It*, 160–67.

120. Smith, *The Christian's Secret of a Happy Life*, 37.

121. Ibid.

122. Ibid., 224.

Webb-Peploe, Bishop Handley Moule, and later on, as nonconformists began to take the stage, Frederick Brotherton Meyer. In one place F. B. Meyer pictures the disc-like red blood corpuscles that flowed in Jesus' veins as the coinage with which Jesus bought mankind.[123] South African revivalist Andrew Murray became known to Keswick-goers in 1882 with the publication of the English edition of his book *Abide in Christ*. He also visited the conference that year as a listener. On the Wednesday of Murray's week at Keswick he had a breakthrough: "I saw it all, Jesus cleansing, Jesus filling, Jesus keeping."[124] Murray insisted that before opening oneself to the Spirit in order to acquire holiness by faith, the blood must be applied to cleanse the heart.[125] Likewise, when the Spirit comes, he points back to the blood and applies its benefits to the heart.[126] So, the blood brings the Spirit, and the Spirit brings the blood.[127] Because of this union of blood and Spirit, both susceptible of the "liquid" terminology of washing, flowing, and flooding, the blood was understood by Murray to be alive, still fresh, still flowing, still efficacious before the throne of God in heaven.[128]

Of all the crucicentric attempts to resolve the objective-subjective, justification-sanctification dialectic that we find in the various types of evangelical holiness movement, it is arguably that of Jessie Penn-Lewis[129]

---

123. Meyer, *From Calvary to Pentecost*, 13.

124. This experience came as a result of hearing the song, "Oh. Wonderful cleansing, oh, wonderful filling, oh, wonderful keeping," (No. 492 in the *Hymns*) and was published in *Life of Faith*. Sloan, *These Sixty Years*, 26.

125. "The sprinkling of the blood, which sanctifies man unto God and takes possession of him for God, bestows at the same time the right of intimacy." Murray, *The Power of the Blood of Jesus*, 93.

126. "Where the blood is honoured, preached, and believed in as the power of full redemption, there the way is opened for the fullness of the Spirit's blessing." Murray, *The Blood of the Cross*, 16.

127. "We must once again notice the two sides of this truth: the blood exercises its full power through the Spirit, and the Spirit manifests His full power through the blood." Murray, *The Blood of the Cross*, 16.

128. Dependence on the Hebrews imagery of the great High Priest sprinkling His own blood in the true and eternal tabernacle of heaven was frequent: "It is as the Holy Spirit reveals this to the soul, *the heavenly power of the blood*, as ministered by our Melchizedek, the minister of the heavenly sanctuary, that we see what power that blood must have, as so sprinkled on us from heaven, in the power of the Holy Spirit." Murray, *The Holiest of All*, 297 (italics original).

129. There are two biographical studies of her life: Gerrard, *Mrs Penn-Lewis: A Memoir*, and Jones, *The Trials and Triumphs of Mrs Jessie Penn-Lewis*, and one study of her theology: Haddad, "The Mystical Theology of Jessie Penn-Lewis."

that is the most worthy of attention. She was born in 1861 into a Calvinistic Methodist home in Neath, South Wales, and was converted in 1882, where-upon she and her husband William moved to Richmond, Surrey. Here they were impacted by the ministry of the chairman of Keswick, Evan Hopkins, leading, in 1884, to Jessie Penn-Lewis making a solemn consecration of her life to Christ's service.[130] Jessie Penn-Lewis had frequent health problems and it became clear from a very early stage that she would not be able to have children.[131] She appears instead to have channeled her motherly in-stincts into caring for wayward and troubled souls via her involvement with the YWCA, and later with the confused and broken Welsh revival preacher Evan Roberts. From 1892, Penn-Lewis became involved with the Keswick Conventions and would later be the tireless organizer of countless local conventions modelled along similar lines. Between 1899 and 1901 was her period of "humiliation"[132] during which her travels across Russia were cur-tailed by a severe bout of respiratory problems. It was out of this time that her theology of the cross reached maturity. She appears to have emerged from this time much stronger and, from 1903, becomes the organizer of Wales's own full-blown Keswick, located at Llandrindod Wells. This con-vention would go on to draw the praise of one who commented, "Now at Llandrindod Wells the doctrines of Rowlands[133] and Keswick have come together. The Cross and the Holy Spirit; Calvary and Pentecost . . . ."[134] Penn-Lewis herself, however, would be increasingly criticized for her "one-tracked" insistence on preaching the cross.[135] She appears to have majored, increasingly, on co-crucifixion.

Examples of this co-crucifixion teaching are found throughout her writings:

> Calvary means that Christ not only bore on that Tree your sins, but that He carried to the Tree the sinner—carried you there. When you come to the point of recognising that God does not patch up the old life, but calls upon you to reckon it crucified, and to take

130. Evans, *The Welsh Revival of 1904*, 29.

131. Jones, *The Trials and Triumphs of Mrs Jessie Penn-Lewis*, 8.

132. Chronicled in Jones, *The Trials and Triumphs of Mrs Jessie Penn-Lewis*, 86–95.

133. Daniel Rowlands was a preacher of the first Welsh revival who dwelt on atone-ment themes.

134. Sermon by Rev. Thomas Phillips at the Welsh Keswick of 1912: Jones, *The Spiri-tual History of Keswick in Wales 1903–1983*, 23.

135. Evans, *The Welsh Revival of 1904*, 30.

from Him a new one, you will find that the new life has in it all the characteristics which belong to it. . . . It is necessary to repeat this message of the Cross again and again, for the truth only lays hold of us "line upon line" until at last it grips us and effectually works in us who believe.[136]

Not surprisingly, her best loved passage was Romans 6:1–14: "The work of deliverance from the guilt and bondage of sin was wrought out at Calvary, and the Apostle calls upon the Roman Christians to enter upon the fruit of Christ's death, by a decisive act of faith. With Christ upon the Cross they died, and in His death they were cut off from their old life."[137]

Haddad fits Penn-Lewis into what she describes as "the classical mystical tradition."[138] This she contrasts with the quietism that was pervasive in the rest of the Keswick movement, which had been channeled via Thomas Upham's account of Madam Guyon. Haddad insists that Penn-Lewis reintroduces the difficult part of the three-fold mystical path of purgation, illumination, union. Penn-Lewis wrested back the purgative stage: "Unlike those in Keswick who defined faith as an experience of rest, Cross Theology was a return to the classical, mystical tradition in which souls participate in the process of purification in the path to holiness or sanctification."[139]

Haddad also portrays Penn-Lewis as being "at odds" with the leadership of Keswick, partly because she was a woman and partly because "they distrusted the mortifications intrinsic to her Cross Theology."[140] The mainstream Keswick route to sanctification, by contrast, was the "shorter path of the Quietists."[141] What is quite distinctive is the moral dimension to her crucicentrism, which is indeed reminiscent of the older mystical traditions. She was deeply aware that, in seeking the baptism in the Holy Spirit, her own selfishness could present a blockage and hence that "Calvary [in the sense of self-denial] must always precede Pentecost."[142] It is well observed that Penn-Lewis' spirituality was "unmistakably coupled with expressions

---

136. Penn-Lewis, *More than Conquerors*, 3.

137. Penn-Lewis, *The Cross of Calvary and its Message*, 33–34.

138. Haddad, "The Mystical Theology of Jessie Penn-Lewis," 3 and elsewhere.

139. Ibid., 23.

140. Ibid.

141. Ibid., 26.

142. Garrard, *Mrs Penn-Lewis: A Memoir*, 26. Also Haddad, "The Mystical Theology of Jessie Penn-Lewis," 87–88, 92.

of self-abnegation."[143] However, to extend this element into a full-blown self-mortification, or even to claim Penn-Lewis as a mystic at all seems to go beyond what she would have said of herself based on the evidence of her copious publications. Though there are elements that are analogous to the mystics of the Middle Ages, it seems clear that she remained deeply rooted within the evangelicalism of her Welsh heritage, but with the added pneumatological and co-crucifixion emphases that Keswick brought. Her outstanding contribution lay in her unique development of this latter emphasis, while her pneumatology prevents her from going down the self-mortification route. For example, she quotes Andrew Murray with approval: "The Cross leads to the Spirit, and the Spirit back again to the Cross."[144] Though she does have a lot to say about the death of self, this is understood to be a dynamic work of the Spirit:

> [T]he Spirit of God shows us that deliverance must come from another source, and that self cannot conquer self or sin. . . . The Spirit of God then leads us again to Calvary and throws light upon the meaning of the death of the Lord for the deliverance of all who trust in him . . . .[145]

In Penn-Lewis, co-crucifixion is primarily a dynamic indicative and only secondarily a moral imperative, a position she doubtless derived from a plain reading of Romans 6 itself: "This is why the Apostle so remarkably interchanges in Romans 6 the Magna Carta of the Church of Christ the words 'HIS DEATH' and 'WE DIED,' as if it meant one and the same thing, which spiritually it does in God's marvelous plan of redemption . . . ."[146]

According to Penn-Lewis, the only thing we can bring to the table is our desire,[147] our will.[148] The willing believer must "sign the death warrant,"[149]

143. Also Haddad, "The Mystical Theology of Jessie Penn-Lewis," 95. Also 96: "Penn-Lewis's North American tour evidenced a consistent theme: Death to self as the pathway to an abundant life in Christ."

144. Penn-Lewis, *The Cross of Calvary*, 52.

145. Penn-Lewis, *Dying to Live*, 30–31.

146. Penn-Lewis, *Dying to Live*, 3–4. Emphasis original.

147. "The Spirit reveals the exceeding sinfulness of sin, and the utter uselessness of the life lived 'after the flesh.' He creates that furnace of intense desire which makes the soul prepared to let Him do His work, and have His way at all costs." Penn-Lewis, *The Pathway to Life in God*, 9.

148. "In Him is the Fulness of God. In us—nothing! We have nothing to offer God, but our *wills*." Penn-Lewis, *The Glorious Secret*, 4.

149. Penn-Lewis, *The Pathway to Life in God*, 4.

which means that they "agree that the death of Christ shall be made really true in experience."[150] When she does have the opportunity to speak of our own self-sacrifice and suffering as cross-bearing,[151] or when she could follow through on a theme of self-abasement before the crucified Christ, such as when she comes to reflect on Job's "self-abhorrence,"[152] she does not do so. Instead, the language tends in the direction of overcoming, of being a conqueror[153] over sin and Satan. She is too triumphalistic to belong in the same category as Catherine of Siena, Teresa of Avila, or any other classical mystics. Magnificent though Haddad's study of Penn-Lewis is, it seems to set out with the purpose of putting Penn-Lewis into the category of a classical, self-mortifying mystic so as to portray her feministically as a woman standing out from the male-dominated crowd, who all advocated a different, easier, approach to sanctification.

Penn-Lewis, though not as widely known as she deserves to be, cast a long shadow, influencing the spirituality of many who came into contact with her teaching. One example would be the famous Welsh revivalist Evan Roberts. After months of astonishing success in which Roberts failed to take enough rest, there seems to have been a turning point in his ministry in the wake of a hostile article about him in the *Western Mail* that appeared on 31 January 1905. This article wrote off his meetings as a "sham" revival. From this time, Roberts was prone to detecting "hindrances" in the meetings, culminating in a meeting on 21 February 1905 in which he professed to have detected a person in the meeting who was damned beyond the point of recovery.[154] It was his increasingly unstable behavior that first provoked the intervention of Penn-Lewis, who was a chronicler of the revival. She met up with him for the first time over this period, apparently to counsel him over how to discern between the genuine guidance of God and counterfeit promptings.[155] Penn-Lewis maintained contact with Roberts

---

150. Ibid.

151. E.g., Penn-Lewis, *The Climax of the Risen Life*, 21–29 where a chapter on "The Sacrifice of the Cross" is followed by a chapter called, "Sons of the Cross."

152. Penn-Lewis, *Opened Heavens*, 14–20.

153. "Christ is the Conqueror, and you are joined in one Spirit with the Conqueror." Penn-Lewis, *More Than Conquerors*, 6.

154. Jones, *Instrument of Revival*, 90–91.

155. Jones, *The Trials and Triumphs of Mrs Jessie Penn-Lewis*, 157. Even before the revival, Penn-Lewis had spoken of the need to "'prove all things' along the line of spiritual experiences," warning of "the possibility of a Christian being deceived." Penn-Lewis, *Life in the Spirit*, 77.

throughout 1905 repeatedly offering him a place in the Penn-Lewis' home, which was now in Leicester, where he could find seclusion and rest, but he refused. Meanwhile, Roberts suffered a series of severe mental breakdowns. By March 1906, the exhausted Evan Roberts finally took up the offer of a home with the Penn-Lewises. He did not become a recluse at this time, however, and appeared, at his own insistence, at an Easter convention organized by Penn-Lewis in Bangor. Attendance was high owing to leaked information about Roberts' planned appearance there. At this convention, Roberts preached two "passionate exhortations" about facing the cross[156] and apologized for all his "unbelief in the power of the Blood."[157] It is here that he publicly adopted Penn-Lewis's theology of the cross.[158] In August at the Llandrindod convention he claimed that it had been the "Father of Lies" that had persuaded him not to preach about the cross, implying, much to the chagrin of those present, that anyone who likewise failed to preach the cross as much as Penn-Lewis did had been listening to the same lying spirit.[159] Unfortunately, the hostile response to him at Llandrindod brought on another severe mental and physical breakdown.

Norman Grubb and his wife Pauline (née Studd) came into contact with Penn-Lewis' cross teaching while serving in the Congo in the early 1920s. Galatians 2:20, another co-crucifixion verse, soon became a key verse for Norman and Pauline Grubb. Pauline entered into an experience of peace and liberty without difficulty on the basis of Penn-Lewis' teaching, but for Norman this proved difficult. He relates that he had to learn not to look for a change within himself but instead to remind himself of who it was that now lived in him and through him: "He in me is the all, the joy, power, wisdom, victory—all. I transfer my attention, my recognition, my affirmation from the human vessel to Him whom it contains."[160]

Timothy George has lamented the "deadly divorce"[161] that has persisted within evangelicalism between theology and spirituality and has postulated that this arises from the fact that justification by faith and union with Christ have not been understood as inseparably linked. And it is, he insists, in the cross that the two come together. This is surely the signifi-

---

156. Jones, *The Trials and Triumphs of Mrs Jessie Penn-Lewis*, 152–53.

157. Ibid.

158. Ibid., 160.

159. Ibid., 161.

160. Grubb, *Once Caught, No scape*, 86.

161. George and McGrath (eds.), *For all the Saints*, 4.

cance of Penn-Lewis in that she intuited to a greater extent than the other Keswick teachers where to find the true solution to the Boardman lament: "Forgiveness did not satisfy me; I wanted the power of sin destroyed." She sees that the cross of Christ invites us into a dynamic union with it in which we become crucified, and we become risen.

Hymn Break

A hymn that was an anthem of the 1904–5 Welsh revival and would have been well known to both Evan Roberts and Jessie Penn-Lewis was *Here is Love*. It is of multiple points of origin: the Welsh version, which originally only had the first two verses, was written by William Rees and set to music by Robert Lowry in 1876. Not until 1900 was this translated into English:

> Here is love, vast as the ocean,
> Lovingkindness as the flood,
> When the Prince of Life, our Ransom,
> Shed for us His precious blood.
> Who His love will not remember?
> Who can cease to sing His praise?
> He can never be forgotten,
> Throughout Heav'n's eternal days.
>
> On the mount of crucifixion,
> Fountains opened deep and wide;
> Through the floodgates of God's mercy
> Flowed a vast and gracious tide.
> Grace and love, like mighty rivers,
> Poured incessant from above,
> And Heav'n's peace and perfect justice
> Kissed a guilty world in love.[162]

Conclusion

Evangelical devotion to the cross and blood of Christ gradually changes over the period so far covered. The first phase is that embodied by the Moravians. In essence it represents only a small development on medieval passion mysticism. Its dominating note is that of personal, heart-felt

162. *The Cyber Hymnal* No. 2322: http://www.hymnary.org/text/here_is_love_vast_as_the_ocean [accessed online 18/03/2016].

devotion. At the dawn of the Enlightenment, at the start of the modern era, the Moravians drank deeply from a pre-modern well. In an age of growing infidelity towards religion, the blood of Christ was calling the Moravians to give themselves utterly to him who gave his life for them. The spirituality of the medieval mystics was now translated into a Lutheran context.

The second phase begins with the Wesleys. Charles provides the devotional language while John supplies the theological framework. Thanks to them, the great theme of being washed in the blood is bequeathed to a huge body of nineteenth-century devotion. The role of the blood in personal holiness was that it cleansed the heart, Wesleyans would say permanently, from "inbred" sin. And it ongoingly removes our guiltiness before God, setting to work as soon as the believer has become conscious of wrongdoing and acknowledges it. This blood was a symbol of Christ's atonement that brought his death within reach. It could be pictured as being applied to the unclean. For this reason, 1 John 1:7 was much proclaimed as the scripture that pointed the way from purely forensic categories to more experiential ones.

A most promising way of appropriating the atonement was offered by Jessie Penn-Lewis within the Keswick tradition. This represents a third phase in the passion piety of evangelicalism: it is the mystical co-crucifixion with Christ. Penn-Lewis took seriously the fact that Romans 6 and Galatians 2:20 offer a crucifixion of self, they promise to deal with sin and not just with our sins. The possibility, which she tirelessly proclaimed, of living a new life in union with the crucified and risen Christ became known as her cross theology.

But what of the extremes? As with medieval passion mysticism, there are some highly irrational moments here, particularly with the Moravians. Stibbs, in his masterful study of the word "blood" in Scripture, concluded his monograph with the insight that blood is "a sign of life either given or taken in death. Such giving or taking of life is in this world the extreme, both of gift or price and of crime or penalty. Man knows no greater."[163]

So the phrase, "the blood of Christ" is by nature susceptible of hyperbolic usage. It is by nature extreme language. No greater gift and no higher price is possible; and no worse a crime or exacting a penalty is conceivable than all that is involved in the death of the Son of God at the hands of sinners on behalf of sinners. Accordingly, over this period, the type and variety of metaphors used in conjunction with the blood is as much an indicator

---

163. Stibbs, *The Meaning of the Word "Blood" in Scripture*, 33.

of an outspoken emphasis upon it as are the bare frequency of references. Over the nineteenth century, there were blood corpuscles used as coinage, spears covered in the blood, arrows dipped in blood, blood-stained banners, and molten brands quenched in the blood, not to mention fountains of blood, rivers of blood, purple floods of blood, and blood-currents, in which people drink, dip, plunge, lie, bathe, wash themselves, and wash their garments.

This nineteenth-century peak in blood mysticism is an extension of evangelicalism's routine crucicentrism recruited in the cause of some specific fight: the fight against inbred sin; or the fight against liberalism and Catholicism. Against the tide of liberal scholarship, Charles Spurgeon declared that he would rather have his tongue cut out than ever agree to stop preaching about the blood.[164] Preaching the once-for-all atoning blood was a way of opposing the perceived watering-down of the gospel that the liberals had brought with their penchant for the life and teachings of Jesus; it was also a way of countering the revival in Catholic sacramentalism that had come about the wake of the Oxford movement. Among all evangelicals therefore, a bloody sacrificial atonement served as an identity marker, identifying evangelicals as anti-liberal and anti-ritualist.[165]

But this fight will grow more intense and take on a further dominant theme. For in early Pentecostalism, the blood becomes a war cry. These believers felt themselves to be no longer battling with human secularization or with the enemy within, now it is Satan himself who is enemy number one. Consequently, they must now be "covered" by the blood. They must stay "under" it. They must loudly and repetitiously invoke the justifying, cleansing accomplishments of the atonement in order to see the devil flee. The desire for purity thus gives way to the desire for victory and power. To the beginnings of Pentecostalism we now turn.

164. Spurgeon, *The Metropolitan Tabernacle* Vol. 32, 129.

165. Rennie, "Fundamentalism and the Varieties of North Atlantic Evangelicalism," in Noll et al. (eds.), *Evangelicalism: Comparative Studies of Popular Protestantism*, 333: "fear of liberalism," and "fear of resurgent Catholicism" were formative of Anglican evangelicalism as early as the 1820s.

Chapter 5

BLACK RELIGION AND THE ORIGINS OF PENTECOSTALISM

Introduction

THE CONTEXT FOR THIS chapter is a sea change within certain sectors of English-speaking evangelicalism that began to be in evidence towards the end of the nineteenth century and came to full fruition with the birth of Pentecostalism. This change consisted in the emergence of what would today be described as "spiritual warfare." Evangelicals had often seen themselves as locked in moral combat, but it seems clear that by the tail end of the holiness movement in the late nineteenth century the battle was no longer so much about indwelling sin, or even the sins of society. The theatre of war was now the unknown zone of demonic activity. The fight was with the devil. The whole sanctification project, in both its Wesleyan and non-Wesleyan forms, was failing and a new enemy was needed to pin this failure on. And this enemy, whether manifested through human agency or not, was the devil.

This shift to a more demonological worldview was of a piece with the rise of the premillennial outlook and the conviction that these were the Last Days. The tribulation was just around the corner. The imminent rise of the antichrist provided the milieu in which the devil was much more likely than before to be blamed for a variety of evils. He could be blamed for disruption and fanaticism in meetings, persecution from the wider church, and bodily sickness.[1]

The atoning death of Jesus became the focus of this war, and within that, the blood of Jesus—previously a symbol of sanctification—occupied a central place in conjunction with the Holy Spirit. In other words, the same two agents of Wesleyan sanctification: the blood and the Spirit, were now the agents of spiritual warfare. In the context of the celebrated Los Angeles birthplace of global Pentecostalism, Azusa Street, the heritage of slave religion, with its strong attachment Israelite slavery motifs, was influential in the way these Wesleyan symbols were deployed. Hence, the evocative image of Passover night became the rallying point for all those who sought shelter "under the blood," and deliverance from Pharaoh's Egypt.

William Seymour and the Azusa Street Revival

Born in 1870 in Louisiana, William Seymour was the son of freed slaves. The forms of Christianity that developed among the slaves were heavily tinged with West African spirituality. Indeed, similarities have been noted between the Pentecostal concept of baptism in the Holy Spirit and the West African concept of spirit possession.[2] African American Christianity generally has been noted for its strong syncretistic tendencies.[3]

Seymour was converted at an African Methodist Episcopal church in Indianapolis but soon joined the Evening Light Saints, a radical Wesleyan holiness group with strong interracial ideals.[4] He was invited in 1905 by Lucy Farrow to pastor a holiness mission near Houston. There, in Houston, he was introduced for the first time to Charles Parham and his Bible school. Early in 1906, Seymour was permitted, thanks to Lucy Farrow's mediation, to attend Parham's all-white Bible school by sitting outside the window of the classroom. Seymour soon fell under the spell of Parham's teaching on tongues as the initial evidence of baptism in the Holy Spirit, although nei-

---

1. Robert Mapes Anderson comments: "The extraordinary activity of evil spirits, Pentecostals believed, was evidence of a wholesale counter-movement of the demonic world against its impending destruction." This would seem to support the idea that Pentecostal demonology was bound up with their eschatology. Anderson, *Vision of the Disinherited*, 96.

2. Lovett, "Black Origins of the Pentecostal Movement," in Synan (ed.), *Aspects of Pentecostal-Charismatic Origins*, 123–41.

3. See Terrell, *Power in the Blood?* 35–70 for a sympathetic exploration of this.

4. Sanders, *Saints in Exile*, 26–28.

ther he nor Parham had experienced the gift at this stage. Lucy Farrow had this gift, however, and was able to help convince Seymour of its reality. This latter-day restoration of the gift of tongues to the church was described by Parham as the "Apostolic Faith." The faith and practice of the churches of the New Testament apostles was being restored in preparation for the return of Christ. Parham styled himself as the projector of this Apostolic Faith Movement.[5]

Parham soon arranged for Seymour to do some preaching in Houston, being particularly keen that Seymour should be used to reach the African Americans with the Apostolic Faith message. Seymour's competent preaching in Houston was witnessed by Neely Terry, a member of a small black-majority holiness group that was based in Los Angeles. This group was under the provisional leadership of Julia Hutchins. Wishing to appoint a male leader, Hutchins promptly invited Seymour to leave Houston to become the pastor of the group. Joseph Smale, a zealous Baptist preacher determined to bring the Welsh Revival to Los Angeles, and Frank Bartleman, the earliest chronicler of the Azusa Street revival, had both previously preached to this small gathering of nine families. When Seymour came, however, he brought a traditional Wesleyan holiness message combined with Parham's tongues emphasis, stating overtly that unless one spoke in tongues one could not claim to be baptized in the Spirit. A number in Hutchins's congregation were quite willing to accept this message. Hutchins herself, however, considered herself to be already baptized in the Spirit because she had experienced entire sanctification. She had no need of a confirming sign. Still less did she want to be told that, without this sign, she was not in fact baptized in the Spirit at all. She was so offended by Seymour's teaching that she famously padlocked the door to him in time for his return for the evening service.[6]

Seymour then began his own work with a handful of sympathetic followers, beginning with a nightly prayer meeting at 214 North Bonnie Brae Street. On April 6, 1906 a ten-day fast was inaugurated. On April 9, Edward Lee was healed and spoke in tongues. On the same day, Jennie Evans Moore (later to become Seymour's wife) spoke in tongues and miraculously played the piano. Soon, the meetings at North Bonnie Brae Street were attracting the attention of the whole neighborhood.

5. Robeck, *Azusa Street Revival and Mission*, 45.

6. His text had been Acts 2:4: Cox, *Fire From Heaven*, 45; Synan, *Century of the Spirit*, 46–47.

On April 12 Seymour himself spoke in tongues. By April 14, owing to all the publicity, the group had grown so large that it had to move to an abandoned building: 312 Azusa Street. The first of many less-than-flattering newspaper reports appeared on April 18, 1906, the day of the portentous San Francisco earthquake. In a matter of months, this old fly-ridden building became a world center for Pentecostal activity, and was open for prayer and preaching around the clock for three years until 1909. The publication of *The Apostolic Faith* helped spread the Pentecostal message throughout the USA and the world. Beginning with a distribution list of ten thousand addressees,[7] *The Apostolic Faith* reached a readership of fifty thousand within three years.[8]

When, in October 1906, Charles Parham came to see the mission for himself, he was disgusted at the racial intermingling and the unbridled fanaticism. Parham tried to take over the work, but Seymour's followers were loyal. Parham then started a competing mission nearby. By June 1908, Clara Lum, the editor of *The Apostolic Faith,* appears to have stolen the mailing list[9] and moved to Portland, Oregon, where she teamed up with a former church member, Florence Crawford. There they ran an independent mission claiming the paper as their own. In 1911, while Seymour was away preaching, William Durham attempted to take over the Mission, but was repelled by Seymour's board of trustees and was locked out by Seymour himself.[10] Like Parham before him, Durham then also started his own mission nearby. In 1913, Seymour was not invited to the Arroyo Seco camp meeting—the meeting of the very organization he had founded, the Apostolic Faith Mission. In 1915, Seymour concluded that, since all these people who had sought to undermine his ministry were white, the problem was racism.[11] As a result, he developed a policy of forbidding anyone white

7. Anon., *Apostolic Faith* 1.4, December 1906, 15.

8. Cauchi, "William J. Seymour and the History of the Azusa Street Mission," in Cauchi (ed.), *The Apostolic Faith: The Original Azusa Street Editions*, 15.

9. This was initially under the guise of taking the mailing list with her to a conference so that she could continue her editorial responsibilities while away from the mission.

10. Bartleman, *Azusa Street*, 143, 150–52.

11. Seymour seldom publicly resisted anyone, however, and frequently invited his enemies to take the pulpit. Liardon points out that this might not have been down to his humility so much as his belief that if he lost the right attitude and became angry, he would lose his salvation. He cites this extract from the *Apostolic Faith:* "If you get angry, or speak evil, or backbite, I care not how many tongues you may have, you have not the baptism with the Holy Spirit. You have lost your salvation." Anon., *Apostolic Faith* 1.9, June 1907, 12; Liardon, *God's Generals,* 159.

from being appointed to leadership. The congregation gradually dwindled. Seymour himself died in 1922. One more takeover attempt was made by Ruthford Griffith in 1930, resulting in a protracted legal battle, in the middle of which the mission was demolished in 1932. After the loss of their building, the original Azusa Street congregation returned to their original home at North Bonnie Brae Street. Mrs Seymour died in 1936.[12]

The Apostolic Faith Magazine

The impression that visitors had that the blood of Jesus was emphasized a lot at Azusa Street meetings is supported by even a cursory reading of the early issues of *The Apostolic Faith*, a magazine first issued in September 1906. So great was the spontaneous prayer and financial support of all those on the mailing list that the transfer of all but the local mailing list to Portland in the June of 1908 is credited with sucking the life out of the Azusa Mission, leading to the cooling off of the revival by early 1909.[13]

The blood and the Spirit were together in the experience of Pentecost as far as the Azusa Street worshippers were concerned. To mention the one was to imply the other. This conjoining of Christology and pneumatology can be seen in such pithy sayings as this: "After we get the Holy Ghost on our souls, we need the Blood just as much, because the Blood brings life and sweetness,"[14] and this: "the only way to get right is to be born of the Spirit through the Blood of Calvary."[15] The same principle works in reverse: the Spirit brings a new realization of the importance of the blood: "I seemed to have a conception of the mighty efficacy of the Blood of Christ, and His omnipresence in Spirit as never before."[16] And, quoting from a British testimony: "The Holy Spirit came upon me on Sunday night, showing me the mighty power in the blood of Jesus."[17]

In terms of composition, cleansing is, in true Wesleyan holiness tradition, top of the list of themes, with 1 John 1:7 frequently quoted and

---

12. The only published study devoted to her life is Robeck, "Moore, Jennie Evans (1883–1936)," in Burgess (ed.), *NIDPCM*, 906–7.

13. Cauchi, "William J. Seymour," 15–16.

14. Anon., *Apostolic Faith* 1.6, February-March 1907, 47.

15. Ibid., 55.

16. Mead, "New-Tongued Missionaries for Africa," *Apostolic Faith* 1.3, November 1906, 20.

17. Anon., "Testimony of a Yorkshire Farmer," *Apostolic Faith* 1.11, January 1908, 8.

paraphrased throughout. Thus, 19 percent (sixty-four instances) of all references to the blood in the Azusa Street *Apostolic Faith* are about being cleansed and washed. Sayings like "How I worship Him today. How I praise Him for the all-cleansing blood!"[18] were common at Azusa Street services: "A colored brother arose and sang the verses of a hymn, the people joining in the chorus: 'The Blood, the Blood, is all my plea; Hallelujah, it cleanseth me.'"[19]

The theme of sanctification is also very prominent in references to the blood. The second blessing of sanctification was clearly separated from the third blessing of "Baptism in the Holy Spirit":

> So in the first chapter of Acts, Jesus taught His disciples to wait for the promise of the Father. This was not to wait for sanctification. His blood had been spilt on Calvary's cross. He was not going to send His blood to cleanse them from carnality but His Spirit to endue them with power.[20]

Yet both the Holy Spirit and the blood are sanctifying agents: "The next step for us is to have a clear knowledge, by the Holy Spirit, of the second work of grace wrought in our hearts by the power of the blood and the Holy Ghost.[21] And, as with traditional Wesleyanism, this second blessing of sanctification was sought and remembered as a nameable, datable experience: "The 30th day of October 1897, I was wholly sanctified through faith in the blood of Jesus Christ."[22]

"Under the Blood" and Exodus

A distinguishing mark of Azusa Street spirituality is the recurring imperative to stay "under" or "covered" by the blood. References to being covered by or being under the blood comprise 10.5 percent (thirty-five instances) of the total in the first twelve issues of *The Apostolic Faith*: "As long as we live under the Blood we will have life and be preserved . . . ."[23] Readers are

18. Anon., *Apostolic Faith* 1.3, November 1906, 14.

19. Anon., *Apostolic Faith* 1.7, April 1907, 12. This was the "hymns of improvisation" phase in the development of Black sacred music, just prior to the emergence of Black Gospel: Walker, *Somebody's Calling my Name*, 97–125.

20. Anon., *Apostolic Faith* 1.4, December 1906, 23.

21. Anon., *Apostolic Faith* 1.5, January 1907.

22. H. M. Turney of San Jose, *Apostolic Faith* 1.4, December 1906.

23. Anon., *Apostolic Faith* 1.6, February-March 1907, 47.

exhorted to "Tell the saints to love one another and keep united in love, and under the Blood every day, and humble."[24] "Under the blood" becomes a standard way for contributors to sign off their articles by issue number 5 (January 1907).

Another distinguishing mark, besides this "covering" theme, and one that would come to dominate Pentecostal blood mysticism, is the victory theme. Azusa Street references to the blood are steeped in combative terminology almost to the same extent that they are steeped in nineteenth-century holiness terminology.

The number of times the blood is described specifically as a victory over "Satan," "the enemy," or the "devil" is considerable, amounting to 10 percent of the total (thirty-three occurrences): "The blood of Jesus prevails against every force and power of the enemy. Glory to God."[25] Readers are assured that, "Satan is not able to make his way through the blood,"[26] and may be confident that, "The Blood conquers all the forces of hell."[27]

There seems to have been a real fear amongst some that a counterfeit miracle might take place when they were seeking the baptism in the Holy Spirit with the sign of tongues. This was when it became useful to know that one was covered by the blood. Inspired by Luke 11:9–13, Seymour reassures his readers: "Do you think when I get down covered with the blood of Jesus, and seek Him to baptize me with the Holy Ghost that He is going to give me a serpent?"[28] In a later edition, he says again: "Never let the hosts of hell make you believe that while you live under the blood, honoring the blood, and pleading through the blood for blessings from the throne, that God will let Satan get through the blood, and put a serpent into you."[29]

In later issues, the imagery becomes more defiant: "We can stand before the very gatling guns of hell and tell them that the Blood cleanseth."[30] The October 1907—January 1908 issue (1.11) contains what might be the first recorded use of the phrase "plead the blood" within Pentecostalism, the suggestion of a practice that would soon become very popular within British Pentecostalism for a time.

24. Andrew G. Johnson of Sweden, *Apostolic Faith* 1.7, April 1907.

25. Anon., *Apostolic Faith* 1.4, December 1906, 3.

26. Ibid., 16, another possible reference to the Red Sea.

27. Anon., *Apostolic Faith* 1.6, February-March 1907, 47.

28. Anon., *Apostolic Faith* 1.2, October 1906, 30.

29. Anon., *Apostolic Faith* 1.4, December 1906, 37.

30. Anon., *Apostolic Faith* 1.12, January 1908, 17.

> Remember, when the Lord works, the devil works too, but when Satan presents anything to you, just tell him you are under the Blood. Just plead the Blood, and he will flee. . . . So, when the Holy Ghost is working, keep your eyes centered upon Jesus, and when the devil presents a thought just rebuke him and plead the Blood.[31]

Throughout the magazine, Passover, Red Sea, and exodus language occurs alongside many of the other themes. The malicious presence of Satan and his hosts (typified by Pharaoh and the Egyptians) is something of a common denominator among such references, though in some cases the thought has more to do with salvation from a sinful past: "The Passover Lamb was a type of Christ. . . . The blood stood for salvation to save them from the destroyer. So the blood of Jesus saves us from sin, for Satan is not able to make his way through the blood.[32]

> [E]vil spirits cannot come under the Blood any more than the Egyptians could pass through the Red Sea—the Red Sea represents the Blood of Jesus Christ. The Blood gives you power over all the power of the enemy.[33]

> . . . and the passing over the Red Sea, which was a type of the Blood of Jesus Christ that gives us victory over all the powers of the enemy.[34]

> The night when they ate the Passover in Egypt was the type of a sinner coming out of darkness, through the Blood of Jesus. Hallelujah![35]

> It was the blood that saved the people from the awful destruction in Egypt, and it takes the Blood to save us today from sin.[36]

The exodus story had been a deeply rooted cultural metanarrative among African Americans since the days of slavery.[37] In fact, the whole

---

31. Anon., "Jesus, O How Sweet the Name!" *Apostolic Faith* 1.11, January 1908, 30.

32. Anon., "Salvation and Healing," *Apostolic Faith* 1.4, December 1906, 16.

33. Anon., "Questions Answered: Can a child of God be Possessed by Evil Spirits?" *Apostolic Faith* 1.11, January 1908, 15.

34. Anon., *Apostolic Faith* 1.10, September 1907, 14.

35. Anon., "Old Testament Feasts Fulfilled in our Souls Today," *Apostolic Faith* 1.9, September 1907, 13.

36. Anon., "Who May Prophesy?" *Apostolic Faith* 1.12, January 1908, 17.

37. E.g., Raboteau, "African Americans, Exodus, and the American Israel," in Murphy

African American story tended to be embedded within the story of the Israelites.[38] The exodus narrative, therefore, is the most likely underlying meaning behind black Azusa Street congregants' use of the phrase "under the blood." This phrase then is rooted in Exodus 12–14, which pictures the Israelites being shielded from the destroying angel because of the blood of the lamb daubed upon their doorposts and lintels. They were "under" the protection of the blood. The Red Sea is further recruited as a type of the blood of Christ, the term Red being especially fitting.[39] Just as the Egyptians were covered by the Red Sea, so the past is under the blood, and just as the Israelites were cut off from the enemy by the sea, so the believer is cut off from sin and Satan by the blood.

It is possible that, at times, the real threat was a very human one and that the image of the Israelites battening down the hatches for a night under the blood followed by their glorious liberation from oppression was reassuring for the readers as they faced persecution. Pentecostals the world over were soon to be denounced by fellow evangelicals as the "last vomit of Satan,"[40] but in the case of Azusa Street there might well have been a racial dimension to the opposition. Most of the opposition, as we saw when we looked at Seymour's life, was white. The blood may have become a symbol of their spiritual emancipation. Doubtless, as Seymour continued to encounter racism throughout his ministry, exodus imagery would have been a comfort. It is worth noting the coded dimension to African American

---

(ed.), *Down by the Riverside*, 20: "no single story captures more clearly the distinctiveness of African American Christianity than that of the Exodus." So too Hoyt, "Interpreting Biblical Scholarship," in Felder (ed.), *Stony the Road We Trod*, 30: "The functional mythology of the Exodus that operated in their lives provided the necessary motivation for the earthly journey of the Jews, and it has provided the same motivation for blacks." Also: Glaude, *Exodus! Religion, Race and Nation in Early Nineteenth-Century Black America*. There have also been a number of studies on African American Pentecostalism, a number of which make reference to the widespread use of the exodus narrative, e.g. "Africans in the 'New World' identified with the Israelites under Egyptian Bondage[;] . . . non-violent victory over enemies and Pentecost, became the theological symbolic imagery for a people with whom God wandered through the desert . . . ." Gerloff, "The Holy Spirit and the African Diaspora," 91.

38. This led to some measure of fellow-feeling between blacks and Jewish immigrants. Black appropriation of the exodus narrative resonated with Jewish immigrants who then went on to defend the interests of blacks against white American discrimination: Kay, "The Exodus and Racism: Paradoxes for Jewish Liberation," 25.

39. *Apostolic Faith* 1.10, September 1907, 14.

40. Nichol, *Pentecostalism*, 70.

speech.[41] Before the Reconstruction Era, Christian imagery had been used by them in a way that sounded similar to white Christian imagery but which had an additional meaning hidden in the only place a black slave knew of that was free of the white man's control—his heart. Originally, of course, the Egyptians would have been a type of the white man, and it is possible that on occasions when invasive, over-ambitious whites threatened to take over the Mission, this typology would have reverted to its original usage. At any rate, all human opposition was read as satanic opposition, and to this the only answer was to take shelter in God's provision: the blood. Exactly how this was supposed to work was never unpacked. The biblical precedent alone sufficed as grounds for seeing a protective power released by placing one's trust in the shed blood of Jesus.

There is, however, with this strong note of warfare and protection from demonic onslaught, a clear break from historic African American uses of the atonement. Historically, slave religion had found in the suffering and death of Christ some strong emblems of victimization which they could identify with as a source of comfort. Terrell writes:

> Through the lens of slavery, African Americans—bond and free—fixed their gaze on the cross of Jesus, deriving from it a way to understand and cope with their own painful experiences of proscribed existence. Jesus' presumed innocence, his betrayal by his friends, and his arrest, torture and execution in occupied Palestine mirrored the brutal conditions the slaves experienced in antebellum America.[42]

Similarly, James Cone writes of how black slaves were "impressed by the Passion,"[43] describing how, in Negro Spirituals such as *Were You There?* black slaves had seen themselves at the cross where they "unleashed their imagination, describing what they felt and saw."[44] The shift in devotional approach that we see at Azusa Street is probably down to the fact that the white threat had now become a more subtle or hidden one. The "intangibles" of "cultural taxonomies, fear, shame, chronic mourning, vulnerabil-

41. Ellis speaks of these double meanings: "Slavemaster Christianity-ism was rejected by most Christian slaves, but under its cover they began to develop an indigenous theological outlook and practice. We began using a 'double-meaning' language which was passed down in our oral tradition." Ellis, *Beyond Liberation*, 43.

42. Terrell, *Power in the Blood?* 13.

43. Cone, *The Spirituals and the Blues*, 52–54. Some further work has been done on black hymnody by Jon Spencer: *Protest and Praise*, and, *Black Hymnody*.

44. Cone, *The Spirituals and the Blues*, 52–54.

ity, social alienation, marginalization and muted despair" were an ongoing source of psychological trauma.[45] The spite that Seymour experienced, for example, was far from the brutality of antebellum America, but was harder to pin down: easier in fact to define as demonic rather than merely human. This change in the nature of the threat was coupled with the African American tendency to "deepen the import of the evangelical focus on the Atonement."[46] Wider evangelicalism had already become more apocalyptic and demonological. At Azusa Street, black evangelicalism took this eschatology and deepened it, making it relevant to its own story.

Conclusion

At Azusa Street it could be said that Pentecostalism was birthed as a theology of liberation. The liberation of the Israelites from slavery in Egypt by the blood of the lamb was a significant biblical precedent. The exodus narrative supplied the focal point for the Christology of early American Pentecostalism, while the Day of Pentecost narrative provided the pneumatology. And this Pentecostal liberation was only understood to work if both theologies were in place. Time and again the early Pentecostals showed themselves to be at pains to maintain that their message was not about the Spirit only, but about the Spirit and the blood together. However distasteful or difficult to understand it may be at times, the blood seems almost as definitive of Pentecostal origins as the Spirit is.

Empowerment continues to be the main selling point of Pentecostalism the world over and the story of the beginning of Pentecostalism reveals a spirituality of empowerment that involved being freed from something as well as being freed for something. The redeeming motif of Christ as Passover Lamb originally provided the means to be freed from everything that disempowers: darkness, sin, the demonic, and human oppression. This was the indispensable preliminary to receiving power for service: Pentecost, gifts, and a missionary anointing. The word "Blood," reverently capitalized and mentioned as often as possible by the pioneers of the Pentecostal vision of life, was more than a mere fetish or incantation. It was, just as it often is in the New Testament itself, a kind of shorthand for experiences of profound

45. Noel and Johnson, "Psychological Trauma, Christ's Passion, and the African American Faith Tradition," 363.

46. Terrell, *Power in the Blood?* 53.

safety in God's presence, encounters of great power, overwhelming love, of cleansing and of liberating non-answerability to human opposition.

Chapter 6

———

GETTING UP TO DATE

Pleading the Blood, A Waning Emphasis, and Mel Gibson

Pleading the Blood

THERE IS A LINK between Azusa Street and the birth of Pentecostalism in Europe. Thomas Ball Barratt, originally a Cornish Methodist who later came to be leading a congregation in Oslo, brought the Pentecostal experience to his Oslo congregation in December 1906 following a visit to New York and some correspondence while there with Azusa Street.[1] Alexander Boddy, a mild-mannered Anglican priest who was vicar of All Saints Church, Monkwearmouth, Sunderland, visited T. B. Barratt's thriving Oslo congregation in March 1907.[2] He wanted what he saw. He finally persuaded Barratt to come to Sunderland in the Autumn of that year. Before long, Sunderland became nationally and internationally significant, associated with the early ministries of such names as Smith Wigglesworth and George Jeffreys. By April 1908, Sunderland was producing its own international magazine called *Confidence*.

Sunderland clearly shared with Azusa Street a fundamental anxiety about Satan. Indeed, it is perhaps surprising that the birth of the most remarkable phenomenon in modern religious history should begin with

---

1. The correspondence has been preserved and is discussed here: Bundy, "Spiritual Advice to a Seeker," 159–60.

2. Boddy, "Some Sacred Memories," *Confidence* 7.2, 1914, 24.

groups of people who at times seemed to be living with a siege mentality. For Azusa Street worshippers, victory was all about making sure that one is in the right position: under the blood. The Sunderland worshippers, who were even more obsessed with the theme of victory, went further and developed a mechanical means of invoking the blood when seeking their baptism in the Holy Spirit, which they termed "pleading the blood." This involved repeating the word "blood" or slightly longer phrases referring to the blood of Christ until the Spirit came, a practice that appears to have an independent point of origin in a revival in Kilsyth, Scotland, in January 1908. This practice was taken up by Sunderland and some prominent leaders associated with Sunderland, such as Wigglesworth, from the Spring of that year.

At Kilsyth was Andrew Murdoch's new Pentecostal assembly in Westport Hall.[3] On January 31, 1908, so the story goes, a man there by the name of John Reid, "raised his hand and cried 'Blood! Blood! Blood!'" Immediately following this, thirteen young people reportedly received a baptism in the Holy Spirit and spoke in tongues.[4] From this point onwards, this repetition of the word blood became standard practice at Kilsyth as people sought this baptism in the Holy Spirit. On one occasion, forty-three people at Westport Hall received the experience over a single weekend of continuously crying out "the Blood!"[5] It was not long before Westport Hall was receiving a flood of visitors from England, Scotland, Wales, Ireland, Africa, and North America. These visitors experienced exactly the same thing: they were filled with the Spirit by "pleading the blood." Meetings were held every day for a period of nine months.[6] Before long, twenty-eight young people had offered themselves for missionary service, causing these events to take their place in local history as the fourth significant revival to have taken place in Kilsyth.[7] Boddy visited Kilsyth at the end of March 1908 and witnessed the now well-established practice of pleading the blood before receiving Spirit baptism. Whilst there he also experienced an intensity of power in the meetings that he described as greater that anything he had

3. This church had initially been founded in 1896 by the Kilsyth United Evangelical Society in an effort to reach local miners with the gospel: Hutchison, "The Kilsyth Religious Revivals." http://kilsyth.org.uk/?page_id=81 [accessed online: 15/03/2016].

4. Weeks, *Chapter Thirty-Two*, 19.

5. Worsfold, *The Origins of the Apostolic Church in Great Britain*, 46.

6. Ibid.

7. The previous three revivals were under John Livingstone, 1627, James Robe 1742–43 and William Chalmers Burns in 1839: Hutchison, "'Kilsyth' Religious Revivals."

seen under T. B. Barratt in Norway.[8] As a result, he carried this doctrine of pleading the blood back to Sunderland where he and his wife Mary began to teach the doctrine as standard practice. One thing that appears to have made an impression on Boddy during his visit to Kilsyth was the "power" of the blood. His wife Mary, having already had a vision of the blood during her experience of the Spirit, was equally convinced of this, and both were happy to promote the practice of pleading the blood in Sunderland for well over a year after Boddy's visit to Kilsyth.

Here is an example of someone pleading the blood who describes his experience in the very first issue of *Confidence:*

> I found I had spiritual enemies hindering my getting through. I felt them. They were like an atmosphere in front of me. I BEGAN TO PLEAD THE BLOOD. I assured myself and Satan that it was the all-atoning Blood, and that Jesus was both Lord and Christ.[9]

Moments later, while flat on his back in his pastor's kitchen, he was swept "in to the sea of Pentecostal Fulness with its unmistakable seal."[10]

However, pleading the blood as a way of clearing away demons so as to be filled with the Spirit was a practice that soon fell out of favor and was never revived. Probably this was because the Apostolic Faith Church—an especially radical wing of early British Pentecostalism—took the idea of pleading the blood to extremes that most Pentecostals were not happy with. William Oliver Hutchinson, the leader of the Apostolic Faith Church, had, for example, developed a sophisticated Old Testament theology in defense of pleading the blood. This theology was based, in particular, on the repetitious blood sacrifices made by Solomon at the dedication of the temple,[11] as well as the story of Abel's righteous blood sacrifice over against Cain's wicked bloodless one. By 1916, most Pentecostals would have wished to distance themselves from Hutchinson and his beliefs. As early as July 1909 there appears in *Confidence* a rather incidental cautionary note:

---

8. White, *Word of God*, 83–85. He had previously said exactly the same thing about T. B. Barratt's ministry in Oslo in comparison to the Welsh Revival: Gee, *Wind and Flame*, 20. This shows either a tendency towards sensational language on his part (something that can be traced to his travel writings if looked for), or else that his experience of Kilsyth was truly quite exceptional, surpassing even the Welsh Revival.

9. John Martin, *Confidence* 1.1, April 1908, 12–13.

10. Ibid., 13.

11. Hathaway, "The Role of William Oliver Hutchinson and the Apostolic Faith Church in the Formation of British Pentecostal Churches," 44.

> He [Anton Reuss of Florence] had learned to plead the Blood—not
> by repetition of the word "Blood," but by presenting the Atone-
> ment to the Father in the power of the Holy Ghost.[12]

However, even Hutchinson wanted to distance himself from the repetition of the word "Blood" as a tongue-twisting device to aid talking in
tongues: "We do not plead the Blood for a tongue, as some suppose, but
we do plead the Blood against the foe which opposes us."[13] There does not
appear to be any evidence that saying the word "blood" again and again
to help bring on tongues was ever a widespread practice, yet the instances
when "blood, blood, blood" would suddenly give way to fluent tongues-
speaking were sufficiently common for observers to deduce that this was
the case.

By the 1957, within classical Pentecostalism, things had changed so
much that Donald Gee could write an article for the American periodical
The Pentecostal Evangel in which he claimed that in the early days of Pentecostalism, exhortations to plead the blood had always "perplexed" him.[14]
The importance that early Pentecostals placed on the blood he sympatheti-
cally put down to the "truculent modernism of fifty years ago"[15] with its
scorn of evangelical "'slaughterhouse religion,'"[16] yet he regarded much of
the reaction to it as a superstitious "fetish."[17] He went on to debunk the
pleading of the blood as a means of invoking God's protection prior to
making a journey by train, car, or boat, or over a house or a person or when
encountering demons. He pointed out that appeals made to the exodus
story, the commonest Scriptural justification adduced by blood-pleaders,
are moot seeing as the protection obtained through the blood on that occasion was from the wrath of God, not from the devil. He goes on to suggest
that the name of Jesus, rather than his blood, ought to be invoked for victory over the devil.[18]

What remains of this idea of pleading the blood has been taken up
by some charismatics, who continue to practice it, but in a different form.

---

12. Boddy et al., "Sunderland International Pentecostal Congress, Whitsuntide 1909:
A Record in Detail," *Confidence* 2.4, July 1909, 159.

13. Hutchinson, *Showers of Blessing* 5, August-September 1910, 5.

14. Gee, "Under the Blood," 4.

15. Ibid.

16. Ibid.

17. Ibid.

18. Ibid.

For Benny Hinn, for instance, pleading the blood has taken the form of a simple daily prayer for his family: "Lord, cover Suzanne, Jessica, Natasha, Joshua and Eleasha with Your blood."[19] He has written in detail about the subject, offering the story of the Passover as his chief biblical precedent. Joyce Meyer has also taught extensively on this subject.[20] For both Hinn and Meyer, the purpose of pleading the blood is clearly the warding off of demonic activity, though not with a view to receiving the Spirit, and not by simply repeating the word "blood."

Hymn Break

Before we move on from the early twentieth century, we must pause for a moment at the hymn that this book is named after: George Bennard's *The Old Rugged Cross*, written in 1912, and, as it happens, a favorite among the older generation of Pentecostals. It takes up many of the themes of glory and shame that we saw in *The Dream of the Rood*, themes that possibly explain its popularity with such a beleaguered and persecuted group as the early Pentecostals:

On a hill far away stood an old rugged cross,
The emblem of suff'ring and shame;
And I love that old cross where the Dearest and Best
For a world of lost sinners was slain.

So I'll cherish the old rugged cross,
Till my trophies at last I lay down;
I will cling to the old rugged cross,
And exchange it someday for a crown.

Oh, that old rugged cross, so despised by the world,
Has a wondrous attraction for me;
For the dear Lamb of God left His glory above
To bear it to dark Calvary.

In that old rugged cross, stained with blood so divine,
A wondrous beauty I see,
For 'twas on that old cross Jesus suffered and died,
To pardon and sanctify me.

To the old rugged cross I will ever be true;

19. Hinn, *Power in the Blood*, 75.
20. E.g., Meyer, *The Word, The Name, The Blood*, 115–38.

Its shame and reproach gladly bear;
Then He'll call me someday to my home far away,
Where His glory forever I'll share.[21]

A Waning Emphasis

It seems that the baton, if there was one, of heavily crucicentric piety was now in the hands of the Pentecostals. In the first half of the twentieth century, if really strong concentrations of passion mysticism were to be found anywhere at all, they were to be found with them. If this was to continue, they would need to maintain it and then pass it on, just as they had received it from the holiness movements. However, it is clear that, along with the immense early emphasis on the second advent within Pentecostalism, the equally monolithic emphasis on the atonement soon subsided in the West.

Inter-war Pentecostals continued to reference the blood, but in a nostalgic way, using nineteenth-century hymnodic phraseology. The purpose of these invocations was to identify themselves, in the face of bitter opposition, as rooted in the old-time gospel. During the 1920s and 30s, they faced almost universal hostility from the churches. In the case of Britain in particular, Donald Gee would later reminisce that he doubted whether any Pentecostals anywhere in the world had to endure hostility that was so "determined, capable and prejudiced."[22] The main role for the blood at this time was therefore as a badge of orthodoxy. The need to prove to the wider evangelical community Pentecostalism's doctrinal legitimacy was an urgent one.[23] Emphasis on a bloody atonement formed part of an apologetic for the baptism in the Holy Spirit: "Let us examine the fruit of the experience that so many reject . . ." suggests Howard Carter. "There is a joy in the Holy Ghost, a love of the Word of God, a magnifying of the precious Blood, and an atmosphere of praise."[24]

21. *United Methodist Hymnal*, No. 504: http://www.hymnary.org/text/on_a_hill_far_away_stood_an_old_rugged [18/03/2016].

22. Gee, *These Men I Knew*, 88–89.

23. So Randall's general thesis that inter-war Pentecostalism was at pains to portray itself as in continuity with traditional evangelicalism: Randall, *Evangelical Experiences*, 206–30. Cf. Randall, "Old Time Power," 57.

24. Howard Carter, "The Fruit of the Land," *Redemption Tidings* 10.16, August 15, 1935, 3.

Mimicking wider evangelicalism, attacks by Pentecostals on blood-less gospel preaching were virulent at this time: "It is damnable to tell a man to save himself by works, and finally be lost, when the Word positively says, 'There is no remission of sins without the shedding of blood.' Such doctrine is as heartless as it is bloodless."[25] Another says: "Pity the poor, polite preachers who are too polite to preach the blood from the pulpit!"[26] D. L. Moody's success in preaching is attributed, on Moody's own admission, to his emphasis on the blood.[27] Billy Bray is also cited for support. On one occasion, Bray reputedly cried out "The Blood!" at the top of his voice three times, resulting in the power of God falling upon the meeting.[28] The frustrated desire for affiliation with wider evangelicalism sometimes rises to the surface: "Evangelical denominations have no quarrel with us over preaching salvation through the blood, immersion of believers, or the breaking of bread . . . ."[29] The only stumbling block was this: ". . . but when we tell them that there is a sign accompanying the baptism of the Holy Spirit, what a change."[30]

The *Elim Evangel* and *Redemption Tidings,* which I quote from above, afford us a very interesting barometer as both of these publications have continued, virtually without interruption, to the present day.[31] Even a cursory glance at their slickly produced present-day counterparts will confirm the relative lack of interest in all matters connected with the atonement. There has been an even more striking loss of interest in the second advent. It seems that, as modern life has become steadily more comfortable, many Western Pentecostals are no longer expecting the Lord to return at any time in the near future.[32] The whole premillennial framework by reference to which the devout were urged to take shelter under the blood as the days

---

25. Fletcher, "The Three Future Judgments," *Elim Evangel* 8.5, March 1, 1927, 71.

26. Lacey, "Where Love and Justice Meet," *Elim Evangel* 14.32, August 11, 1933, 509.

27. Gortner, "The Blood," *Elim Evangel* 14.47, November 24, 1933, 742.

28. Frodsham, "The Blood that Speaketh," *Elim Evangel* 14.21, May 26 1933, 322.

29. Anon, "Signs," *Elim Evangel* 15.9, March 1934, 133.

30. Ibid.

31 Though they have undergone a number of changes of title. They are presently called *Direction* and *Re* respectively: http://www.elim.org.uk/Articles/427141/Direction_Magazine.aspx [accessed online 07/03/2016], http://www.aog.org.uk/resources/re-magazine [accessed online 07/03/2016].

32. Anderson, agreeing with Land (*Passion for the Kingdom*, 76), also cites the upward mobility of Western Pentecostals, who now see the world as getting a little better: Anderson, "Pentecostal and Charismatic Theology," 598.

grew more and more evil has all but vanished. While the picture in global Pentecostalism may be different, it seems that today, the crucicentric heart of Western Pentecostalism that was once preserved so vocally and so ardently, to the tune of "Nothing but the Blood," in which there was "Power, power, wonder-working power" appears not to be beating as strongly as once it did.

However, I am aware that the center of gravity within global Pentecostalism has shifted to the Southern hemisphere and is growing the most strongly in the developing, not the developed, world. Judging from a number of conversations I have had, an emphasis on the blood of Jesus has remained an important feature of Pentecostalism in Sub-Saharan Africa. The West African spirituality in which African American spirituality was rooted has always been a spirituality of conflict in which the realities of Ephesians 6:12 are self-evident long before conversion to Christianity from animism. Sacrificial blood has a role, according to one man I have interviewed, in "spiritual bulletproofing,"[33] and this role is simply transferred to the blood of Christ upon conversion. Clearly some interesting field work could be done on this, but such work would be beyond both the scope and the methodology of this book.

Hymn Break

No book on Christian devotion to the cross would be complete without a hymn from the modern hymn-writing partnership: Keith Getty and Stuart Townend. By far the most popular hymn of theirs, which was sung at the enthronement of Justin Welby as Archbishop of Canterbury in 2013, is *In Christ Alone*, first published in 2001.

> In Christ alone!—who took on flesh,
> Fullness of God in helpless babe.
> This gift of love and righteousness,
> Scorned by the ones He came to save:
> Till on that cross as Jesus died,
> The wrath of God was satisfied -
> For every sin on Him was laid;
> Here in the death of Christ I live.
>
> There in the ground His body lay,
> Light of the world by darkness slain:

---

33. Temi Kpogho, a Nigerian, informal interview, July 31, 2007.

Then bursting forth in glorious day
Up from the grave He rose again!
And as He stands in victory
Sin's curse has lost its grip on me,
For I am His and He is mine -
Bought with the precious blood of Christ.[34]

Mel Gibson's *The Passion of the Christ*

There seems, then, in the West at least, to have been a break in the continuity. Despite a number of modern hymns and songs like the one above, the flow of impassioned blood-soaked evangelical piety that we have seen such a lot of over the previous pages appears to have petered out in the developed world.[35] It is all the more interesting then, that a full-blooded revival of a pre-evangelical, medieval-style piety suddenly took the world by storm in 2004. In keeping with the post-Christendom shift, this new piety did not arise from within a church or monastic setting but on the big screen.

Evaluations of the film *The Passion of the Christ*[36] were as hasty as they were prejudiced. Complaints were hitting the press from the Anti-Defamation League about the film's alleged antisemitism long before the film was released, with many of the most vociferous complainants having never seen any of it.[37] And even after the film's release, critiques of the work based on the assumptions of the critics themselves were legion, while any articles based on the stated intentions and other divulgences of those who actually

---

34. Extract taken from the song 'In Christ Alone' by Stuart Townend & Keith Getty Copyright (c) 2001 Thankyou Music.

35. In its stead has been an upsurge in academic interest in atonement theology. See my *Atonement Theories: A Way Through the Maze*, which attempts to evaluate some of this by reference to the much earlier episodes in the story of atonement theology.

36. Icon Entertainment, 2004.

37. Medved, "The Passion and the Prejudice," 38. Medved, a devout Jew, concludes: "Gibson's critics may resent these elements of the drama, but they must blame Matthew, Mark, Luke, and John rather than Mel," 40. Perhaps the unusually sympathetic portrayal of Pilate did not help matters, however: Ronan, "Mel Gibson's *Passion* and the Many Uses of Christ's Suffering," 378–79, and neither did Gibson's anti-Semitic father and the association of both with Roman Catholic traditionalism, which is considered anti-Semitic because it rejects Vatican II, together with that council's repudiation of historic tendencies to blame the Jews for the death of Jesus: Dinges, "Gibson and Traditionalist Catholicism," 16.

made the film were remarkably scarce.[38] The Christian reception of the film was very surprising. *The Passion* was based on the fourteen Stations of the Cross, with both the actor who played Jesus (James Caviezel) and the producer Mel Gibson being devout Catholics at the time, yet by far the most critical Christian viewers were Catholics. Evangelicals, on the other hand, were able to overlook the inclusion of Veronica wiping the face of Jesus and various other extra-canonical details.[39] Evangelicals loved it so much as to use showings of the film as an opportunity for evangelism.[40] New Testament scholars were also highly critical: the film came out when the Third Quest for the Historical Jesus was in full swing and there seems to have been an unusual sensitivity in the academic community about all matters historical in relation to Jesus. And, in what has now become something of a tradition within academia, there was what can only be described as intellectual overkill. The excess of academic analysis of the Toronto Blessing pales into insignificance when compared to the rash of articles and full-length books analyzing *The Passion* to within an inch of its life.[41]

The Passion stands within a long tradition of graphically bloody artistic representations of the suffering of Christ, such as those of Grünewald, Bosch, and Dürer, and of the passion play. It also stands within a not-so-long but just as remarkable tradition of cinematic renderings both of the historical Jesus of the Gospels, and of various allegorical Christ-figures[42] (plus one film that is a bit of both: *Jesus of Montreal*[43]). However, there are

38. Webb, and many others, are completely sure that the plot is based on the work of the nineteenth-century mystic Anne Catherine Emmerich and her *The Dolorous Passion of Our Lord Jesus Christ*: Webb, "*The Passion* and the Influence of Emmerich's *The Dolorous Passion of Our Lord Jesus Christ*," in Corley and Webb (eds.), *Jesus and Mel Gibson's The Passion of the Christ*, 160–77, yet in an interview at the 2004 Annual Meeting of the Society of Biblical Literature, Benedict Fitzgerald who wrote the screenplay, appeared to deny any direct influence: Shepherd, "From Gospel to Gibson," 324.

39. "Fifty years ago it would have been unimaginable that the Evangelical wing of the Christian community would flock to a film using the template of the Stations of the Cross." Goa, "*The Passion*, Classical Art and Re-presentation," in Corley and Webb (eds.), *Jesus and Mel Gibson's The Passion of the Christ*, 151.

40. Walker, "Witnessing with *The Passion*," *Christianity Today*, April 2004, 23.

41. One book review I found reviews not just one but seven books on the same subject which had all been published between 2004 and 2006: Plate, "Mel Gibson's Bible," 535–39.

42. Telford, "Jesus Christ Movie Star," in Marsh (ed.), *Explorations in Theology and Film*, 122; Baugh, *Imaging The Divine*, 62, 112; Hurley, "Cinematic Transfigurations of Jesus," in May (ed.), *Religion in Film*, 61.

43. I am indebted to Cliff College creative arts student Su Parker for helping me to

two elements to this film that link it more strongly to medieval passion piety than to most of the cinematic portrayals. The first is the very strong element of faith that was invested into both its conception and execution. Benedict Fitzgerald spoke about the childlike faith within him which brought the screenplay into existence and helped him to deal with the immense responsibility that came upon him after Gibson had asked him to write it:

> The first thing I should say was that I was remembering. Nothing to do with screenwriting, but as a human being I was simply remembering how I was brought up and in a sense, I was going back to a time in which all of this was unquestionably credible to me—all of it, everything—I simply opened up to the sort of faith that children have and let that influence me with the added help of years of experience writing screen plays.[44]

He freely describes how his faith was slowly coming back to him while he worked on the film: "really a remarkable experience."[45] And in line with the affective piety that brought forth the great wealth of medieval and Renaissance crucifixion paintings, he speaks about how these last fifteen hours of Christ's life, which are the subject of the film, "can bring a grown man to tears."[46] The film itself he describes as a kind of a Mass, with Gibson as the "altar boy."[47] William Fulco, the theological adviser and biblical language expert employed for the film explains how for cast, crew, and director, there was a growing and unifying desire to "preach Christ crucified," through the film.[48]

Gibson himself, who apparently attended Mass every Sunday during the making of the film,[49] describes his intentions using the Greek word for truth: *alētheia,* which can carry the idea of "unforgetting."[50] He goes on: "It is not merely representative or merely expressive. I think of it as contemplative in the sense that one is compelled to remember (unforget) in a spiritual way which cannot be articulated, only experienced."[51]

---

see this.

44. Shepherd, "From Gospel to Gibson," 323.

45. Ibid., 324.

46. Ibid., 323.

47. Ibid., 328.

48. Ibid., 330.

49. Hutch, "Mel Gibson's Big Gamble: *The Passion of Christ*," 339.

50. Corley and Webb, *Jesus and Mel Gibson's The Passion of the Christ*, 2.

51. Ibid.

The second element relates more to the content of the finished product than to the making of the film, and this is the notoriously graphic violence, which includes a grueling half-hour flagellation scene. An article for *Time* magazine put it aptly: "*The Passion* may be unique in movie history in devoting most of its length to the torture of one man who doesn't fight back. He takes a flaying and keeps on praying. This is Gandhi as Rocky. It's Bloodheart."[52] It is a case of "Nightmare on the Via Dolorosa."[53]

"Images of a violated and bloodied Jesus dominate the screen," observes one, astutely adding, "This is not altogether new in the history of Christianity."[54] Gibson seems to have turned the paintings of the likes of Grünewald into a movie.[55] Gibson himself was deeply impacted by the paintings of Caravaggio, which mostly consist of violent nighttime scenes such as *The Betrayal by Judas,* which especially caught Gibson's eye during a museum visit.[56] The film is claimed to be "in the tradition of Lenten art."[57] However, Krondorfer claims that, despite this, the true context for the film is not theological, as had been the context for the paintings of the Isenheimer Altar for instance. Rather the context is "Hollywood's fondness for violent movies."[58] And Gibson apparently "identifies with the persecuted white, male Christ." The film's downfall seemingly is that it demonstrates too much "heroic masculinity."[59] Apparently, it is a "muscular martyrdom,"[60] coming from a lead actor elsewhere described as "gaunt" and "haunted."[61] Despite this contradiction, it may be that Gibson's use of demonic characters throughout the film creates a villain for the hero Jesus, making him, after all, quite a macho character, in keeping with the kinds of parts Gibson has historically played himself.[62] It is certain that this combination of abject victim with devil-defeating hero with the Stations of the

52. Corliss, "The Goriest Story Ever Told," http://content.time.com/time/magazine/article/0,9171,593580–1,00.html [accessed online 08/03/2016].

53. Zuckerman, "Where Are the Flies? Where Is the Smoke?" 129.

54. Krondorfer, "Mel Gibson's Alter Ego," 17.

55. Ibid., 18.

56. Shepherd, "From Gospel to Gibson," 325.

57. Hittinger and Lev, "Gibson's Passion," 7.

58. Krondorfer, "Mel Gibson's Alter Ego," 18.

59. Ibid.

60. Ibid.

61. Corliss, "The Goriest Story Ever Told."

62. Pizzato, "A Post 9/11 *Passion*," 374.

Cross liturgical structure, has created a heady mixture: "much more than mere entertainment."[63]

Conclusion

Evangelical passion piety began in a way heavily indebted to medieval styles of devotion to the bleeding Lamb and his "lovely side hole," but evangelicalism then began to instrumentalize the atonement as an avenue to a clean heart, a heart that has lost all its guilty stains and is truly sanctified. Paul's teaching about being crucified with Christ was also revisited. As the turn of the twentieth century approached, a more apocalyptic mood prevailed, which brought about a new role for the blood of Jesus: a tool of spiritual warfare. Some early Pentecostals even developed a practice of pleading the blood against Satan while seeking the baptism in the Holy Spirit: an experience that the devil and all his hosts were presumed to be trying to stop.

While no one could deny that evangelicalism still is crucicentric it is coolly so. There are not the fevered invocations of the Moravians, the Salvation Army, of Jessie Penn-Lewis, or the early Pentecostals. The thread seems to peter out somewhere in between the world wars.

Almost out of the blue, then, comes Mel Gibson's passion-fest, in so many ways a throwback to a pre-Reformation world of emotional outpourings and gory portrayals. In true postmodern fashion, instead of anything new coming forth, there is this historical turn, the nostalgic backwards glance. However, the distinctive thing about *The Passion* in a postmodern context is its sincerity. It is not tongue-in-cheek or cynical. It is not a lighthearted brief history. We have come to expect of these of postmodern culture. It is a counter-cultural outpouring of earnestness created for the screen by a crew united by their shameless faith. Such a thing could not be more surprising.

63. Ibid., 376.

CONCLUSION

The Story and Its Golden Moments

This may be self-indulgence on my part, but, as I retell the story, I would like to draw particular attention to the moments that felt like a real discovery to me. They seemed quite marvelous. I will have plenty to say later about the less savory aspect of the story, but here I will be pausing at the golden moments.

As we leave the New Testament world behind and enter the postapostolic era, it is by no means certain that the cross will end up being selected as *the* central symbol of Christianity. Yet, as the history of the church unfolds, in which we see it struggle more and more against the miseries of organized persecution, this emphasis appears to progressively deepen. It is during this early period that we have our first golden moment: staurograms. I found it extraordinary that written into the Greek manuscripts, upon which we still rely today, was this cryptic iconography. In the Gospel narratives, the copyists, instead of writing the word for "crucify" or "crucified" simply wrote a *tau* and then a *rho* over the top of it to create a tiny crucifix with the loop of the *rho* forming the head of Christ on the cross. It was a way of making the reader stop for a moment to remember the price that was paid for their salvation. I thought this was marvelous.

Not until the peace of the church has been secured, though, does the cross finally take over as *the* symbol of Christianity, and when it does the context is very unexpected: a military victory on the part of a Roman emperor. All along the communion table had been the point around which Christians gathered to show their allegiance to Christ. Before long, the wine was holy blood and the bread was sacred flesh. The Western church even went so far as to believe that the laity could not be trusted with the consecrated wine—supposing it spilled? Only the officiating priest was permitted to drink it. The Mass soon became a spectacle and its ritual power was lost.

Other avenues were pursued as the faithful sought ways of appropriating the atonement. The martyr tradition with its relics soon evolved into pilgrimages to find New Testament relics. And here is our second golden moment: the Turin Shroud. It is the most famous historical artefact in existence. Its mystery has not subsided. I was amazed by how much evidence there is to support the possibility that this might even be a genuine relic. Even the case for doubting the carbon dating (the samples were only taken from the edge) appears strong. I never thought I would find myself so ready to believe in a relic.

There was soon a body of devotional literature all about the passion. The suffering human Christ stumbling as he carries his cross through the streets of Jerusalem was an image that caught the imaginations of the devout across medieval Europe, but before we even get to that, there is, if you like, an opening song. It is the first of its kind, and I would say the best. It comes just as the sun is setting on Anglo-Saxon civilization, yet, in its masterful understatements and dignified restraint, it outshines all the medieval passion poetry that is to come, and still moistens my eyes when I read it. It is *The Dream of the Rood*:

> Then the young Hero laid his garments by,
> He that was God Almighty, strong and brave;
> And boldly in the sight of all He mounted
> The lofty cross, for he would free mankind.[1]

With the dawn of the age of affective piety—the origins of which remain mysterious—there was a flood of emotional outpourings to the suffering human Christ. This human Christ perhaps served as a welcome and accessible counterbalance to the divine and exalted Christ of late antiquity, though it is the writers who most ardently hold the two together that seem to create the most powerful devotional writings about the cross. Here is Bonaventure:

> The Just One fell in love with the iniquitous, the Beautiful One
> with the vile, the only God and the Holy One with the sinful and
> unholy. Oh tremendous condescension![2]

---

1. Stevens, *The Cross in the Life and Literature*, 71–72.
2. Bonaventure, *The Mystical Vine*, XVI.1.

And Catherine of Siena:

> Life is grafted onto death, so that we mortals have gained life through this union. And because God has been grafted onto the human being, this God-and-human-being has plunged, love-smitten, to the opprobrious death of the cross.[3]

All of the Reformers, of course, emerged from a Catholic tradition already steeped in passion meditation. Luther was no exception, forming his own *theologia crucis* that insisted on the absolute merit and centrality of the blood of Jesus.[4] The man described as "Luther come back to life" was Count Zinzendorf, whose Moravian community went on to acquire a degree of notoriety due to the vulgarity with which they gloried in the blood and wounds of Christ. The Moravians in turn, influenced the Wesleys, Charles Wesley in particular, adopted much of their devotional language in his hymns but refined it and enriched it with more biblical content. The greatest and most popular of his atonement hymns is *And Can It Be?*—a marvelously rich and intense explosion of gratitude for the saving power of the cross, looked at from a variety of different angles, including the Bunyan-esque allegory about a rescue from a dungeon, which is packed in alongside federal union with Adam and Christ. This hymn qualifies as a golden moment.

> He left his father's throne above –
> So free, so infinite his grace –
> Emptied himself of all but love,
> And bled for Adam's helpless race.[5]

For John Wesley, the cleansing of the blood was part of a datable crisis event subsequent to conversion that he called entire sanctification, terminology he would spend his life debating and defending. In the hands of Phoebe Palmer and the American holiness movement, Wesleyan concepts of sanctification were simplified and mechanized into a three-step altar theology, a way of obtaining sanctification by faith without the need for any evidence that it had happened. Under the influence of American holiness teachers, Britain raised up two significant holiness movements of its own: Keswick and the Salvation Army. Both of these movements placed great emphasis on the cleansing power of the blood of Christ. The blood,

---

3. *Letters* 2: 120.

4. *Atonement Theories*, 64–73.

5. *Methodist Hymnbook*, No. 371.

in the minds of the devout, had now progressed from an awesome mystery and catalyst of deeper devotion into something that does something. It "cleanseth." Using this motif many individuals found ways of subjectivizing penal substitution. Within the Keswick tradition, Jessie Penn-Lewis applied herself in a different way to the quest to overcome the dialectic between a justified status and a powerless state. She proposed co-crucifixion:

> When you come to the point of recognising that God does not patch up the old life, but calls upon you to reckon it crucified, and to take from Him a new one, you will find that the new life has in it all the characteristics which belong to it.[6]

As the twentieth century approached, premillennial eschatology promised to explain the unrest of nations and the apostasy of the church: the Lord was about to come, but first there would be one final outpouring of the Spirit, one last, great, big revival. Yet Christians would need to be on their guard: these were perilous times. The devil was very active and the Christian's only sure defense was the blood of Christ, daubed on the lintel and doorposts of the heart. The blood of the Lamb would overcome the accuser. The Welsh Revival happened: could this be the final outpouring? Azusa Street happened. This time there were spiritual gifts, as foretold in Joel's prophecy. Soon, thanks to T. B. Barratt, the phenomena experienced at Azusa Street travelled across the Atlantic to Norway. From thence, thanks to the persuasiveness and enthusiasm of Alexander Boddy, it came to Sunderland. It was there that the blood as a tool of spiritual warfare, was finally honed and perfected. In time, the effervescence subsided, and along with it the millennial fever—and the blood mysticism. Inter-war Pentecostals preserved the blood mystical tradition in a nostalgic way, seeking to identify themselves, in the face of bitter opposition, as rooted in the old-time gospel.

The next concentration of passion piety comes from Hollywood in 2004. It is that totally unexpected and beautifully filmed movie *The Passion of the Christ*. When a symbol has lost its power, whether through over-familiarity or through total ignorance, one strategy is shock. Viewers of this film were deeply shocked. There were not many indifferent responses.

---

6. Penn-Lewis, *More than Conquerors*, 3.

Disconnect and Dialectic

Most of the passion piety that we have considered falls either within Roman Catholicism or within evangelicalism. It is interesting to note that, within both confessions, there seems to have been a disconnect between official positions and the way things look on the ground. Within Roman Catholicism, the official position was that the faithful were to expect to be able to fully appropriate for themselves the benefits of the atonement simply by attending Mass. The reality was that "hearing the Mass" soon became a spectacle rather than a participation in the body and blood of the Lord, and so other avenues were pursued by which to achieve this participation: relics, pilgrimages, stations, new feasts, paintings, poems, and so on. Similarly, in evangelicalism, the party line was a celebration of a once-and-for-all atoning work that was entirely objective. In fact, the more evangelicals reacted against the subjective turn within liberal Protestantism, the more objective their penal substitutionary doctrine became. Evangelical atonement theory became super-objective;[7] a transaction that took place over our heads that secures our eternity and should never be participated in for fear that we might be tempted to add to it something of our own meriting. However, the Reformers had originally conceived of the atonement as working hand-in-hand with the mystical union with Christ. By the nineteenth century, the work of Christ on the cross in many theological portrayals had become abstracted from just about everything else apart from justification, to which it had become intimately wedded. To compensate for this we see a change of language from "cross" to "blood" in order to make the subjective appropriation of atonement more easily imaginable. And we also see moves to bring sanctification into the matrix of Christian beginnings, wresting it from its perpetual gradualism. This too affected the way atonement was conceived of, opening the way not only to language about being washed in blood but also to recoveries of the Pauline doctrine of a co-crucifixion with Christ, thus bringing the mystical union with Christ back into the center of passion piety.

No one would have said that they found the Mass inadequate and so were seeking an alternative, and no one would have said that they found penal substitution insufficient and so were on a quest to compensate for its shortcomings, and, far be it from me to now say, "Yes, but that's what you meant." It is simply interesting to note that the people of God instinctively

---

7. On which see my discussion of Charles Hodge in *Atonement Theories*, 85–87.

feel the need to participate in as intimate a way possible with the historic death of Christ. I am calling this the participation imperative. They instinctively know that it was not a bare historical event but that it is to be appropriated, and these pages are a record of that effort. This provides a note-to-self for us theologians that we should be more intentional about facilitating this appropriation in the way we articulate our theories and how we help to shape the official positions of the denominations we serve. The alternative is that we will be sidelined. When our theories fail to be, in the language of Dewey, a "plan of action," the people of God will make plans of action without our help.

A Word about the Weirdness

Building on what I have said above, I also want to close the loop on contrasts I began to outline in the Introduction between the atonement theologies of the theologians and the outpourings of the devout. It seems that, while the biblical legacy is singular: it is a single, already interpreted crucifixion, the church's celebration of it has been in stereo. There are two distinct voices with which we tend to speak of the old rugged cross. I could say that it is a masculine voice and a feminine voice—the theologians and the devout respectively—but would fall foul of essentializing male and female. I could speak instead of a logical voice and an emotional voice and be mainly correct but mostly uninteresting. I could speak neurologically of the left hemisphere way of looking at the cross and the right hemisphere way of looking at it and probably come at least a little closer to a defensible appraisal of these two very different ways of attending to the cross.

In atonement theology the quest is to interpret the cross in supposedly objective and abstract ways, with the need to appropriate it not normally taken very seriously: it's someone else's concern. In Christian devotion, the quest is precisely to appropriate it, with the need to interpret it taken less seriously and when it does happen it happens in a subjective, contextual way. Very few lines are drawn by anyone all the way from the theologizing of the theologians to the outpourings of the devout. In fact, the last time this kind of joined-up thinking happened on a significant scale was during the Middle Ages when lines were very clearly drawn that joined up the thinking of Anselm with Bonaventure, or Anselm with himself for that matter. The hymns of Charles Wesley, too, are full of the theology of Protestantism. But with the onset of theological liberalism in various forms, there seems to have been a growing alienation between the voices speaking theology putatively to the church, mostly about the newly sanitized and modernized ways of looking at the cross, and the voice of church continuing to sing of the cleansing flood of blood.

It seems to me that, following McGilchrist,[8] the right hemisphere ought certainly to be allowed to be the master, with the left as its emissary. Let the right preserve the mystery and ever reinvent the wonder, but with the important caveat that the left hemisphere be allowed to keep everything intelligible and useful. If such were the case I would not have had to write quite such a weird book as this one. Much as we have celebrated the golden moments in the history, we must also admit that this book is stock full of devotional weirdness: quasi-erotic ramblings, spontaneously oozing foreheads, palms, and feet, embarrassing crying and roaring at the Golgotha pilgrimage site, side-holes that give birth to the church, red blood corpuscles as metaphors for coinage and cries of "Blood! Blood! Blood!" to ward off the devil. I have written about only one voice here, the right hemisphere voice, and it has not always struck very harmonious sounds with the other, more rational, voice of the theologians who dominated my first volume. I would have preferred to write of a church with a singular, intelligent, and intelligible voice of worship that is directed, nonetheless, at a Redeemer whose descent into humanity and into humanity's deepest death leaves great swathes of mystery yet untrammeled.

Theory That Supports Practice

You can probably predict the kind of thing I will say next. It is a plea for more joined up thinking between the spontaneous devotional urges of the devout and the thinking of theologians and denominational leaders. My view is that, as far as possible, our theorizing about atonement ought to start with, not vaguely hope to finish with, the worshipping church. Hopefully, we are conscious that culture has significantly moved on and that some (though not all) ways of conceptualizing the work of Christ have begun to jar with people. If so, then we rightly want an atonement theory for our age and books have been coming out thick and fast over the past twenty years that try to meet that need. Everyone wants to be the person who comes up with the new atonement theory for postmodernity. Everyone wants to go down in history and be the next Anselm, or the next Calvin. I do too! Who

---

8. McGilchrist, *The Master and His Emissary*.

wants to languish in obscurity? My suggestion is this: if you want to be that person, listen to the worshipping church. Hearken to its longings.

The good news is, what the Bride of Christ longs for has not changed much. She wants what she has always wanted. She just wants to get too close for words to that magnificent person who came and died and rose and lives for her rescue and restoration. The church is only as beautiful as her heavenly King is lovely. She derives her entire vitality and power from being one spirit with him. With this in view, we could do a lot worse than explore the writings of those who saw that, whatever else we say about what the death of Christ was for, what we do with it must have a loving participation in Christ as its central point. The recapitulation and theosis, therefore, of Irenaeus and Athanasius—especially if renewed and reinvented by passing their ideas afresh through a New Testament filter—seems to be the right place to begin suggesting an atonement theory that is not only postmodern but could stand the test of time itself.

BIBLIOGRAPHY

Aalen, L. *Die Theologie des jungen Zinzendorf.* Berlin: Lutherisches Verlagshaus, 1966.

Adams, Edward. *The Earliest Christian Meeting Places: Almost Exclusively Houses?* London: Bloomsbury, 2013.

Aers, David. "The Humanity of Christ." In *Powers of the Holy: Religion, Politics, and Gender in Late Medieval English Culture,* edited by David Aers and Lynn Staley, 15–42. University Park, PA: Pennsylvania State University Press, 1996.

Aldis, W. H. *The Message of Keswick and Its Meaning.* London: Marshall, Morgan & Scott, nd.

Allen, John. "Pope Francis and the Shroud of Turin." *National Catholic Reporter,* April 1, 2013; Accessed 21 December 2015. http://ncronline.org/blogs/ncr-today/pope-francis-and-shroud-turin.

Anderson, Allan. "Pentecostal and Charismatic Theology." In *The Modern Theologians,* edited by David Ford, 589–607. Oxford: Blackwell, 2005.

Anderson, R. M. *Vision of the Disinherited: The Making of American Pentecostalism.* New York: Oxford University Press, 1979.

Andreopoulos, Andreas. *Art as Theology: From the Postmodern to the Medieval.* London: Routledge, 2006.

Armstrong, Regis, and Ignatius Brady, trans. *Francis and Clare: The Complete Works.* New York: Paulist.

Atkinson, Clarissa. *Mystic and Pilgrim: The Book and World of Margery Kempe.* Ithaca, NY: Cornell University Press, 1983.

Atwood, Craig. *Community of the Cross: Moravian Piety in Colonial Bethlehem.* University Park, PA: Pennsylvania State University Press, 2004.

———. "The Mother of God's People: The Adoration of the Holy Spirit in the Eighteenth-Century Brüdergemeine." *Church History* 68.4 (1999) 886–909.

———. "Understanding Zinzendorf's Blood and Wounds Theology." *Journal of Moravian History* 1 (2006) 31–47.

———. "Zinzendorf's Litany of the Wounds of the Husband." *Lutheran Quarterly* 11 (1997) 189–214.

Augustine of Hippo. *Confessions.* Translated by R. S. Pine-Coffin. London: Penguin, 1961.

Babington, Eleanor. *Selections from the Poems of Charlotte Elliot.* London: Religious Tract Society, 1873.

Baert, Barbara. *A Heritage of Holy Wood: The Legend of the True Cross in Text and Image.* Translated by Lee Preedy. Leiden: Brill, 2004.

Baillie, Donald. *The Theology of the Sacraments.* London: Faber & Faber, 1957.

Baker, F. *From Wesley to Asbury: Studies in Early American Methodism*. Durham, NC: Duke University Press, 1976.

Balthasar, Hans Urs von. *Prayer*. Translated by A. V. Littledale. London: Chapman, 1961.

Barber, Richard. *The Holy Grail: Imagination and Belief*. Cambridge: Harvard University Press, 2004.

Barrington Bates, J. "The Holy Eucharist in the Early Church: Material for a Small-Group Discussion, an Adult Forum, or a Reading Course." *Anglican Theological Review* 84.2 (2002) 391–410.

Bartleman, Frank. *Azusa Street: The Roots of Modern-day Pentecost*. South Plainfield, NJ: Bridge, 1980.

Baugh, Lloyd. *Imaging The Divine*. Franklin, WI: Sheed and Ward, 1997.

Bebbington, David. "Holiness in the Evangelical Tradition." In *Holiness Past and Present*, edited by Stephen Barton, 298–315. Edinburgh: T. & T. Clark, 2003.

———. *Holiness in Nineteenth-Century England*. Didsbury Lectures. Carlisle, UK: Paternoster, 2000.

Beckwith, Sarah. *Christ's Body: Identity, Culture and Society in Late Medieval Writings*. London: Routledge, 1996.

Begbie, Harold. *Life of William Booth, the Founder of the Salvation Army*, Vol. 1. London: MacMillan, 1920.

Begbie, Jeremy. *Voicing Creation's Praise: Towards a Theology of the Arts*. Edinburgh: T. & T. Clark, 1991.

Bennet, J. A. W. *Poetry of the Passion: Studies in Twelve Centuries of English Verse*. Oxford: Clarendon, 1982.

Bernard of Claivaux. *On Loving God*. Translated by H. Martin. London: SCM, 1959.

Bestul, Thomas. *Texts of the Passion: Latin Devotional Literature and Medieval Society*. Philadelphia: University of Pennsylvania Press, 1996.

Beyreuther, E. *Studien zur Theologie Zinzendorfs*. Neukirchen-Vluyn: Neukirchener Verlag der Buchhandlung des Erziehungsvereins, 1962.

———. *Zinzendorf und die Christenheit*. Marburg an der Lahn: Francke, 1961.

Bhattacharji, Santha. "Tears and Screaming: Weeping in the Spirituality of Margery Kempe." In *Holy Tears: Weeping in the Religious Imagination*, edited by Kimberley Patton and John Hawley, 229–41. Princeton: Princeton University Press, 2005.

Biddick, Kathleen. "Genders, Bodies, Borders: Technologies of the Visible." *Speculum* 68.2 (1993) 389–418.

Bihl, M. "St. Leonard of Port Maurice." In *The Catholic Encyclopedia*. New York: Appleton, 1910. Accessed January 7, 2016. http://www.newadvent.org/cathen/09178c.htm

Bitton-Ashkelony, Brouria. *Encountering the Sacred: The Debate on Christian Pilgrimage in Late Antiquity*. Berkeley: University of California Press, 2005.

Boardman, William. *The Higher Christian Life*. Boston: Hoyt, 1859.

Bonaventure. *Breviloquium, The Mystical Vine, The Soul's Journey into God*, and *The Tree of Life*. In *Opera Omnia*. 10 vols. Translated by Iosé de Vinck. Quaracchi, Italy: Collegium S. Bonaventurae, 1882–1902.

Borgehammar, Stephan. *How the Holy Cross Was Found: From Event to Medieval Legend*. Stockholm: Almquist & Wiksell, 1991.

———. "Heraclius Learns Humility: Two Early Latin Accounts Composed for the Celebration of Exaltatio Crucis." *Millennium* 6 (2009) 145–201.

Bortin, Virginia. "Science and the Shroud of Turin." *Biblical Archeologist*, Spring 1980, 109–17.

Bradford, Clare. "Julian of Norwich and Margery Kempe." *Theology Today* 35.2 (1978) 153–58.

Bradshaw, Paul. *Eucharistic Origins*. London: SPCK, 2004.

———. *The Search for the Origins of Christian Worship: Sources and Methods for the Study of Early Liturgy*. Oxford: Oxford University Press, 2002.

Brand, Hilary, and Adrienne Chaplin. *Art and Soul: Signposts for Christians in the Arts*. Downers Grove, IL: IVP, 1999.

Braswell, Mary. "The Search for the Holy Grail: Arthurial Lacunae in the England of Edward III." *Studies in Philology* 108.4 (2011) 469–87.

Brintnall, Kent. "Tarantino's Incarnational Theology: *Reservoir Dogs*, Crucifixions and Spectacular Violence." *Crosscurrents* 54.1 (2004) 66–75.

Brown, Stephanie. *Religious Painting: Christ's Passion and Crucifixion*. New York: Mayflower, 1979.

Buck, Lorraine, P. "Voluntary Martyrdom Revisited." *The Journal of Theological Studies* 63.1 (2012) 125–35.

Bundy, David. "Spiritual Advice to a Seeker: Letters to T. B. Barratt from Azusa Street, 1906." *Pneuma* 1.14 (1992) 159–70.

Burns, J. Patout. "The Concept of Satisfaction in Medieval Redemption Theory." *Theological Studies* 36 (1975) 285–304.

Busfield, Lucy. "Women, Men and Christ Crucified: Protestant Passion Piety in Sixteenth Century England." *Reformation and Renaissance Review* 15.3 (2013) 217–36.

Bynum, Caroline Walker. "The Blood of Christ in the Later Middle Ages." *Church History* 71.4 (2002) 685–714.

———. *Holy Feast and Holy Fast: The Religious Significance of Food to Medieval Women*. Berkeley: University of California Press, 1987.

———. *Jesus as Mother: Studies in the Spirituality of the High Middle Ages*. Berkeley: University of California Press, 1982.

———. *Jesus as Mother: Studies in the Spirituality of the High Middle Ages*. Berkeley: University of California Press, 1982.

Calvin, John. *A Treatise on Relics*. Translated by Valerian Krasinski. Edinburgh: Johnstone, Hunter & Co., 1870.

Camporesi, Piero. *Juice of Life: The Symbolic and Magic Significance of Blood*. London: Continuum, 1995.

Carwardine, R. *Transatlantic Revivalism: Popular Evangelicalism in Britain and America 1790–1865*. 1978. Reprint. Studies in Evangelical History and Thought. Carlisle, UK: Paternoster, 2007.

Casabianca, Tristan. "The Shroud of Turin: A Historiographical Approach." *The Heythrop Journal* 54.3 (2013) 414–23.

Castagna, Valentina. *Re-Reading Margery Kempe in the 21st Century*. Bern: Lang, 2011.

Caswell, Edward. *Hymns and Poems, Original and Translated*. London: Burns & Oates, 1873.

Cauchi, Tony, ed. *The Apostolic Faith: The Original Azusa Street Papers*. Bishops Waltham, UK: Revival Library CD-ROM, nd.

———, ed. *Confidence: Britain's First Pentecostal Magazine, 1908–1926*. Bishops Waltham, UK: Revival Library CD-ROM, nd.

———, ed. *The Elim Evangel: 1919–1934*. Bishops Waltham, UK: Revival Library CD-ROM, nd.

———, ed. *Redemption Tidings: 1924–1938.* Bishops Waltham, UK: Revival Library CD-ROM, nd.

———. "William J. Seymour and the History of the Azusa Street Mission." In *The Apostolic Faith: The Original Azusa Street Papers*, edited by Tony Cauchi, 15–16. Bishops Waltham, UK: Revival Library CD-ROM, nd.

Caughey, James. *Revival Sermons and Addresses.* London: Dickinson, 1891.

Chase, Christopher. "A Note on the Theological Origins of the Iconography of the Dead Christ." *The Greek Orthodox Theological Review* 14 (1980) 58–64.

Chilton, Bruce. "Eucharist: Surrogate, Metaphor, Sacrament of Sacrifice." In *Sacrifice in Religious Experience*, edited by Albert Baumgarten, 175–88. Leiden: Brill, 2002.

Clare Kirchberger, trans. *The Goad of Love.* London: Faber and Faber, 1952.

Cohn-Sherbok, Dan. *The Crucified Jew: Twenty Centuries of Christian Anti-Semitism.* London: Fount, 1993.

Columba, Stewart. "Christian Spirituality during the Roman Empire (100–600)." In *The Blackwell Companion to Christian Spirituality*, edited by Arthur Holder, 73–89. Oxford: Wiley, 2011.

Cone, James. *The Spirituals and the Blues.* San Francisco: Harper & Row, 1972.

Copelan, R. "Stigmata: Passion and Punishment: A Modern Case History." *Journal of the American Society of Psychosomatic Dentistry and Medicine* 22 (1975) 85–90.

Corley, Kathleen, and Robert Webb. *Jesus and Mel Gibson's The Passion of the Christ: The Film, the Gospels and the Claims of History.* London: Continuum, 2004.

Corliss, Richard. "The Goriest Story Ever Told." *Time*, February 23, 2004. Accessed 8 March 2016. http://content.time.com/time/magazine/article/0,9171,593580–1,00.html

Cousins, Ewert, trans. *Bonaventure: the Soul's Journey into God, the Tree of Life, the Life of St Francis.* New York: Paulist, 1978.

Coutts, F. *The History of the Salvation Army.* 7 Vols. London: Salvation Army, 1979.

Cox, Harvey. *Fire from Heaven: The Rise of Pentecostal Spirituality and the Reshaping of Religion in the Twenty-First Century.* London: Cassell, 1996.

Cracknell, K., and S. J. White. *An Introduction to World Methodism.* Cambridge: Cambridge University Press, 2005.

Cumming, J. Elder. "What We Teach." In *Keswick's Triumphant Voice*, edited by H. F. Stevenson, 17–25. London: Marshall, Morgan & Scott, 1963.

Cummings, Owen. *Eucharist and Ecumenism: The Eucharist across the Ages and Traditions.* Eugene, OR: Pickwick, 2013.

———. "The Liturgical Margery Kempe." *Worship* 79.4 (2005) 341–57.

Currie, Lloyd. "The Remarkable Metrological History of Radiocarbon Dating [II]." *Journal of Research of the National Institute of Standards and Technology* 109.2 (2004) 185–217.

Daly, Robert. "Eucharistic Origins: From the New Testament to Liturgies of the Golden Age." *Theological Studies* 66 (2005) 3–22.

Dam, Raymond van. *Remembering Constantine at the Milvian Bridge.* Cambridge: Cambridge University Press, 2011.

Damon P. E., et al. "Radiocarbon Dating of the Shroud of Turin." *Nature* 337, February 16, 1989, 611–15.

Davie, D. *Christian Verse.* Oxford: Oxford University Press, 1981.

Dayton, Donald. "From 'Christian Perfection' to the 'Baptism in the Holy Ghost." In *Aspects of Pentecostal-Charismatic Origins*, edited by Vinson Synan, 39–54. South Plainfield, NJ: Logos, 1975.

———. *Theological Roots of Pentecostalism*. Grand Rapids: Baker, 1987.

De Gregorio, Scott. "Affective Spirituality: Theory and Practice in Bede and Alfred the Great." *Essays in Medieval Studies* 22 (2005) 129–39.

De Jong, Mary G. "'I Want to be Like Jesus': The Self-Defining Power of Evangelical Hymnody." *Journal of the American Academy of Religion* 54.3 (1986) 461–93.

De Liguori, Alphonsus. *The Way of the Cross*. Accessed January 7 2016. http://www.ecatholic2000.com/liguori/stations/cross.shtml#__RefHeading___Toc362635538.

De Santa Teresa, P. Silverio, and E. Allison Peers, trans. *The Complete Works of Saint John of the Cross*. 3 vols. London: Burns & Oates, 1943.

Dearborn, Kerry. "The Crucified Christ as the Motherly God: The Theology of Julian of Norwich." *Scottish Journal of Theology* 55.3 (2002) 283–302.

Dearmer, Percy, and Ralph Vaughan Williams. *The English Hymnal*. London: Oxford University Press, 1906.

Delio, Ilia. *Crucified Love: Bonaventure's Mysticism of the Crucified Christ*. Quincy, IL: Franciscan, 1998.

———. *Simply Bonaventure: An Introduction to his Life, Thought, and Writings*. Hyde Park, NY: New City, 2001.

Devlin, Dennis. "Corpus Christi: A Study in Medieval Eucharistic Theory, Devotion and Practice." PhD diss., University of Chicago, 1975.

Dieter, Melvin. *The Holiness Revival of the Nineteenth Century*. Lanham, MD: Scarecrow, 1996.

Dinges, William. "Gibson and Traditionalist Catholicism." *Religion in the News,* Fall 2003, 16–22.

Dix, Gregory. *The Shape of Liturgy*. Westminster, UK: Dacre, 1945.

———, trans. *The Treatise on the Apostolic Tradition of St. Hippolytus of Rome*. London: SPCK, 1968.

Dreyer, Elizabeth. "A Condescending God: Bonaventure's Theology of the Cross." In *The Cross in Christian Tradition: From Paul to Bonaventure*, edited by Elizabeth Dreyer, 192–210. New York: Paulist, 2000.

———. "Mysticism Tangible through Metaphor: Bonaventure's Spirituality of the Cross." In *The Cross in Christian Tradition*, edited by Elizabeth Dreyer, 211–35. New York: Paulist, 2000.

Drijvers, Willem Jan. *Helena Augusta: The Mother of Constantine the Great and the Legend of Her Finding of the True Cross*. Leiden: Brill, 1992.

Early, L. F., and J. E. Lifschutz. "A Case of Stigmata." *Archives of General Psychiatry* 30 (1974) 197–200.

Edwards, Jonathan. *Sinners in the Hands of an Angry God*. Phillipsburg, NJ: P & R., 1992.

Elim Alliance, *Redemption Hymnal*. London: Elim, 1951.

Ellis, Carl. *Beyond Liberation: The Gospel in the Black American Experience*. Downer's Grove, IL: IVP, 1983.

Engen John Van, ed. *Devotio Moderna: Basic Writings*. Mahwah, NJ: Paulist, 1988.

Erb, Peter, ed. *Pietists: Selected Writings*. Mahwah, NJ: Paulist, 1983.

Ervine, John. *God's Soldier: General William Booth*, Volume 1. New York: Macmillan, 1935.

Eusebius. *Life of Constantine.* Translated by Averil Cameron and Stuart Hall. Oxford: Clarendon, 1999.

Evans, E. *The Welsh Revival of 1904.* Bridgend, UK: Evangelical Press of Wales, 1969.

Faithful, George. "A More Brotherly Song, a Less Passionate Passion: Abstraction and Ecumenism in the Translation of the Hymn 'O Sacred Head Now Wounded' from Bloodier Antecedents." *Church History* 82.4 (2013) 779–811.

Fassetta, Raffaele. "The Christocentric and Nuptial Mysticism of Saint Bernard." *Cistercian Studies Quarterly* 49.3 (2014) 347–65.

Faull, K. M. "Faith and Imagination: Nikolaus Ludwig von Zinzendorf's Anti-Enlightenment Philosophy of Self." In *Anthropology and the German Enlightenment: Perspectives on Humanity,* edited by K. M. Faull, 23–56. Lewisburg, PA: Bucknell University Press, 1995.

Fessler, Daniel. "Starvation, Seratonin, and Symbolism: A Psychobiocultural Perspective on Stigmata." *Mind and Society* 6.3 (2002) 81–96.

Flynn, Maureen. "The Spiritual Uses of Pain in Spanish Mysticism." *Journal of the American Academy of Religion* 64.2 (1996) 257–78.

Forest, Jim. "Through Icons: Word and Image Together." In *Beholding the Glory: Incarnation through the Arts,* edited by Jeremy Begbie, 83–97. London: Darton, Longman and Todd, 2000.

Forwell, G., trans. *Zinzendorf: Nine Public Lectures on Important Subjects in Religion.* Iowa City: University of Iowa Press, 1973.

Foster, Kenelm, and Mary John Ronayne, trans. *I, Catherine: Selected Writings of St. Catherine of Siena.* London: Collins, 1980.

Frale, Barbara. *The Shroud of Jesus of Nazareth.* Meath, Ireland: Maverick House, 2011.

Frantzen, Allen J. "Spirituality and Devotion in the Anglo-Saxon Penitentials." *Essays in Medieval Studies* 22 (2005) 117–28.

Freeman, A. *An Ecumenical Theology of the Heart: The Theology of Count Nicholas Ludwig von Zinzendorf.* Bethlehem, PA: The Moravian Church in America, 1998.

Freze, Michael. *They Bore the Wounds of Christ.* Huntingdon, IN: One Sunday Visitor, 1989.

Fuller, Reginald. "The Double Origin of the Eucharist." *Biblical Research* 8 (1963) 60–72.

Fulton, Rachel. *From Judgment to Passion: Devotion to Christ and the Virgin Mary, 800–1200.* New York: Columbia University Press, 2002.

Gallyon, Margaret. *Margery Kempe of Lynn and Medieval England.* Norwich, UK: Canterbury, 1995.

Garrard, M. *Mrs Penn-Lewis: A Memoir.* Westbourne, UK: Overcomer Book Room, 1947.

Gatta, Julia. "Julian of Norwich: Theodicy as Pastoral Art." *Anglican Theological Review* LXIII.2 (1981) 173–81.

Gee, Donald. *These Men I Knew.* Nottingham, UK: Assemblies of God, 1965.

———. "Under the Blood." *The Pentecostal Evangel,* December 8, 1957, 4.

———. *Wind and Flame.* Croydon, UK: Heath, 1967.

George Timothy, and Alister McGrath, eds. *For all the Saints: Evangelical Theology and Christian Spirituality.* Louisville, KY: Westminster John Knox, 2003.

Gerloff, Roswith. "The Holy Spirit and the African Diaspora: Spiritual, Cultural and Social Roots of Black Pentecostal Churches." *Journal of the European Pentecostal Theological Association* 14 (1995) 85–100.

Gerrard, Mary. *Mrs Penn-Lewis: A Memoir.* Westbourne, UK: Overcomer Book Room, 1947.

Gilson, E. *The Mystical Theology of St. Bernard*. Kalamazoo, MI: Cistercian, 1990.

Girón-Negrón, Luis M. "Dionysian Thought in Sixteenth-Century Spanish Mystical Theology." *Modern Theology* 24.4 (2008) 693–706.

Glaude, Eddie. *Exodus! Religion, Race and Nation in Early Nineteenth-Century Black America*. Chicago: University of Chicago Press, 2000.

Goa, David. "*The Passion*, Classical Art and Re-presentation." In *Jesus and Mel Gibson's The Passion of the Christ*, edited by Kathleen Corley and Robert Webb, 151–59. London: Continuum, 2004.

Gollin, G. L. *Moravians in Two Worlds: A Study of Changing Communities*. New York: Columbia University Press, 1967.

Gonzalez, Justo. *The Story of Christianity, Volume 1: The Early Church to the Dawn of the Reformation*. San Francisco: HarperCollins, 1984.

Gougaud, Louis. *Devotional and Ascetic Practices in the Middle Ages*. London: Burns and Oates, 1927.

Gough, Michael. *The Origins of Christian Art*. London: Thames & Hudson, 1973.

Graham, Gordon. "Liturgy as Drama." *Theology Today* 64 (2007) 71–79.

Grubb, Norman. *Once Caught, No Escape: My Life Story*. London: Lutterworth, 1969.

Gutgsell, Jessie. "The Gift of Tears: Weeping in the Religious Imagination of Western Medieval Christianity." *Anglican Theological Review* 97.2 (2015) 239–53.

Haddad, M. R. "The Mystical Theology of Jessie Penn-Lewis (1861–1927)." PhD diss., Durham University, 2005.

Halwachs, Maurice. *La Topographie Légendaire des Evangile en Terre Sainte: Étude de Mémoire Collective*. Quadrige: Presses Universitaire de France, 2008.

Hamilton, J. and K. *History of the Moravian Church: The Renewed Unitas Fratrum 1722–1957*. Bethlehem, PA: Moravian Church in America, 1967.

Hamilton, J. *A History of the Church Known as the Moravian Church during the Eighteenth and Nineteenth Centuries*. Bethlehem, PA: The Moravian Church in America, 1900.

Harbus, Antonina. *Helena of Britain in Medieval Legend*. Cambridge: Brewer, 2002.

Harrison, Anna. "'Jesus Wept': Mourning as Imitation of Christ in Bernard's Sermon Twenty-Six on the Song of Songs." *Cistercian Studies Quarterly* 48.4 (2013) 433–67.

Harrison, Ted. *Stigmata: A Medieval Mystery in a Modern Age*. New York: St. Martin's, 1994.

Hathaway, Malcolm. "The Role of William Oliver Hutchinson in the Formation of British Pentecostal Churches." *Journal of the European Pentecostal Theological Association* XVI (1996) 50–57.

Hattersley, Roy. *Blood and Fire: William and Catherine Booth and Their Salvation Army*. London: Little, Brown & Co., 1999.

Hayes, Zachary. *The Hidden Center: Spirituality and Speculative Christology in St. Bonaventure*. New York: Paulist, 1981.

Heckman, Christina M. "Imitatio in Early Medieval Spirituality: The Dream of the Rood, Anselm, and Militant Christology." *Essays in Medieval Studies* 22 (2005) 141–53.

Heitzenrater, R. P., ed., *The Works of John Wesley*. 27 vols. to date. Nashville: Abingdon, 1970–.

Hempton, D. *Methodism: Empire of the Spirit*. New Haven: Yale University Press, 2005.

Henriksen, Erin. *Milton and the Reformation Aesthetics of the Passion*. Leiden: Brill, 2010.

Hindmarsh, Bruce. *The Evangelical Conversion Narrative: Spiritual Autobiography*. Oxford: Oxford University Press, 2005.

Hinn, Benny. *Power in the Blood: The Biblical Significance of the Blood from Genesis to Jesus to the Modern Believer*. Lake Mary, FL: Creation House, 1993.

Hittinger, Russell, and Elizabeth Lev. "Gibson's Passion." *First Things*, March 2004, 3–4.

Hodges, Doris. *The Story of Hymns*. Bath, UK: Kingsmead, 1979.

Hoffke, Suzanne, trans. *Catherine of Siena: The Dialogue*. London: SPCK, 1980.

Hogg, David. *Anselm of Canterbury: The Beauty of Theology*. Aldershot, UK: Ashgate, 2004.

Hollywood, Amy. *The Soul as Virgin Wife: Mechthild of Magdeburg, Marguerite Porete, and Meister Eckhart*. Notre Dame, IN: University of Notre Dame Press, 1995.

Holmes, Michael, trans. *The Apostolic Fathers: Greek Texts and English Translations*. Grand Rapids: Baker, 1992.

Holweck, F. G. "Five Sacred Wounds, The." In *The Catholic Encyclopedia*. New York: Robert Appleton, 1912. Accessed November 10, 2015. http://www.catholic.com/encyclopedia/five-sacred-wounds-the

Horan, Daniel. "Christcentricity, Unity and Ethics in Bonaventure's Theology of the Eucharist." *Worship* 85 (November 2011) 503–20.

Houghton, W. E. *The Victorian Frame of Mind, 1830–1870*. New Haven: Yale University Press, 1957.

Hoyt, Thomas. "Interpreting Biblical Scholarship." In *Stony the Road We Trod: African American Biblical Interpretation*, edited by Cain Hope Felder, 17–39. Minneapolis: Fortress, 1991.

Huelin, Gordon. *The Cross in English Life and Devotion*. London: The Faith, 1972.

Hurley, Neil. "Cinematic Transfigurations of Jesus." In *Religion in Film*, edited by John May and Michael Bird, 61–78. Knoxville: University of Tennessee Press, 1982.

Hurtado, Larry. *The Earliest Christian Artifacts: Manuscripts and Christian Origins*. Grand Rapids: Eerdmans, 2006.

Hutch, Richard. "Mel Gibson's Big Gamble: *The Passion of Christ*." *Pastoral Psychology* 53.4 (2005) 337–40.

Hutchison, James. "The Kilsyth Religious Revivals." Accessed March 15, 2016. http://kilsyth.org.uk/?page_id=81.

Hutton, James. *A History of the Moravian Church*. London: Moravian Publication Office, 1909.

James, Montague Rhodes, trans. *The Apocryphal New Testament: Being the Apocryphal Gospels, Acts, Epistles, and Apocalypses*. Oxford: Clarendon, 1924.

James, William. *Pragmatism*. London: Longmans, Green & Co., 1907.

Jantzen, Grace. *Julian of Norwich*. London: SPCK, 2000.

Jensen, Robin. "The Suffering and Dead Christ in Early Christian Art." *Arts* 8.1 (1995) 22–28.

Johnson, Adam. "The Crucified Bridegroom: Christ's Atoning Death in St. John of the Cross and Spiritual Formation Today." *Pro Ecclesia* XXI.4 (2012) 393–94.

Johnson, Maxwell. "Worship, Practice and Belief." In *The Early Christian World*, Volume 1, edited by Philip Esler, 480–84. London: Routledge, 2000.

Jones, Brynmor. *An Instrument of Revival: The Complete Life of Evan Roberts 1878–1951*. South Plainfield, NJ: Bridge, 1995.

———. *The Spiritual History of Keswick in Wales 1903–1983*. Cwmbran, UK: Christian Literature Press, 1989.

———. *The Trials and Triumphs of Mrs Jessie Penn-Lewis*. North Brunswick, NJ: Bridge-Logos, 1997.

Jones, John. "The Metaphor That Will Not Perish: 'The Dream of the Rood' and the New Hermeneutic." *Christianity and Literature* 38.2 (1989) 63–72.

Julian of Norwich. *Showings*. Translated by Edmund Colledge and James Walsh. New York: Paulist, 1978.

Kane, Harold, ed. *The Prickynge of Love*. Salzburg: Institut für Anglistik und Amerikanistik der Universität Salzburg, 1983.

Karnes, Michelle. *Imagination, Meditation, and Cognition*. Chicago: University of Chicago Press, 2011.

Kay, Judith. "The Exodus and Racism: Paradoxes for Jewish Liberation." *Journal for the Society of Christian Ethics* 28.2 (2008) 23–50.

Kempe, Margery. *The Book of Margery Kempe*. Translated by B. A. Windeatt. Harmondsworth, UK: Penguin, 1994.

Kennedy, Charles, trans. *The Poems of Cynewulf*. London: Routledge, 1910.

Kent, J. *Holding the Fort: Studies in Victorian Revivalism*. London: Epworth, 1978.

Kille, Andrew. "More Reel than Real: Mel Gibson's *The Passion of the Christ*." *Pastoral Psychology* 53.4 (2005) 341–50.

Kilmartin, Edward. "Sacrificium Laudis: Content and Function of Early Eucharistic Prayers." *Theological Studies* 66 (2005) 268–87.

Kinkel, G. S. *Our Dear Mother the Spirit: An Investigation of Count Zinzendorf's Theology and Praxis*. New York: University Press of America, 1990.

Kirchberger, Clare, ed. *The Goad of Love*. London: Faber and Faber, 1952.

Knowles, David. *The English Mystical Tradition*. London: Burns and Oates, 1961.

Krondorfer, Björn. "Mel Gibson's Alter Ego: A Male Passion for Violence." *Crosscurrents* (Spring 2004) 16–21.

Kupfer, Marcia, ed. *The Passion Story: From Visual Representation to Social Drama*. University Park, PA: Pennsylvania State University Press, 2008.

Lactantius, Lucius. *On the Deaths of the Persecutors*. In *The Minor Works*, translated by Mary McDonald, 137–203. Washington, DC: Catholic University of America Press, 1965.

Land, S. *Pentecostal Spirituality: A Passion for the Kingdom*. Sheffield, UK: Sheffield Academic Press, 1993.

Larsen, Matthew. "Addressing the Elephant That's Not in the Room: Comparing the Eucharistic Prayers in *Didache* 9–10 and the Last Supper Tradition." *Neotestamentica* 45.2 (2011) 252–74.

Leclercq, Jean. "Introduction to Saint Bernard's Doctrine in the Sermons on the Song of Songs." *Cistercian Studies Quarterly* 43.3 (2008) 309–25.

Lewis, A. J. *Zinzendorf: The Ecumenical Pioneer: A Study in the Moravian Contribution to Christian Mission and Unity*. London: SCM, 1962.

Liardon, Roberts. *God's Generals: Why They Succeeded and Why Some Failed*. New Kensington, PA: Whitaker House, 1996.

Liftin, Bryan. "Eusebius on Constantine: Truth and Hagiography at the Milvian Bridge." *Journal of the Evangelical Theological Society* 55.4 (2012) 773–92.

Linyard, F., & P. Tovey, *Moravian Worship*. Bramcote: Grove Books, 1994.

Loewe, Andreas. "Proclaiming the Passion: Popular Drama and the Passion Tradition in Luther's Germany." *Reformation & Renaissance Review* 12.2–3 (2010) 235–82.

Lord, R. A. "A Note on Stigmata." *American Imago* 14 (1957) 299–302.

Louth, Andrew. "'Beauty Will Save the World:' The Formation of Byzantine Spirituality." *Theology Today* 61 (2004) 67–77.

Lovett, L. "Black Origins of the Pentecostal Movement." In *Aspects of Pentecostal-Charismatic Origins*, edited by Vinson Synan, 123–42. South Plainfield, NJ: Logos, 1975.

Lynch, Joseph. *The Medieval Church: A Brief History*. London: Longman, 1992.

Mabillon, John. Preface to *Cantica Canticorum: Eighty-Six Sermons on the Song of Solomon by Saint Bernard*. Edited by Samuel Eales. London: Stock, 1895.

Mak, Phyllis. *Heart Religion in the British Enlightenment: Gender and Emotion in Early Methodism*. Cambridge: Cambridge University Press, 2008.

Marrow, James. *Passion Iconography in Northern European Art of the Late Middle Ages and Early Renaissance: A Study of the Transformation of Sacred Metaphor into Descriptive Narrative*. Kortrijk, Belgium: Van Ghemmert, 1979.

Mason, J. C. S. *The Moravian Church and the Missionary Awakening in England, 1760–1800*. Woodbridge, UK: Boydell, 2001.

Maternus, Julius Firmiens. *The Error of the Pagan Religions*. Translated by Clarence Forbes. New York: Newman, 1970.

McFadden, M. "The Ironies of Pentecost: Phoebe Palmer, World Evangelism, and Female Networks." *Methodist History* 31.2 (1993) 63–75.

McGilchrist, Iain. *The Master and his Emissary: The Divided Brain and the Making of the Western World*. New Haven: Yale University Press, 2009.

McGinn, Bernard, ed., *Christian Spirituality I: Origins to the Twelfth Century*. New York: Crossroad, 1987.

———. "Love, Knowledge, and Mystical Union in Western Christianity: Twelfth to Sixteenth Centuries." *Church History* 56 (1987) 7–24.

McGonigle, Herbert. *Sufficient Saving Grace: John Wesley's Evangelical Arminianism*. Studies in Evangelical History and Thought. Carlisle, UK: Paternoster, 2001.

McGowan, Andrew. "Rethinking Eucharistic Origins." *Pacifica* 23 (June 2010) 173–90.

McKenna, Stephen, trans. *The Fathers of the Church: Saint Hilary of Poitiers, the Trinity*. Washington, DC: Catholic University of America Press, 1968.

McNamer, Sarah. *Affective Meditation and the Invention of Medieval Compassion*. Philadelphia: University of Pennsylvania Press, 2011.

McPherson, Claire. "Spiritual Combat: The Dream of the Rood." *Anglican Theological Review* 71.2 (1989) 166–75.

Medved, Michael. "The Passion and the Prejudice: Why I Asked the Anti-Defamation League to Give Mel Gibson a Break." *Christianity Today*, March 2004, 38–41.

Meer, F. van der. *Early Christian Art*. Chicago: Chicago University Press, 1967.

Meier, John. "The Eucharist and the Last Supper: Did it Happen?" *Theology Digest* 42 (Winter 1995) 335–51.

Merritt, John, ed. *Historical Dictionary of the Salvation Army*. Lanham, MD: Scarecrow, 2006.

Methodist Conference. *Hymns and Psalms*. London: Methodist Publishing House, 1983.

Meyer D., and P. Peuker, eds. *Graf Ohne Grenzen: Leben und Werk von Nikolaus Ludwig Graf von Zinzendorf*. Herrnhut, Germany: Unitätsarchiv im Verlag der Comeniusbuchhandlung, 2000.

Meyer, D. *Bibliographisches Handbuch zur Zinzendorf-Forschung*. Düsseldorf: privately printed, 1987.

Meyer, Joyce. *The Word, The Name, The Blood*. Lebanon, KY: Time Warner, 2003.

Middleton, Paul. "Early Christian Voluntary Martyrdom: A Statement for the Defence." *The Journal of Theological Studies* 64.2 (2013) 556–73.

————. *Martyrdom: A Guide for the Perplexed.* London: T. & T. Clark, 2011.

————. *Radical Martyrdom and Cosmic Conflict in Early Christianity.* London: T. & T. Clark, 2006.

Mitchell, Nathan. "Washed Away by the Blood of God." In *The Cross in Christian Tradition: From Paul to Bonaventure,* edited by Elizabeth Dreyer, 51–71. New York: Paulist, 2000.

Mize, Britt. "The Mental Container and the Cross of Christ: Revelation and Community in The Dream of the Rood." *Studies in Philology* 107.2 (2010) 131–78.

Molnár, E. "The Pious Fraud of Count Zinzendorf." *Iliff Review* 11 (1954) 29–38.

Monk, William Henry, ed. *Hymns Ancient and Modern.* London: Clowes, 1861.

Montgomery, James. *The Moravian Hymn Book.* London: Moravian Publication Office, 1911.

Mueller, Jane, ed., *Katherine Parr: Complete Works and Correspondence.* Chicago: University of Chicago Press, 2011.

Muessig, C. "Signs of Salvation: The Evolution of Stigmatic Spirituality Before Francis of Assisi." *Church History* 82:1 (March 2013) 40–68.

Murdoch, N. H. "Evangelical Sources of Salvation Army Doctrine." *Evangelical Quarterly* 59.3 (1987) 235–44.

————. "Female Ministry in the Thought and Work of Catherine Booth." *Church History* 53.3 (1984) 348–62.

————. *Origins of the Salvation Army.* Knoxville, TN: University of Tennessee Press, 1994.

Murphy-O'Connor, Jerome. "Tracing the Via Dolorosa." In *Keys to Jerusalem: Collected Essays,* edited by Jerome Murphy-O'Connor, 107–17. Oxford: Oxford University Press, 2012.

Murray, Iain. *Revival and Revivalism: The Making and Marring of American Evangelicalism 1750–1858.* Edinburgh: Banner of Truth, 1994.

Musser, Benjamin, editor. *Kyrie Eleison :Two Hundred Litanies.* Manchester, NH, The Magnificat, 1944.

Nichol, J. T. *Pentecostalism.* New York: Harper & Row, 1966.

Nickell, Joe. *Looking for a Miracle: Weeping Icons, Relics, Stigmata, Visions and Healing Cures.* New York: Prometheus, 1993.

Noel, James, and Matthew Johnson. "Psychological Trauma, Christ's Passion, and the African American Faith Tradition." *Pastoral Psychology* 53.4 (2005) 361–69.

Nugent, Donald Christopher. "What Has Wittenberg to Do with Avila? Martin Luther and St. Teresa." *Journal of Ecumenical Studies* 23.4 (1986) 650–58.

O'Loughlin, Thomas. *The Eucharist: Origins and Contemporary Understandings.* London: Bloomsbury T. & T. Clark, 2014.

Origen. *An Exhortation to Martyrdom, Prayer, First Principles: Book IV, Prologue to the Commentary on the Song of Songs, Homily XXVII on Numbers.* Translated by Rowan Greer. New York: Paulist, 1979.

Ousterhout, Robert. "The Church of Santa Stefano: A 'Jerusalem in Bologna.'" *Gesta* 20.2 (1981) 311–21.

Palmer, Phoebe. *Faith and its Effects, or, Fragments from my Portfolio.* London: Heylin, 1856.

The Passion of the Christ. Directed by Mel Gibson. Los Angeles; Icon Entertainment, 2004.

Peirce, C. S. *The Essential Peirce,* Volume 2. Bloomington, IN: Indiana University Press, 1992–99.

Pelphrey, Brant. *Christ Our Mother: Julian of Norwich.* London: DLT, 1989.

Penn-Lewis, Jessie. *The Climax of the Risen Life*. Poole, UK: Overcomer Publications, nd.

———. *The Cross of Calvary and Its Message*. London: Morgan & Scott, 1903.

———. *The Cross of Calvary*. Poole, UK: Overcomer Publications, nd.

———. *Dying to Live*. Alresford, UK: Christian Literature Crusade, 2013.

———. *The Glorious Secret*. Poole, UK: Overcomer Publications, nd.

———. *Life in the Spirit*. Fort Washington, MD: Christian Literature Crusade, 1991.

———. *More Than Conquerors*. Poole, UK: Overcomer Literature Trust, nd.

———. *Opened Heavens*. 1903. Reprint. Poole, UK: Overcomer Publications, nd.

———. *The Pathway to Life in God*. Poole, UK: Overcomer Publications, nd.

Percy, Martyn. "Sweet Rapture: Subliminal Eroticism in Contemporary Charismatic Worship." *Theology and Sexuality* 6 (1997) 71–106.

Peterson, Ingrid. *Clare of Assisi: A Biographical Study*. Quincy, IL: Franciscan Press, 1993.

Petroff, Elizabeth. *Body and Soul: Essays on Medieval Women and Mysticism*. Oxford: Oxford University Press, 1994.

Peucker, Paul. *A Time of Sifting: Mystical Marriage and the Crisis of Moravian Piety in the Eighteenth Century*. University Park, PA: Pennsylvania State University Press, 2015.

Piggin, Stuart. *Firestorm of the Lord*. Carlisle, UK: Paternoster, 2000.

Piper, John. *Counted Righteous in Christ*. Leicester, UK: IVP, 2002.

Pizzato, Mark. "A Post 9/11 *Passion*: Review of Mel Gibson's *The Passion of the Christ*." *Pastoral Psychology* 53.4 (2005) 371–76.

Plate, S. Brent. "Mel Gibson's Bible: Religion, Popular Culture, and *The Passion of the Christ*." *Christianity and Literature* 56.3 (2007) 535–39.

Podmore, C. *The Moravian Church in England 1728–1760*. Oxford: Clarendon, 1998.

Pohlsander, Hans. *Helena: Empress and Saint*. Chicago: Ares, 1995.

Pollock, J., *The Keswick Story*. London: Hodder & Stoughton, 1964.

Poulain, Augustin. "Mystical Stimata." In *The Catholic Encyclopedia*. New York: Robert Appleton, 1912. Accessed July 3, 2015. http://newadvent.org/cathen/14294b.htm

Polanyi, Michael, and Harry Prosch. *Meaning*. Chicago: Chicago University Press, 1975.

Pugh, Ben. *Atonement Theories: A Way through the Maze*. Eugene, OR: Cascade, 2014.

———. "'Under the Blood' at Azusa Street: Exodus Typology at the Heart of Pentecostal Origins." *Journal of Religious History* 39.1 (2015) 86–103.

———. "The Wesleyan Way: Entire Sanctification and Its Spin-offs—A Recurring Theme in Evangelical Devotion." *Evangelical Review of Theology* 38.1 (2014) 4–21.

Quennell, Peter. *A History of English Literature*. London: Ferndale, 1973.

Raboteau, Albert. "African Americans, Exodus, and the American Israel." In *Down by the Riverside: Readings in African American Religion*, edited by Larry Murphy, 20–25. New York: New York University Press, 2000.

Randall, Ian. *Evangelical Experiences: A Study in the Spirituality of English Evangelicalism 1918–1939*. Studies in Evangelical History and Thought. Carlisle, UK: Paternoster, 1999.

———. "Old Time Power: Relationships between Pentecostalism and Evangelical Spirituality in England." *Pneuma* 19.1 (1997) 53–80.

———. "Recovering Evangelical Spirituality." *Evangelical Journal of Theology* 19.1 (2010) 33–44.

Reid, George. "Acta Pilati." In *Catholic Encyclopedia*. New York: Robert Appleton Company. 1913. Accessed March 23, 2016. http://www.newadvent.org/cathen/01111b.htm

Reinhard, Kathryn. "Joy to the Father, Bliss to the Son: Unity and the Motherhood Theology of Julian of Norwich." *Anglican Theological Review* 89.4 (2007) 629–45.

Rennie, Ian, S. "Fundamentalism and the Varieties of North Atlantic Evangelicalism." In *Evangelicalism: Comparative Studies of Popular Protestantism in North America, The British Isles, and Beyond 1700-1990*, edited by Mark Noll, David Bebbington, and George Rawlyk, 333-50. Oxford: Oxford University Press, 1994.

Riani, Marco, et al., "Regression Analysis with Partially Labelled Regressors: Carbon Dating of the Shroud of Turin." *Statistics and Computing* 23.4 (2013) 551-61.

Ricoeur, Paul. "The Metaphorical Process." *Semeia* 4 (1975) 75-106.

Robeck, Cecil. *Azusa Street Revival and Mission: The Birth of the Global Pentecostal Movement*. Nashville: Thomas Nelson, 2006.

————. "Moore, Jennie Evans (1883-1936)." In *New International Dictionary of Pentecostal and Charismatic Movements*, edited by Stanley Burgess and Eduard van der Maas, 906-7. Grand Rapids: Zondervan, 2002.

Roberts, Alexander, and James Donaldson, trans. *Ante-Nicene Christian Library: The Writings of Quintus Sept. Flor. Tertullianus* 1. Edinburgh: T. & T. Clark, 1869.

————, trans. *Ante-Nicene Christian Library: The Writings of Cyprian*. Edinburgh: T. & T. Clark, 1868.

Rock, Daniel. *The Church of Our Fathers*, Volume 3. London, 1853.

Rohling, Joseph. *The Blood of Christ in Christian Latin Literature before the Year 1000: A Dissertation*. Washington, DC: Catholic University of America, 1932.

Ronan, Marian. "Mel Gibson's *Passion* and the Many Uses of Christ's Suffering." *Pastoral Psychology* 53.4 (2005) 377-80.

Ross, Ellen. *The Grief of God: Images of the Suffering Jesus in Late Medieval England*. Oxford: Oxford University Press, 1997.

Rubin, Miri. *Corpus Christi: The Eucharist in Late Medieval Culture*. Cambridge: Cambridge University Press, 1991.

Sanders, Cheryl J. *Saints in Exile: The Holiness-Pentecostal Experience in African American Religion and Culture*. New York: Oxford University Press, 1996.

Saunders, S. *Cross, Sword and Lyre: Sacred Music at the Imperial Court of Ferdinand II of Habsburg, 1619-1637*. Oxford: Clarendon, 1995.

Schiller, Gertrud. *Iconography of Christian Art, Volume 2: The Passion of Jesus Christ*. Translated by Janet Seligman. Greenwich, CT: New York Graphic Society, 1972.

Schmidt, Herman. *Hebdomada Sancta*, Volume 1. Rome: Herder, 1956.

Sebeok, Thomas. *Signs: An Introduction to Semiotics*. Toronto: University of Toronto Press, 2001.

Sergeev, Mikhail. "Crucifixion Painting: Historical Considerations and Twentieth-Century Expressionism." *Arts: The Arts in Religious and Theological Studies* 18.1 (2006) 26-36.

Sheeb, Mercedes, and Timothy Jordan. "Effects of Contextual Information on Seeing Pareidolic Religious Inscriptions on an Artifact: Implications for the Shroud of Turin." *Perception* 44 (2015) 1427-30.

Shepherd, David. "From Gospel to Gibson: An Interview with the Writers Behind Mel Gibson's *The Passion of the Christ*." *Religion and the Arts* 9.3-4 (2005) 321-31.

Sheppard, W. J. Limmer. *Great Hymns and Their Stories*. Guildford, UK: Lutterworth, 1979.

Sherry, Patrick. *Spirit and Beauty: An Introduction to Theological Aesthetics*. London: SCM, 2010.

Shoemaker, Stephen J. "Mary at the Cross, East and West: Maternal Compassion and Affective Piety in the Earliest *Life of the Virgin* and the High Middle Ages." *The Journal of Theological Studies* 62.2 (2011) 570–606.

Siker, Jeffrey. "Christianity in the Second and Third Centuries." In *The Early Christian World*, Volume 1, edited by Philip Esler, 231–57. London: Routledge, 2000.

Sloan, W. *These Sixty Years: The Story of the Keswick Convention.* London: Pickering & Inglis, 1935.

Sloyan, Gerard. "The Popular Passion Piety of the Catholic West." *Worship* 69.1 (1995) 2–28.

Smith, Dennis. *From Symposium to Eucharist: The Banquet in the Early Christian World.* Minneapolis: Fortress, 2003.

Smith, Hannah Whitall. *The Christian's Secret of a Happy Life.* Westwood, NJ: Fleming H. Revel, 1952.

Soskice, Janet. *Metaphor and Religious Language.* Oxford: Clarendon, 1985.

Southern, Richard. Foreword to *The Prayers and Meditations of St. Anselm*, translated by Benedicta Ward. London: Penguin, 1973.

———. *The Making of the Middle Ages.* London: Pimlico, 1993.

———. *Saint Anselm: A Portrait in a Landscape.* Cambridge: Cambridge University Press, 1990.

Sox, H. D. "Authenticity of the Turin Shroud." *Clergy Review* 63 (1978) 250–56.

———. *File on the Shroud.* Sevenoaks, UK: Coronet, 1978.

Spencer, Jon. *Protest and Praise: Sacred Music of Black Religion.* Minneapolis: Augsburg Fortress, 1990.

Spinks, B. D. *Do This in Remembrance of Me: The Eucharist from the Early Church to the Present.* London: SCM, 2013.

Spurgeon, Charles Haddon. *The Metropolitan Tabernacle* Volume 32. Edinburgh: Banner of Truth, 1991.

Staley, Lynn. *Margery Kempe's Dissenting Fictions.* University Park, PA: Pennsylvania State University Press, 1994.

Staniforth, Trevor, *The Methodist Pentecost: Personal Testimonies and Eyewitness Accounts of Revival in the 1760s and the Doctrine of Entire Sanctification.* Ilkeston, UK: Moorley's, 2010.

Ste Croix, Geoffrey de. "Aspects of the Great Persecution." *Harvard Theological Review* 47 (1954) 75–113.

———. *Christian Persecution, Martyrdom, and Orthodoxy.* Oxford: Oxford University Press, 2010.

Stead, G. "Moravian Spirituality and Its Propagation in West Yorkshire during the Eighteenth-Century Evangelical Revival." *Evangelical Quarterly* 71.3 (1999) 233–59.

Stead, G., and M. Stead. *The Exotic Plant: A History of the Moravian Church in Great Britain 1742–2000.* Peterborough, UK: Epworth, 2003.

Stein, Edith. *The Science of the Cross: A Study of St. John of the Cross.* Translated by Hilda Graef. London: Burns & Oates, 1960.

Sterrick, E. "Mährische Brüder, böhemische Brüder, und die Brüdergemeine." *Unitas Fratrum* 48 (2001) 106–14.

Stevens, William. *The Cross in the Life and Literature of the Anglo-Saxons.* New York: Holt, 1904.

Stibbs, Alan. *The Meaning of the Word 'Blood' in Scripture.* London: Tyndale, 1948.

Stoeffler, F. *German Pietism during the Eighteenth Century.* Leiden: Brill, 1973.

———. Preface to *Pietists: Selected Writings*, edited by Peter Erb. London: SPCK, 1983.

Storme, Albert. *The Way of the Cross: A Historical Sketch.* Translated by Kieran Dunlop. Jerusalem: Franciscan, 1976.

Stringer, Martin. *Rethinking the Origins of the Eucharist.* London: SPCK, 2011.

Sweet, Anne. "'Participating in the Passion of Christ': Benedict's View of the Monastic Life." *Cistercian Studies Quarterly* 37.3 (2002) 279–96.

Synan, Vinson. *The Century of the Holy Spirit.* Nashville: Thomas Nelson, 2001.

———. *The Pentecostal-Holiness Tradition: Charismatic Movements in the Twentieth Century.* 1971. Reprint. Grand Rapids: Eerdmans, 1997.

Syndacus, E. *Early Christian Art.* Translated by J. R. Foster. New York: Hawthorn, 1962.

Tappert, T., trans. *Pia Desideria by Philip Jacob Spener.* Philadelphia: Fortress, 1964.

Telford, William. "Jesus Christ Movie Star: The Depiction of Jesus in the Cinema." In *Explorations in Theology and Film*, edited by Clive Marsh, 115–41. New York: Wiley, 1997.

Teresa of Avila, *Interior Castle.* Translated by Allison Peers. Garden City, NY: Image, 1961.

Terrell, JoAnne. *Power in the Blood? The Cross in the African American Experience.* Eugene, OR: Wipf & Stock, 1998.

Thiede, Carsten, and Matthew D'Ancona. *The Quest for the True Cross.* New York: Palgrave, 2002.

Thorpe, Benjamin, trans. *Aelfric of Eynsham: The Homilies of the Anglo-Saxon Church. The First Part, Containing the Sermones Catholici, or Homilies of Ælfric Volume 1.* London: Richard and John E. Taylor, 1844.

Thurstan, Herbert. *The Stations of the Cross: An Account of their History and Devotional Purpose.* London: Burns & Oates, 1906.

———. *The Physical Phenomena of Mysticism.* Chicago: Regnery, 1952.

Tobin, Frank, trans. *Henry Suso: The Exemplar, with Two German Sermons.* Mahwah, NJ: Paulist, 1989.

Tomlin, G. *The Power of the Cross: Theology of the Death of Christ in Paul, Luther and Pascal.* Carlisle, UK: Paternoster, 1999.

Tongeren, Louis van. *Exaltation of the Cross: Towards the Origins of the Feast of the Cross and the Meaning of the Cross in Medieval Liturgy.* Leuven: Peeters, 2000.

Towlson, C. *Moravian and Methodist: Relationships and Influences in the Eighteenth Century.* London: Epworth, 1957.

Turner, Denys. *Julian of Norwich: Theologian.* New Haven: Yale University Press, 2011.

Turner, Steve *Imagine: A Vision for Christians and the Arts.* Leicester, UK: IVP, 2001.

Upham, Thomas C. *Life, Religious Opinions and Experience of Madam De La Mothe Guyon.* New York: Harper & Brothers, 1857.

Vandenbroucke, Francois. "New Milieux, New Problems: From the Twelfth to the Sixteenth Century." In *The Spirituality of the Middle Ages: A History of Christian Spirituality, Volume II*, edited by Jean Leclercq, Francois Vandenbroucke, and Louis Bouyer, 141–67. London: Burns and Oates, 1968.

Voragine, Jacobus de. *The Golden Legend, Volume I: Readings on the Saints.* Translated by William Ryan. Princeton: Princeton University Press, 1995.

Walker, Ken. "Witnessing with *The Passion.*" *Christianity Today,* April 2004, 23.

Walker, P. J. *Pulling the Devil's Kingdom Down: The Salvation Army in Victorian Britain.* Berkeley: University of California Press, 2001.

Walker, Wyatt Tee. *Somebody's Calling My Name: Black Sacred Music and Social Change.* Valley Forge, PA: Judson, 1979.

Walsh, Christopher. "Stations of the Cross." In *The New SCM Dictionary of Liturgy and Worship*, edited by Paul Bradshaw, 450. London: SCM, 2002.

Walsh, Kilian, trans. *The Works of St. Bernard of Clairvaux, Volume 3: On the Song of Songs II*. London: Mowbray, 1976.

Walsh, Kilian, and Irene Edmonds, trans. *Bernard of Clairvaux on the Song of Songs III*. Kalamazoo, MI: Cistercian, 1979.

Ward, Benedicta, trans. *The Prayers and Meditations of St. Anselm*. London: Penguin, 1973.

Ward, W. R. "The Renewed Unity of the Brethren: Ancient Church, New Sect, or Transconfessional Movement." *Bulletin of the John Rylands Library* 70 (1988) ixvii–xcii.

Warfield, B. B. *Perfectionism*. Philadelphia: Presbyterian & Reformed, 1858.

Watkins, Renee Neu. "Two Women Visionaries and Death." *Numen* 30.2 (1983) 174–98.

Watson, J. R. *The English Hymn: A Critical and Historical Study*. Oxford: Oxford University Press, 1999.

Webb, Robert. "*The Passion* and the Influence of Emmerich's *The Dolorous Passion of Our Lord Jesus Christ*." In *Jesus and Mel Gibson's The Passion of the Christ: The Film, The Gospels and the Claims of History*, edited by Kathleen Corley and Robert Webb, 160–72. London: Continuum, 2004.

Weeks, Gordon. *Chapter Thirty-Two—Part Of*. Barnsley, UK: Weeks, 2003.

Weinlick, J. R. *Count Zinzendorf*. New York: Abingdon, 1956.

Westerholm, Stephen. *Perspectives Old and New on Paul: The "Lutheran" Paul and His Critics*. Grand Rapids: Eerdmanns, 2004.

White, C. E. *The Beauty of Holiness: Phoebe Palmer as Theologian, Revivalist, Feminist, and Humanitarian*. Grand Rapids: Francis Asbury, 1986.

White, Ellen, G. *Present Truth* 1 August and 1 December 1849. Accessed March 22, 2016. https://egwwritings.org/?ref=en_PT.August.1.1849.par.14&para=517.18 .

White, Kent. *The Word of God Coming Again*. Bournemouth, UK: Apostolic Faith Church, 1919.

Whitlock, F. A., and J. V. Hynes. "Religious Stigmatization: An Historical and Psychophysiological Enquiry." *Psychological Medicine* 8 (1978) 185–202.

Whittle, Donald. *Christianity and the Arts*. Oxford: Mowbray, 1966.

Wiles, Maurice. *The Christian Fathers*. London: Hodder & Stoughton, 1966.

Williams, Rowan. *Lost Icons: Reflections on Cultural Bereavement*. Edinburgh: T. & T. Clark, 2000.

Wood, A. Skevington. *The Inextinguishable Blaze: Spiritual Renewal and Advance in the Eighteenth Century*. Exeter, UK: Paternoster, 1960.

Wood, Juliette. "The Holy Grail: From Romance Motif to Modern Genre." *Folklore* 111 (2000) 169–90.

Worsfold, J. *The Origins of the Apostolic Church in Great Britain*. Wellington, NZ: Julian Literature Trust, 1991.

Yarnold, Edward, *Cyril of Jerusalem*. London: Routledge, 2000.

Yarom, N. *Body, Blood, and Sexuality: A Psychoanalytic Study of St Francis' Stigmata and Their Historical Context*. New York: Lang, 1992.

Zeman, J. K. *The Anabaptists and the Czech Brethren in Moravia 1526–1628: A Study of Origins and Contacts*. The Hague: Mouton, 1969.

Zuckerman, Bruce. "Where Are the Flies? Where Is the Smoke? The Real and Super-Real in Mel Gibson's *The Passion*." *Shofar: An Interdisciplinary Journal of Jewish Studies* 23.3 (2005) 129–36.

INDEX

Printed in Great Britain
by Amazon

38818687R00128